FOODS OF THE
HUDSON

FOODS OF THE HUDSON

A SEASONAL SAMPLING OF THE REGION'S BOUNTY

·····

PETER G. ROSE

THE OVERLOOK PRESS

WOODSTOCK · NEW YORK

First published in 1993 by
The Overlook Press
Lewis Hollow Road
Woodstock, New York 12498

Library of Congress Cataloging-in-Publication Data

Rose, Peter G.
    Foods of the Hudson / Peter G. Rose
      p.   cm.
    Incudes Index.
    1. Cookery, American.   2. Cookery, Dutch.   3.Cookery—Hudson River Valley (N.Y. and N.J.)   4. Hudson River Valley (N.Y. and N.J.)—Description and travel.   I. Title.

TX715.R8336   1993
641.59747'3—dc20   92-35040
                                                   CIP

Typesetting by AeroType, Inc.
Design by Bernard Schleifer

ISBN: 0-87951-489-2

To:
My parents—for the past
Don—for the present
Peter Pamela—for the future

Contents

•:

•:•:•:•:•:•:•:•:•:

Acknowledgments

MANY thanks to all who contributed to this book. Not one person I asked for information or a recipe let me down, and everyone was as delighted with the idea of a book about this exciting region as I am. Credit is given as appropriate in the various chapters. The book contains several recipes of friends no longer with us. Cooking their wonderful food will be a way of remembering them.

In addition to those who helped me so much by giving me information and recipes I have to thank some others. First my dear friend Dr. Elisabeth Paling Funk, who continues to be my mentor. It was a very good day indeed for me when we met at a Washington Irving Conference nine years ago. We both come from the Netherlands, and we share a great pride in our heritage. It is very hard to imagine that it was only such a short time ago that we met, and yet she has come to mean as much to me as if she were a sister, the kind of sister anyone wishes for. She was the reader and critic for this book; her help was essential for the final product.

My sincere thanks go to Dr. Charles T. Gehring, director of the New Netherland Project, who is always willing to answer questions and contributes so much to the understanding of the Dutch-American period.

I am deeply indebted to He Who Stands Firm, who reinforced my respect for Native Americans and their culture. His course

Ethnobotany of the Eastern Woodland Indians was very significant to me and to the way I came to see the Hudson region.

Special thanks must go to Joe DiMauro, proprietor of Mount Kisco Seafood in Mount Kisco, New York, for his advice and for finding fish not in season.

I feel extremely fortunate to live in the little town of Lewisboro, New York, where the "white church"—the major edifice, if you will—is shared by the Presbyterian, the Roman Catholic, and the Jewish congregations. It speaks for its people.

I express my deep appreciation to all those others who helped and encouraged me in various ways: Elizabeth S. Armstrong, Daniel Berman, Elizabeth Berman, Agaath Brandt, Edo Brandt, Barbara Bucklin, Andrea Candee, Gail Daigle, Patrick Daigle, Dr. Charles Danowski, Christine Danowski, Peter De Jong, Cara De Silva, Marie Louise Donarski, Ray Donarski, my determined agent Jane Dystel, Howard Funk, Marge Harper, Liesbeth Kalff, Monique Martens, Donald F. Pember, Dr. Steven M. Rosman, everyone at the South Salem Library, William A. Starna, Radiah Sumler, and Laura Ten Eyck.

I am most sincerely grateful to my best friend and husband Don for his constant help, especially with the fireplace recipes, and for his reassurance and encouragement. Without him none of this would be possible. Our wonderful daughter Peter Pamela continues to enchant me with her love, talent, and tenacity.

SPECIAL ACKNOWLEDGMENTS

Cherry bounce
  Clermont State Historic Site, New York State Office of Parks, Recreation and Historic Preservation, Taconic Region.

Fish chowder
  New York State Office of Parks, Recreation & Historic Preservation Olana State Historic Site, David Huntington Archives.

Hard bread and peas porridge
  Knox's Headquarters State Historic Site, Palisades Interstate Park Commission, New York State Office of Parks, Recreation and Historic Preservation.

•.•.•.•.•.•.•.

Hudson Valley Camembert Crisp with Fresh Apple-Pear Conserve
Copyright Chef Larry Forgione, 1983, all rights reserved.

Interview with Alfred Martin
United States Department of the Interior, National Park Service, Roosevelt-Vanderbilt National Historic Sites.

Information on Martin Van Buren
U.S. Dept. of the Interior, National Park Service, Martin Van Buren National Historic Site.

Information on dining practices at Lyndhurst
Lyndhurst, a property of the National Trust for Historic Preservation.

Martha Washington's crab soup
Nesbitt, Henrietta. *The Presidential Cookbook*. New York: Doubleday, 1951.

Shaker ginger bread
The Ladies Guild, Church of Our Savior (Episcopal),Lebanon Springs, New York 12114.

Tea cookjes
On the Score of Hospitality: Selected Receipts of a Van Rensselaer Family, Albany, New York 1785 - 1835, and the collection of Historic Cherry Hill, Albany, New York.

Introduction

EVERYTHING I have done professionally since I moved to the Hudson region seventeen years ago has led up to writing this book. I was born in the Netherlands and grew up close to another majestic river, the Rhine. My background, then, provides two good reasons for my fascination with and passion for this region, one that is filled with evidence of its Dutch past, with a river that reminds me of home. It was not until we moved to the Hudson Valley that I could combine my love for history and food. I studied the ethnobotany and culture of the Native Americans of the area. I explored the region's many historical places, its festivals, and its fairs, and I have written many articles on these subjects. Furthermore, the research for my latest book, *The Sensible Cook: Dutch Foodways in the Old and the New World,* has contributed immeasurably to my understanding of the Hudson's European heritage.

More than a dozen years ago, I started writing a column on seasonal family food for readers in Westchester, Rockland, and Fairfield counties. Testing three or four recipes for my article each week ensures that dinner is never dull in our house. My husband even came up with a family slogan: "You eat it today; you read it tomorrow!" In those many years I have used far more than a thousand recipes, some of which are included here.

Recipes for seasonal foods, recipes for locally produced food and foodstuffs, recipes from those chefs who work together with the growers in a sincere effort to support the agriculture of the region, recipes from the people who grow or produce those foods, recipes from special festivals, country fairs or other food happenings, and recipes for holiday treats or other favorites from the twelve largest ethnic groups in the region are all part of *Foods of the Hudson*. All together, the chapters give a representative sampling of the region's foodways, past and present.

An agricultural region richly filled with history deserves a book of its own to document its culinary opulence. Such a region is the Hudson, from its source at tiny Lake Tear of the Clouds to the Statue of Liberty in New York Harbor. To avoid the impression that this is a guidebook and to connect *Foods of the Hudson* with the farmland from which the recipes spring, the chapters' organization follows the seasonal cycle. Each tested recipe begins with a description of its source, its content, or, where necessary, its use, or with suggestions for appropriate accompaniments. Most of the recipes are quick and easy. Above all these recipes—all made from scratch—are for delicious foods that can be served with pride.

Foods of the Hudson reflects the Dutch heritage of the region and, at the same time, its present-day diversity. A look behind the scenes in the great historic houses provides culinary insights into the past, yet the book is firmly rooted in the present. It is a snapshot taken in the early 1990s of the beguiling riches of one of America's first agricultural regions.

The Hudson river is about 315 miles long and begins on the highest peak in the Adirondacks, Mount Marcy, at Lake Tear of the Clouds, gathers momentum just below Troy, where it becomes navigable, and ends in New York Bay. From the bay to about Troy, the Hudson is also an estuary—Native Americans called it "river that flows both ways." The Dutch named it "River of Prince Mauritius," or Mauritius river; some maps identify it as the North River, but eventually it received the name of its early explorer. Canals were dug to connect the largest river in New York State with other points such as the Great Lakes, Lake Champlain, or the Pennsylvania districts. Bridges and tunnels connect one side of the river with the other.

For the present purpose I have defined the Hudson region to include the following counties: Essex, Warren, Washington, Saratoga, Albany, Rensselaer, Greene, Columbia, Ulster, Dutchess,

■·■·■·■·■·■·■·■·■

Orange, Putnam, Rockland, and Westchester in New York State, and Bergen and Hudson in New Jersey. The book includes a recipe from Newcomb, New York, as the northernmost town in the region and recipes from Jersey City, New Jersey, and the Hudson River Club in New York City as the southernmost anchoring points. Manhattan and the boroughs were not further explored as a source of recipes, as they could easily warrant a book of their own.

Native Americans have gathered their food or cultivated their crops in the Hudson region for thousands of years, as archaeological excavations have shown. They were Mohawks, part of the Iroquois Confederacy; and Delaware, who call themselves Lenni Lenape or The Common People. Former New York State archaeologist William A. Ritchie muses on their agricultural practices:

> Whereas the way of the white man centers on the technological domination of his environment, on its mastery and control, and he constantly seeks to improve his environment and usually phrases his ideals in economic terms, the Indian on the other hand was content to adjust himself harmoniously into the scheme of nature, to its seasonal cycles and mystical order of life. The Indian was sensitive to ecological relationships existing between plants and animals and even inanimate objects.

Information on Native American agricultural practices, where appropriate, is included in the chapter introductions. Most of that information is derived from a course called Ethnobotany of the Eastern Woodland Indians, conducted by He Who Stands Firm at the New York Botanical Garden in the Bronx, New York. An adopted Lenape, he studied under medicine woman Touching Leaves and others, and is well known for his extensive research on Native American life and culture.

In September 1609, when Henry Hudson explored the river and its surrounding area, he called it in his journal ''a beautiful and fruitful place.'' Settlers found him to be right. Fruit, vegetable, and dairy farms have thrived in this region for centuries. New York State ranks among the top five states in apples, pears, strawberries, grapes, tart cherries, carrots, cauliflower, celery, onions, sweet corn, apple cider, grape juice, maple syrup, and wine, and the Hudson region contributes its share. Recipes for all these products are included.

•.•.•.•.•.•.•.

It is only rather recently that Hudson region farms have begun declining, as they have elsewhere in the nation. Leonard Clarke, whose family apple farm has been in production since the early 1700s, says somberly: "I think it's possible that a working farm as we know it now will become a thing of the past." Agriculture is vital to New York State, however, and the Department of Agriculture and Markets is aiding farmers to find new outlets for their products. Various publications from the Department were used for this book. "Niche farming," which means that the farmer grows a specific product for a specific customer, is another way of keeping the farms operating. A big boost to the Hudson region agriculture has been a privately funded program, called Greenmarket, which operates out of the New York City Mayor's Office. These New York City open-air markets give farmers of the surrounding areas an opportunity to sell their products directly to the consumer.

While Giovanni da Verrazano is believed to have been the first European to see the river, in 1524, it was not until after the explorations of Henry Hudson, in the employ of the Dutch East India Company, that the area was settled by Europeans. The New Netherland period spanned only five brief decades, from 1614 to 1664, but the Dutch influence was long-lasting and is still felt today. The sturdy Dutch houses, many now museums, and ample barns still dot the region's landscape, thanks in part to such organizations as the Dutch Barn Preservation Society, which work to preserve them. Other physical evidence is found in area museums, which are filled with gleaming silver, furniture—especially the large, typically Dutch *kast*, sometimes called *Kas* or cupboard— china, and decorative art objects, donated by descendants of Dutch settlers. Many Dutch recipes are included in the book.

During the Revolution, the Hudson was enormously important. By winning the area, the English hoped to separate New England from the South. Emphasizing the significance of the river for the transport of cumbersome army supplies, their general John Burgoyne, later defeated in the famous battle of Saratoga, wrote in 1775: "[This] is precisely the route that an army ought to take for the great purposes of cutting the communications between the Southern and Northern Provinces, giving confidence to the Indians, and securing a junction with the Canadian forces."

What rations were given for such a battle to the Continental soldiers? Dick Beresford, technician at Saratoga National Historical Park, gives some insights, but remarks that payments and allowances were wishful thinking on the part of Congress. Many of the soldiers' diaries, letters, and journals tell of the starving condition of the Continental soldier. Yet ''he remained faithful to the cause.'' The records in the archives of the Saratoga National Historical Park show that the rations as intended were as follows:

Each soldier was entitled to a daily ration of one pound of fresh beef or salt fish, or three-quarters of a pound of pork; one pound of bread or flour, one pint of milk, one quart of spruce beer or cider. He was also to receive a weekly allowance of peas, beans, or other vegetables along with rice, molasses, candles, soap and vinegar. In addition to these daily and weekly rations, each soldier, when in the field, was to receive an additional daily ration of one pound of beef or pork and one pound of hard bread. In cold or wet weather he was entitled to a gill of rum or whiskey.

It is interesting to compare these rations with the ones for modern-day warfare. The Public Affairs Office of the U.S. Army Combined Arms Support Command at Fort Lee, Virginia, supplied the following information on Operation Desert Storm, in which many Hudson region women and men participated:

Soldiers on the front lines during Desert Storm ate Meals-Ready-to-Eat (MREs). A typical menu of a MRE would include chicken and rice, fruit, cheese spread, crackers, and cookie. An accessory packet issued with a MRE would include coffee, chewing gum, hot sauce, and towelette.

After the Revolution, New York City became the capital for a brief period, drawing attention to the entire area. By 1807, steamboats had started to travel up and down the Hudson, while the sturdy, single-masted sloops remained in business and became the market boats, carrying lighter goods such as produce. Proximity to the river and therefore access to markets was an important factor in the success of the region's agriculture. Later the railroad took over this function. Nowadays, most boats on the Hudson are pleasure craft, either privately owned or belonging to such cruise companies as Dutch Apple Cruises, Hudson Highland Cruises, or Hudson River Cruises, giving visitors, who are part of a $2 billion travel industry, a view of the river at its best. There are even some stationary boats in the Hudson, such as the old ferry the Binghampton (now a restaurant) or a museum boat (the *Half Moon*, a recently finished replica of Henry Hudson's ship). The ride by train, right along the Hudson, from New York City to Albany is one of the most scenic rides in the nation.

The nineteenth century was an era of prosperity for the region. Washington Irving described the satisfying life of the Dutch in the Hudson Valley in his Knickerbocker folk tales, and the romantic Hudson River School, the first American school of painting, glorified its landscape. Towns like Newburgh, Hudson, and Poughkeepsie became prosperous settlements, thanks to their whaling fleets. Many great estates, now mostly museums, were built along the river. Though I contacted all of them for period recipes, not all had appropriate material in their archives. Those that did are included in the book.

Toward the end of the nineteenth century, the great lumber camps were created. Timbering then became a way of life in the northern parts of the region, although there is evidence of lumbering in northern New York dating as far back as the mid-eighteenth century. Log hauling started around New Year's and did not let up until spring. One of the factors that made a logging contractor's reputation was the quality of the food served. As the saying went, "good cooks make satisfied lumberjacks," and the competition for cooks was keen. There are still cooks up north who can reminisce about feeding fifteen to twenty (or far more) hungry men three meals a day, seven days a week. Such meals included two meats and several kinds of vegetables, always potatoes, coffee, and tea. The weekly baking produced twenty loaves of regular bread, twenty loaves of lumberjack bread (made with lard and molasses), cookies, cakes, puddings, doughnuts, and fried cakes. Lumberjack cook Rita Chiasson, who worked for such big loggers as Gordon LaPorte or Marcel Pinard, recalls that she made 500 doughnuts every two days. An old lumberjack said, "We always got real good food. There was always more than we wanted." That was the positive side; however, conditions, especially sanitation, were far from ideal. Many remember the bunkhouses full of lice, "as big as my fingernail," and the bedbugs.

Information on those bygone days of the lumberjack is kept in the library of the Adirondack Museum in Blue Mountain Lake, a museum that captures the experience of living in what is now 6 million acres of Adirondack Park, much of which has been declared "forever wild." You will see beautiful artifacts from the summer "camps" of the rich and from the hotels that served them. Menus, such as the one from the Loon Lake House in Loon Lake, New York, testify that good food was served and that there was plenty of it. For July 4, 1923, the menu included a choice of soups and relishes, main courses such as boiled salmon, boiled tongue, or various roasts with Irish, sweet, or mashed potatoes, and vegetables. Fritters, breads, and many different desserts were among the other offerings, including different kinds of tea. Nevertheless, when, nearly seven decades later, I asked a staff member at the Adirondack Interpretive Center, "Do you know of any good cooks in the area?" her answer was, "Gosh, no, they all died." Luckily, I found a good baker alive in Newcomb, New York. Her recipe appears in the final chapter.

In the twentieth century, the region continued to prosper, but to the detriment of the river. Fortunately, dedicated people banded together to save it from succumbing to pollution. Folk singer Pete Seeger and the sloop *Clearwater* became the focal points for the clean-up-the-river movement.

The best-remembered Hudson region event of the twentieth century was Woodstock, as the 1969 music festival became called, which actually took place in the hamlet of Bethel in the town by that name. About 300,000 people attended the three-day festival, where bands such as The Who from England and The Grateful Dead from San Francisco played day and night. Facilities and food were extremely limited. A participant tells, "I ate a hot dog Saturday morning and some potato chips over the weekend." Art Vassmer, who has a general store three miles from the site, became known as the "peanut butter and jelly man," and says, "That's what they lived on for three days." In spite of the lack of amenities, and partially because of it, those who were there will never forget that wondrous weekend.

The population of the region is as varied as its past. The 1980 census figures show an assortment of ethnic groups in the region, which has its greatest population diversity in the southern counties. Relatively few Native Americans remain, but the Dutch are still among the twelve largest ethnic groups. They are joined by African-Americans, English, French, Germans, Hispanics, Hungarians, Irish, Italians, Jews, Poles, and Russians. Together they create the appealing diversity of the region, to which the recipes collected in the final chapter pay tribute.

Well-known artists, writers, actors, musicians, and other famous people live or have lived in the region, including two American presidents, not surprisingly both of Dutch descent: Franklin D. Roosevelt and Martin Van Buren. The Franklin D. Roosevelt Library, the first of the presidential libraries, contains two books written about the foods of the Roosevelt family. A recipe from one of them can be found in Chapter 3. "Martin Van Buren received harsh criticism during his political career for being a bon vivant," writes Michael D. Henderson, museum curator of the Martin Van Buren National Historic Site, Lindenwald, in Kinderhook, New York. No recipes remain from this nineteenth-century president's kitchen, but here is a description of a Van Buren dinner as observed by one of his guests:

> The Dish before him contained a fine ham: then comes two side dishes of potatoes and peas: then an enormous one of fricassee: then potatoes and peas with a sprinkling of butter, cucumber, Beans, Corn and Beets, and then in front of John another supply of fricassee. Four bottles of champagne completed the carte for the first course. The second was pies, custard, jelly of excellent make. [sic] and the third of fine-flavored seegars.

With such an interesting and lavishly documented history, it will come as no surprise that the region can boast of many "firsts"; for example, it has the oldest pulpit in the nation. This carved wooden lectern, equipped with an hourglass to time the service, dates back to 1656. It cost the members of the First Church in Albany 25 beaver skins to have it imported from Amsterdam together with a weathercock, also still preserved, for their new church. Fans know that Goshen, New York, can boast of the oldest harness race track in the nation. But one of the most significant contributions that the region made to the rest of America was to give it Santa Claus.

The seventeenth-century Dutch settlers brought the celebration of the feast day of Saint Nicholas to the Hudson River region. In the early nineteenth century, Washington Irving, a native New Yorker who later built his home, Sunnyside, in Tarrytown, New York, transformed the traditional tall, stern Dutch Saint Nicholas into a jolly person, clad in breeches, thereby providing the origin of the American Santa Claus. Others, such as Clement Moore, in his famous poem "A Visit from Saint Nicholas," adopted that image and amplified the portrait and nineteenth-century illustrators further rounded it out. Other ethnic groups added their traditions, and a new figure was created who became the secular component of the American Christmas celebration.

The region can boast not only many historic firsts, but also many culinary firsts. The Dutch brought to it—and to the nation's table—"olie-koecken," the forerunner of today's doughnut. They also introduced pretzels, pancakes, waffles, wafers, coleslaw, and—above all—cookies.

Many stories have been written about the origins of America's favorite snack food, the potato chip. The generally accepted version is that Saratoga, New York, cook George Speck, better known as George Crum, invented them in a fit of anger when a customer kept complaining that his chips were not crisp enough. He then cut the potatoes very thin and cooked them very crisp. They immediately met with approval. David R. Mitchell, Executive Director of Brookside Saratoga County Historical Center, who has researched the potato-chip story, believes differently. He credits Kate Wicks, George Speck's sister and also a cook, with the discovery of the chip. He adds: "Both Kate Wicks and Speck . . . were of African-American ancestry, a fact that most published sources do not mention, but census records prove."

Another first for the region is the serving of pie with ice cream or, as it became known, "pie à la mode." In 1896, the story goes, a Mr. Townsend was eating pie with ice cream at the Cambridge Hotel in Cambridge, New York, when socialite Mrs. E. Berry Wall was a guest as well. She ordered the same dessert and christened it "pie à la mode." Some time later, when Mr. Townsend ate in New York's famous Delmonico restaurant, he ordered his dessert by that name. When Delmonico's staff did not know what to bring him, the horrified manager assured Mr. Townsend that henceforth they would put pie à la mode on the menu. It has been on the menus of restaurants across the nation ever since.

It seems appropriate that peanut butter sandwiches feature in the story of the region's most famous recent event, Woodstock, because legend has it that peanut butter sandwiches were invented in the Hudson region, in the small town of Alligerville, New York. Eleanor Rosakranse, president of the local historical association, tells that probably some time between 1840 and 1850, in the Peterskill House, near the D&H canal, lived a family named Davis. Their son Ross traveled quite a bit, and on one of his journeys he went to Cuba. During a later journey he was shot and killed there. While in Cuba, he saw women grind peanuts and smear the paste on bread. He wrote to his mother about the practice and she started doing the same, using the peanut butter for sandwiches.

The region has not only interesting food stories but many interesting food products as well. Some manufacturers use local fruit or vegetables for chutneys, jam, jellies, preserves, mustard, and dressing. One of these is Babcock & Babcock, Inc., who tell the story of Sarah Jane Babcock on their labels.

> In the late 1800's Sarah Jane Babcock realized the potential for herb cultivation in the fertile soil of her valley region. Known as "Aunt Jenny" by her family and friends, she became famous for her home cooking by blending those herbs into her recipes.

Her great-grandson continued the tradition and created his company in Craryville, New York.

The Monks and Nuns of New Skete in Cambridge, New York, offer "fine foods for giving and feasting." These include bacon, sausages, smoked poultry, maple syrup, and cheeses. Their kitchens produce cakes such as brandied fruitcake, but they are especially known for their cheesecakes in assorted flavors, which are now even made into wedding cakes.

Honey has been produced at Widmark Honey Farms, in Gardiner, New York, for more than one hundred years. Beekeepers in the area are occasionally bothered by bears invading their bee yard, but Widmark Farms have trained their own bears, which perform at many local events and have become quite famous.

The history of the G. H. Ford Tea Company in Poughkeepsie, New York, is another one of those engaging culinary gems of the region. Gertrude H. Ford, who established her company in 1909 and led it until 1963, is credited as being one of the inventors of the ball-shaped tea bag, still used by the company today. She not only imported, selected, and blended fine teas, but at one time even made her own deliveries. When she was visiting Indian tea plantations, "a wise Indian sage told Miss Ford that purple was her color and would bring her success." Apparently believing him, she always wore shades of lavender and used the color in her packaging. A delicious sampling of some of the fifteen or so blends of tea is available in a lavender tin. The company is now owned by Alfred and Alice Bogad, who continue Miss Ford's traditions.

Tea is not the only drink for which the region is known. The Hudson Valley proper, the area below Albany, is dotted with wineries. Like those in California's Napa Valley, they can be visited for wine tastings. Some wineries use hybrid grapes, others vinifera; fruit wines and meads are also made in the region. As of this writing, these are the vineyards and wineries in the Hudson River Region as listed by the New York State Wine and Grape Foundation. Call before you visit, because not all of these are open to the public.

Starting on the west side of the river, from the north (all in New York):
Johnston's Winery, Ballston Spa
Larry's Vineyard and Farm Winery, Altamont
Woodstock Winery, West Shokan
El Paso Winery, Ulster Park
West Park Wine Cellars, West Park
Adair Vineyards, New Paltz
Rivendell Winery, New Paltz
Royal Kedem Wine Company, headquartered in Brooklyn
Windsor Vineyards, Marlboro
Benmarl Wine Company, Marlboro
Walker Valley Vineyards, Walker Valley
Brimstone Hill Vineyard, Pine Bush
Baldwin Vineyards, Pine Bush
Magnanini Winery, Wallkill
Ashkol Wine Company, Middletown
Brotherhood America's Oldest Winery, Ltd., Washingtonville

On the east side of the river, from the north (also in New York):
The Meadery, Greenwich
Cascade Mountain Winery, Amenia
Clinton Vineyards, Clinton Corners
Millbrook Vineyards, Millbrook
North Salem Vineyard, North Salem

Naturally there are many wine lovers in a region where wine has been made for centuries. One of the most famous wine cellars not only of the region but of the country, must be Dudley Olcott's cellar at the Ten Broeck House in Albany, which remained unopened for almost a century. This Federal-style mansion was built in

1798 by Brigadier General Abraham Ten Broeck (1734–1810). In 1848, Thomas Olcott purchased the property. Four generations of Olcotts occupied the house until the current generation gave the grounds and buildings to the Albany County Historical Association in 1948.

It was Thomas Olcott's son Dudley who assembled the wine collection between 1860 and 1900. Subsequent generations did not add to the cellar, and no vintages were laid down after 1900. When the house was donated, the existence of the cellar was known, but access to it was denied by an influential member of the Historical Society's board. The cellar was opened in 1977, after he died, and eventually the contents were sold so that the proceeds could be used for the continued restoration of the mansion. The cellar was carefully restocked, however, so it can lay claim to the title of one of the oldest wine cellars continuously in use in the country. A. C. McNally, from whose notes I took the above information, was present at the opening of the cellar. Here are some of his observations on "a rainy day in August, 1977":

> It was blocked by double doors so warped against the Eighteenth Century brick floor as to allow opening less than eight inches. We squeezed by to behold within, among the disarray of hundreds of loose binned and ullaged bottles [bottles which have lost wine through evaporation or leakage], original unopened wooden shipping cases with attached steamship tags and notes indicating exact details of purchase, transportation and delivery. My heart was beating as if I had been entering King Tut's Tomb. Our flashlights illuminated sufficiently only to take superficial inventory. It was decided to remove the cases . . . for more clinical examination. . . . Dramatic is hardly descriptive of the scene when prying open for the first time cases packed more than a century ago. The bottles were wrapped in paper tissue and sheathed in straw sleeves, some packed twenty-four to the case. Miraculously, more than half of the corks had held and live wine of good appearance emerged. Upon tasting, even some deeply ullaged bottles contained good wine, the best *great* wines faithful to their famous vintage origins.

Nature provides its own drama in the Hudson region as those who ever were part of the shad runs or shad festivals along the river can testify. It is still possible here to eat a fish a stone's throw away from where it was caught. Native Americans cooked shad on hot stones right at the shore, and even George Washington had shad bakes when he was in the region.

Shad, crab, cheeses, beefalo, chicken and other poultry, game, and especially the large variety of fruits and vegetables make up the regional specialties. Recipes for all of them and many more culinary treasures can be found in *Foods of the Hudson.*

My best effort went into this attempt to touch on all the region's culinary highlights. If you believe I have overlooked a good story or a great source for a recipe, however, I would surely like to hear about it. Please write to me c/o The Overlook Press, Woodstock, New York, 12498.

1. Early Spring

 The subjects of the spring chapter are eggs, fish, lamb and goat, maple syrup, vegetables, herbs and edible flowers.

Eggs

"Fresh eggs for sale" signs join those for shad in season in the Hudson region. In earlier days, eggs were not mostly thought of as breakfast food; they were also a favorite luncheon or dinner course, as is clear from the notes in the files of Alice Delafield Clarkson Livingston (1872–1964) and from the reminiscences of Alfred Martin, second butler employed from 1909–1938 in Hyde Park by Frederick W. Vanderbilt. (Courtesy National Park Service, Roosevelt-Vanderbilt National Historic Sites.)

In a taped interview on December 8, 1947, Martin tells about the routines of the Vanderbilt household. He explains that for a family luncheon the menu would contain three courses; "fish for a first course and then the main course, lamb or whatever they might prefer, dessert, fruit and candies." For dinner, "eggs would be the first course and probably an entrée. The main course would be chicken or turkey or some kind of game and then dessert, fruit and candies."

Fish

Shad is the number one food fish of the Hudson River. According to Andy Kahnle of the Department of Environmental Conservation there are no advisories against the eating of Hudson shad or, for that matter, herring or alewifes. There are shad runs from the St. John's river in Florida to the Connecticut river in Connecticut, but the Hudson seems to have the largest stock at the moment. In 1990, about 380,000 pounds of shad were caught in the river.

Shad are an anadromous fish, returning each year from the ocean to spawn in the Hudson River, where they were hatched. Males return after the age of 3 to 5; females after the age of 4 to 6. Naturalist Christopher Letts points out that this "homecoming" coincides with the flowering of the forsythia.

Most of these fish, if not caught, live up to 12 years of age. Shad is caught with either anchored nets, stake or pole nets, or drift nets. Many people are familiar with the sight of the nets of Bob Gabrielson, just below the Tappan Zee Bridge. Gabrielson, who calls the shad "the queen of the Hudson," and other commercial fishermen, such as Tom Turk and Tom Lake, have been fishing shad for most of their lives, although since the seventies there is not enough money to be made in commercial Hudson fishery to make this a full-time job. It might be a dying occupation in any event, because few young people want to work such long and cold hours to catch fish.

Not only shad is caught in the early spring. Trout season opens April 1. Trout and other fish are caught in the many streams, lakes, and reservoirs in the Hudson region. Farther north, the roads are not easily passable quite so early; lakes are still frozen until early May. The upper Hudson region boasts several aquaculture facilities that grow and sell trout.

When the shad run in April and May, fishermen from all over the area come to catch their share. Roadside stands quickly sell their stock of this delicious fish and its plump roe. Shad weigh between 5 and 7 pounds and are about 22–24 inches long. They are sold as fillets, with or without bones, and fresh or smoked; some people pickle the fish as you would pickle herring. A recipe for pickled shad is included in Chapter 1. Shad with its 769 bones should be purchased boned. Boning them requires a great deal of skill and practice. It is said that even in the Fulton Fish Market, only a few fish cutters possess this skill. They are kept very busy in the season. No wonder native Americans called shad "porcupine turned inside out."

Shad bakes and festivals, held up and down the river from Fort Lee, New Jersey, to Fort Crailo, New York, give the public a chance to participate in a truly regional festival and taste this firm-textured fish either pickled, smoked, or planked. The planked method is traditional: Two boned fillets of shad are placed on an oak, maple, or birch plank about a foot wide and a foot and a half long. Do not use a soft wood plank, such as spruce, which will impart a nasty flavor. Crisscross the fish fillet with several strips of bacon, and then tack the bacon to the board with nails. Prop the board up close to a fire at an angle of 60 degrees, being careful not to let the bacon or the board char. Move the plank away and toward the fire as necessary. It takes about an hour to cook the fish this way.

Lamb and Goat

The large variety of early spring foods of the Hudson region includes lamb and goat. General instructions and remarks regarding their preparation are included in this chapter.

Maple Syrup

"The sap runs!" is the warning cry of the first agricultural activity of the year. It takes 40 gallons of sap to make one gallon of syrup. Other maple products are maple sugar, soft and hard maple candy, and maple spread. The following maple facts were gathered over the years by Jane Smith, of Smith's Maple Products in Napanoch, New York: maple syrup, at 99 calories an ounce, not only is delicious on pancakes, waffles, biscuits, porridges, baked apples, and sweet potatoes but also tastes great in a cake or combined with baked beans. Grade A, sold in New York State, which is usually the nation's first or second maple syrup producer, is subdivided by color. Light amber syrup, with its delicate flavor, is the best to use undiluted on items such as pancakes. Medium amber or, better yet, dark amber, with a stronger maple flavor, is excellent for mixing with other ingredients or for use in baking. To substitute maple syrup for sugar, use three-quarters of a cup of maple syrup for each cup of sugar and reduce the liquid in the recipe by three tablespoons for each cup of syrup. As you would with honey, heat the syrup to redissolve the sugar if crystallization occurs. Keep maple syrup in unopened containers in a dry, cool place. Once opened, store in the refrigerator.

Vegetables, Herbs, and Edible flowers

According to the Metro New York Harvest calendar, issued by the New York State Direct Marketing Program, radishes, spinach, and asparagus are some of the early crops. Some farms in the region harvest broccoli di rabe in April or have baby lettuces in greenhouses ready for picking even earlier.

Pokeweed is one of the early wild shoots mentioned by Jane Colden (1724–1766), America's first woman botanist, who grew up in Orange County about ten miles west of Newburgh. She meticulously describes the plant and adds that the root is "very useful in the use of cancirs[;] some curious persons in England have endeavoured to propogate [sic] this plant by the Seed braigth from America, but could not produce any plant from the Seed."

In today's herb gardens, small blades of sorrel will grow in March under last year's dry leaves and small sprouts of chives will peek through. Only two handfuls of sorrel leaves are needed for a refreshingly tart soup to celebrate the resumption of the growing season.

In May, violets dot lawns in the Hudson region. These edible flowers can be preserved for dreary days in winter by brushing them with egg white and sugar, or they can be used fresh as colorful accents in salads and other dishes.

Native American Customs

The first greens, signaling spring for the Native Americans of the area, were skunk cabbage and marsh marigold, among others. Native Americans watched the bears come out of hibernation to eat these shoots. They felt that for them, too, eating the early greens was purifying, "as if one steals some of that fresh energy of nature," according to He Who Stands Firm.

For his class on the edible-plant gathering cycle of the Eastern Woodland Indians, he cooked mouth-puckering dishes of skunk cabbage and marsh marigold and prepared an enchantingly fragrant and soothing tea from spicebush twigs. The edible parts of skunk cabbage are the reticulate leaves, which are rolled like a cigar in early spring. It is necessary to change the cooking water three or four times to get rid of their astringency. Some of the students still complained that the dish made their mouths burn. Marsh marigold, which grows very close to the flat lowland streams, requires only one change of water when cooked. The buds can be eaten, and the settlers used to pickle the flowers. These are only a few of the early spring plants that were gathered to be eaten or used for medicine. As we see here and in later chapters, Native Americans were quite aware of each plant's properties and were adept in using them.

RECIPES FEATURING:

Eggs
Poached Eggs on Potato Pancakes with
 Spicy Beer-and-Cheddar Sauce

Fish
Baked Shad in Cream
Fish Chowder
Marinated Shad with Ginger and Honey
Christopher Letts' Pickled Shad
Pickled Shad or Herring Salad
Shad Roe
Shad with Honey, Mustard, and Dill
Stuffed Fillet of Shad
Trout Package
Trout Pâté

Lamb and Goat
Lamb Loin with Hudson Valley Stuffing

Maple Syrup
Maple Baked Beans
Maple Syrup Cake with Maple Butter Frosting

Vegetables, Herbs, and Edible Flowers
Asparagus, Ham, and Egg Platter
Asparagus Marinara Sauce for Fettuccine
Asparagus Vinaigrette with Violets
Baked Fish with Yogurt and Chives
Blamensier (Chicken with Rice, Almonds and Violets)

Broccoli di Rabe Sandwiches
Candying of Violets and Other Flowers
Peter's Beer Soup with Spinach, Cheese, and Sausage
Radish Salad
Reuben Soup
Sorrel Soup

EGGS

Poached Eggs on Potato Pancakes with Spicy Beer-and-Cheddar Sauce

▪▪

Alice Delafield Clarkson Livingston (1872–1964) was the last owner of Clermont, in Germantown, New York, now a State Historic Site and since 1973 a National Historic Landmark. She, as well as her husband, John H. Livingston, were descendants of Robert R. Livingston (1746–1813), one of the five drafters of the Declaration of Independence.

It is quite clear from looking through Mrs. Livingston's recipe book, which she started compiling in 1910, that she enjoyed being a hostess. She copied lists of dishes to be served for lunch or dinner from fashionable magazines of the time, such as Vogue, *and kept an extensive handwritten cookbook. One such list shows different ways of preparing and serving eggs:*

> *Creamed, with nutmeg sauce; stuffed with mustard; scrambled with bacon; timbales, Hollandaise sauce; poached in ramekins with chopped olives, or with spinach, or in a half shell of pastry with olives, or en cocotte; [eggs served] with olives; poached with Bechamel sauce; egg timbales [with] mushroom centre or with tomato sauce.*

How she would have loved to add the following recipe to her book! It comes from the Culinary Institute of America in Hyde Park, New York, and represents current and past offerings from the American Bounty Restaurant. One of the Institute's four student-staffed public restaurants, the American Bounty is the final class for all students. It features American food and wine and celebrates our nation's diverse culinary heritage. Suggested accompaniments are fruit salad and steamed asparagus.

At the time of this writing, there is a growing concern regarding salmonella bacteria in eggs. I questioned the Institute on this matter and here is the response:

▪▪▪▪▪▪▪▪▪▪▪▪▪▪

A true ''poached'' egg should be cooked to an internal temperature of 140° F. However, people with particular concerns regarding salmonella bacteria should cook the egg to an internal temperature of 160° F. Clean, uncracked eggs, kept refrigerated at a temperature of 40° F or below pose very little risk of salmonella danger. Always avoid keeping raw or cooked eggs out of the refrigerator for more than two hours (including preparation and serving time).

SERVES 4

PREPARATION TIME: *about 30 minutes*

COOKING TIME: *about 30 minutes altogether for the different components*

POTATO PANCAKES

- 4 *baking potatoes*
- 1 *egg, lightly beaten*
- 1 *tablespoon prepared horseradish*
- ¼ *cup grated onion*
- ¾ *teaspoon salt*
- ¼ *teaspoon freshly ground black pepper*
  Clarified butter, butter, or vegetable oil for frying

SPICY BEER-AND-CHEDDAR SAUCE

- 2 *tablespoons butter*
- ¼ *cup all-purpose flour*
- ¾ *cup milk*
- ¾ *cup dark beer*
- 8 *ounces yellow sharp cheddar cheese, grated*
- 2 *ounces (about ½ cup) grated Parmesan cheese*
- ½ *teaspoon Worcestershire sauce*
  Tabasco to taste
  Salt to taste
  Freshly grated white pepper to taste

PEPPER GARNISH

½   each of a red, yellow, and green bell pepper
     stemmed, cored, and seeds removed
1–2 jalapeño chilies, stemmed, cored, and
     seeds removed, finely julienned
1–2 tablespoons butter

POACHED EGGS

   Cider vinegar
8 eggs

Make the potato pancakes: Peel the potatoes and coarsely grate them. Place in a double thickness of cheesecloth, or a clean kitchen towel, and squeeze to remove any excess moisture. In a large bowl combine potatoes, egg, horseradish, onion, salt, and pepper. Toss to mix well. Heat butter or oil in a large frying pan. For each pancake, spoon about ½ cup of the potato mixture into the hot butter or oil and flatten with a spatula. Cook until golden brown; turn and cook the other side. Drain on paper towels and keep warm, together with the serving plates, in a 275° F oven.

In the meantime, prepare the sauce: Heat the butter in a saucepan over medium heat. Add the flour and cook, stirring until smooth. Combine the milk and beer. Whisk into the flour mixture one-third at a time, bringing the mixture to a simmer after each addition. When all of the liquid has been added, simmer 5 minutes. Add the cheeses and stir until incorporated. Remove from the heat. Add the Worcestershire, Tabasco, salt and white pepper. You can hold the sauce in a covered double boiler over simmering water, but I simply cover the pan and keep it on the stove—the sauce is still nicely warm when needed.

Prepare the pepper garnish: Cut the bell peppers into ½-inch diamonds. Blanch in boiling water until colors are bright; drain, drop in ice water, and drain again. Combine pepper diamonds with julienned jalapeño and set aside.

Prepare the poached eggs: Place 3 inches of water in a large sauté pan and add 1 teaspoon cider vinegar per quart of water used. Heat the water to 180° F, a very slow simmer. Crack each egg into a small bowl; then slide it into the simmering water. Poach until the whites are firm but the yolks are still runny, see remarks above. While the eggs are cooking, reheat the pepper garnish in butter just to warm through.

Place 2 potato pancakes on each plate. When the eggs are done, remove them from the water with a slotted spoon; trim off any ragged edges, and place them on top of the potato pancakes, two eggs per plate. Ladle the cheese sauce over the eggs. Sprinkle the tops of the eggs with the pepper garnish. Serve immediately.

FISH

Baked Shad in Cream

This recipe is from the hand of Joe DiMauro, owner of Mount Kisco Seafood in Mount Kisco, New York, an inspired and inspiring teacher of fish cookery. Carefully follow his suggested cooking times for this dish.

SERVES 4

PREPARATION TIME: *3 minutes*

BAKING TIME: *15–17 minutes*

---

6 tablespoons butter, divided
2 boned shad fillets, about 1 pound each
   Salt to taste
   Freshly ground pepper to taste
1 cup heavy cream
3–4 tablespoons fresh dill, chopped

Preheat the oven to 375° F.

Butter a shallow baking dish with 2 tablespoons of the butter. Place the shad fillets side by side in the baking dish, skin side down. Dot with pats of butter and season with salt and pepper. Bake for 10 minutes, pour in the heavy cream, and sprinkle the chopped dill all over the dish. Bake for another 5–7 minutes. Baste with the sauce at least three times while baking.

Serve hot, straight from the dish. Accompany with boiled new potatoes and tiny peas.

Fish Chowder

Isabel Carnes Church (1836–1899) was the wife of painter Frederic Edwin Church (1826–1900), who built the Moorish villa Olana, overlooking the Hudson river. In its archives one finds many accounts of how the Churches entertained, among them a letter from Miss Grace King, a visitor from New Orleans, who made several visits to Olana and wrote of the hospitality extended to her:

> *Such a nice supper was prepared[:] . . . boiled chicken, green peas, new corn, potatoes, wild berries and cream and cake—all the curious old silver things on the table & napkins with open work hem stitching and the big silver candlabras with the best candles!—I would have felt better if they had just taken off the pretty napkins, but we were too elegant for that.*

Among Mrs. Church's recipes I found one for a nice straightforward fish chowder, a soup we do not see often enough any more. The following is my adaptation. It can be used for the many kinds of fish caught in the small streams, lakes, and reservoirs in the Hudson region, or with store-bought fish.

SERVES 4

PREPARATION TIME: *about 15 minutes*

COOKING TIME: *about 25–30 minutes*

1–1½ *pounds firm-fleshed fish, such as*
        scrod, with bones
        Milk
  6 *slices bacon, chopped*
  1 *large onion, chopped*
  3 *tablespoons flour*
  2 *cups diced raw potatoes*
        Salt to taste

Freshly ground (preferably white)
  pepper to taste
Chopped parsley for garnish
Crackers, optional

Carefully take the fish off the bone and set aside. Place the bones in a small saucepan, cover with water, and boil gently for about 15 minutes. Remove and strain. Discard bones and pour fish broth in a measuring cup, add milk to make 4 cups.

In the meantime, in a large saucepan or Dutch oven, fry the bacon and onion until the bacon is brown and crisp. Drain off fat, if necessary. Sprinkle the mixture with the flour, then slowly stir in the milk/fish broth. Stir constantly until thickened. Add the potatoes and cook for about 5 minutes, until they are barely done, then add the fish pieces. Cook until the fish is done to your liking, but do not overcook. Taste and season with salt and pepper. Sprinkle each serving with a little parsley for color.

Serve with or without crackers, or with some hot garlic bread and butter.

NOTE: If fish with bones are not available, omit the step of making fish broth and just use milk for the liquid.

Marinated Shad with Ginger and Honey

Joe DiMauro, fish cookery teacher for the last five years in the Chappaqua and North Salem school districts, offers another shad recipe. The freshly grated ginger in the marinade gives the fish a wonderful tangy flavor. Watch the cooking time carefully; do not overcook.

SERVES 2

PREPARATION TIME: *5 minutes*

MARINATING TIME: *about 2 hours*

BROILING OR GRILLING TIME: *10–12 minutes*

---

 3 tablespoons vegetable oil
 3 tablespoons soy sauce (low-salt if you prefer)
 2 tablespoons honey
 2 tablespoons freshly grated ginger
   Freshly ground pepper to taste
 1 shad fillet, about 1 pound

Combine the oil, soy sauce, honey, ginger, and pepper. Marinate the shad fillet in this mixture for about 2 hours. Broil, skin side down, about 5–6 inches from the heat source for about 12 minutes, longer if the fillet is very thick. Keep basting the fillet with the marinade. Do not turn. Serve with rice and a spinach salad.

Christopher Letts's Pickled Shad

▪▪▪

Christopher Letts is the Hudson River Educator for the Hudson River Foundation. He loves to share his enthusiasm for the river with the public in many different events that are organized to bring people to the river. He is rightfully proud of the following recipe and makes it with the freshest fish available. He waits for the boats to come in and chooses the best fish, which he then transports home, packed in an ice slurry. You can eat the pickled shad as is, or use it in the herring salad recipe that follows. Here is a chance to use the fish with the bones. The pickling brine will dissolve them.

PREPARATION TIME: *about 45 minutes to 1 hour*

STANDING TIME: *3 days*

---

 1 or 2   shad
           Ice water

▪▪▪▪▪▪▪▪▪▪▪▪▪

PICKLING BRINE

½   gallon distilled vinegar
1¼ cups salt
1   cup sugar

PACKING SOLUTION

1   cup water
    distilled vinegar
½   cup salt
½   cup sugar
2   tablespoons pickling spices
2   bay leaves
4   whole cloves

Fillet and skin the shad, and cut into bite-sized pieces. In pickling, most of the remaining bones will dissolve. Soak the shad in ice water for 15 minutes. Drain well.

In the meantime, prepare the pickling brine: Combine the vinegar, salt, and sugar in a stainless steel or nonmetallic pan and heat to dissolve the sugar. Add the shad in a loose pack. Agitate gently every few hours for the first day so that all sides of the fish contact the brine. After the third day, drain and rinse in cold water. The smaller bones will have dissolved, and the shad is now edible.

Prepare the packing solution: In a stainless steel or nonmetallic pan, combine 3 pints of water, vinegar, salt, sugar, pickling spices, bay leaves, and cloves. Cover and simmer for 15 minutes; then cool.

Pack the shad in clean jars, which have been rinsed with boiling water, and pour in the packing solution to cover. Cover the jars and place in the refrigerator. The shad will keep for several weeks.

Pickled Shad or Herring Salad

Use pickled shad or store-bought pickled herring for this recipe. I always serve this salad on New Year's Eve.

SERVES *6–8*

PREPARATION TIME: *about 30 minutes*

COOKING TIME: *15–20 minutes*

1½ pounds pickled shad or pickled herring,
    drained and cut into small cubes
2 Granny Smith apples, peeled, cored, and
    cut into small cubes
¾ pound boiled beets, peeled, drained and
    cut into small cubes
1½ pounds potatoes (4 to 6), peeled, boiled,
    and cut into small cubes
1 cucumber, peeled, seeded, and cut into
    small cubes
1 medium onion, peeled and chopped
2 eggs, hard-boiled and peeled
    Salt to taste
    Freshly ground pepper to taste
½ cup mayonnaise, or more

FOR GARNISH

    Boston lettuce leaves
2 hard-boiled eggs, whites and yolks
    mashed separately
    Parsley
2 hard-boiled eggs, cut in eighths
    Pickled pearl martini onions

Combine the herring, apples, beets, potatoes, cucumber, and onion. Mash the eggs, add salt and pepper to taste, and bind with ½ cup of mayonnaise. Stir. Then add this mixture to the herring and vegetables. Combine thoroughly. You probably will need more mayonnaise to bind the mixture nicely but do not overdo. Refrigerate until serving time.

At serving time, mound the salad on a platter and surround it with the lettuce leaves. Cover one side of the mound with mashed egg white and the other side with the mashed egg yolk. Where they meet in the middle, place small parsley bouquets. Surround the salad with the 2 cut eggs. Neatly surround the base with the pearl onions.

Shad Roe

According to Joe DiMauro, you should serve one pair of shad roe sacs per person, if the roe is medium in size. Make sure the roe sacs are not punctured when you purchase them. In this recipe, the roe sacs are fried plain, but they can also be dredged in flour first and then fried. Joe warns that, while frying, the roe will ''pop like popcorn.''

SERVES 2

PREPARATION TIME: *about 5 minutes*

COOKING TIME: *about 10 minutes*

½ *stick (4 tablespoons) butter*
2 *tablespoons light olive oil*
2 *cloves garlic, minced*
1 *small onion, finely chopped*
2 *pairs shad roe*
   Salt to taste
   Freshly ground black pepper to taste

In a frying pan that is large enough to hold both roe sacs, heat the butter and oil until the butter is melted and lightly brown; add the garlic and onion and brown lightly. Carefully place the two roe sacs in the pan and cook over a medium flame. Turn after 3–4 minutes, cover the pan, and cook the other side for the same amount of time. Season to taste with the salt and pepper. Serve with wild rice and steamed asparagus.

Shad with Honey, Mustard, and Dill

Every shad fisherman has a favorite recipe for shad. For example, Bob Gabrielson likes it best the way his wife Joan prepares it, with lemon pepper and garlic and broiled in the toaster oven. Here is Joe DiMauro's favorite way. Heed his warning: "The worst fish in the world is the overcooked shad."

SERVES 2

PREPARATION TIME: *3 minutes*

COOKING TIME: *about 12 minutes*

SAUCE

4–5	tablespoons Dijon mustard
2	tablespoons honey
1	tablespoon dark brown sugar
1	tablespoon chopped fresh dill
	Freshly ground pepper to taste
1	shad fillet, about 1 pound

Combine the sauce ingredients and spread liberally across the top of the fillet. Broil the fillet, skin side down, about 5–6 inches from the heat source for about 12 minutes, longer if the fillet is very thick. Do not turn. This method can be used for the barbecue grill as well, but keep the top of the grill closed while cooking. Serve with boiled, small, red potatoes and asparagus vinaigrette.

Stuffed Fillet of Shad

Robert H. Boyle, President of the Hudson River Fisherman's Association, has written a fascinating book called The Hudson River: A Natural and Unnatural History. *It gives a vivid account of the river's marine life and of those involved in saving or spoiling it. When asked for shad recipes, he said: "Ask Joe Hyde. He is one of the great chefs of the world." Joe Hyde of Palisade, New York, an area caterer, has been cooking for thirty-nine years and prepares the shad for the yearly Hudson River Fishermen's Shad Festival. Here is one of his recipes.*

SERVES 2

PREPARATION TIME: *about 10 minutes*

BAKING TIME: *15–17 minutes*

---

3   *tablespoons toasted bread crumbs*
1   *stick (8 tablespoons) butter, melted*
    Shad roe
1   *shallot, minced*
1   *fillet of boned shad, not thicker than 1 inch*
    Salt to taste
    Freshly ground pepper to taste
    More bread crumbs for sprinkling on top
1   *medium onion, thinly sliced*

Preheat the oven to 375° F.

In a small bowl, mix 3 tablespoons bread crumbs, 2–3 tablespoons of the melted butter, about a cupful of roe, and the minced shallot. Place the fillet in an oven-to-table casserole skin-side down. Gently spread apart the opening from which the bones have been removed from the fillet and fill with the stuffing mixture. Season the fillet with salt and freshly ground pepper. Sprinkle lightly with bread crumbs, top with the thinly sliced onion, and over this carefully pour the rest of the melted butter. Bake for about 15–17 minutes. Baste occasionally with the butter. When done, the skin will stick to the pan, so that the flesh can easily be removed with a flat spatula.

Trout Package

....

Fernwood-Limne, Inc. is a private aquaculture facility in Gansevoort, New York, that has been "growing and selling trout for over 50 years." It is located within the big loop of the Hudson River near Glens Falls and is fed by springs and wells on the property. Products are sold primarily to recreational and whole-sale customers. The hatchery is not open to the public. President Thomas C. Field chose the following two recipes to represent Fernwood Trout Hatchery as part of our parade of superb Hudson region products.

SERVES 1–2

PREPARATION TIME: *3–5 minutes*

BAKING TIME: *15 minutes*

---

  1 **fresh dressed trout**
  1 **tablespoon dry white wine**
  1 **teaspoon olive oil**
  1 **teaspoon lemon juice**
 ¼ **teaspoon dried basil**
   Salt to taste
   Freshly ground pepper to taste

Preheat the oven to 450° F.

Place the trout and other ingredients on a sheet of aluminum foil and seal into a package. Be sure to double-fold the edges of the foil to ensure a tight seal. Place the package on a baking sheet. Bake for 15 minutes. Serve as is or in the following recipe.

Trout Pâté

....

SERVES 4–6

PREPARATION TIME: *about 10–15 minutes*

....

6   ounces flaked trout
3   ounces cream cheese
1   tablespoon minced onion
2–3 drops Tabasco, or more, to taste
½   teaspoon dried basil
½   teaspoon minced parsley
    Salt to taste
    Freshly ground pepper to taste
    Accumulated juices from the package
       (see above)

Flaked trout is prepared by following the recipe above; water may be substituted for the wine and the basil may be omitted, if desired.

After the trout has been cooked and cooled, it is slit down the backbone. Peel the skin from the meat and discard the skin. Flake the meat from the upper side of the fish with a fork. Next, remove the head and skeleton by gently raising them, head first, and flaking the meat downward from the lower side of the fish. A whole undressed trout will yield approximately 35 percent of its weight as flaked trout. A dressed trout with head yields about 50 percent of its weight as flaked trout.

Combine all ingredients in a blender and process at high speed until well blended. Add the juice a little at a time, as needed. Refrigerate for several hours and serve with a variety of crackers.

LAMB AND GOAT

Frances Szasz of Legend West Farm—so named after a village in Hungary—in Germantown, New York, who breeds sheep and goats mainly for milk and wool, gave me some general pointers about preparing both meats.

She thinks the Hudson region is fortunate to have quite a few excellent butchers who cut up the meat according to customer's preference, while local smokehouses can smoke meat and fish that is brought to them. She is very partial to smoked "lamb-ham."

Frances Szasz prefers to cook the flavorful goat and lamb meat as plainly as possible. Goat is very lean and has a bright flavor, but needs to be cooked with moisture, as in braised dishes or stews. Or marinate the meat in an oil-based dressing for shish kebabs or other grilled dishes. Add a grated carrot and some onion to ground goat meat to give it some moisture. Certain ethnic groups are fond of goat and serve it traditionally on special holidays, but more and more people are becoming interested in trying goat because of its leanness.

"Lamb barbecues beautifully," says Frances. One-inch-thick lamb burgers or chops are grilled rare to medium-rare and served with steak sauce, Worcestershire sauce, or even Marmite. Frances also makes her own horseradish sauce as an accompaniment. She peels the roots like a carrot, then chops them in a food processor, outfitted with the steel blade, and she mixes the chopped horseradish with Chinese rice vinegar because of its clean vinegar flavor.

Lamb stew, the cubes of meat dredged in flour and browned, consists of the traditional components of carrots, potatoes, and onions. Sometimes she fixes it the "Long Island way" with the addition of tomatoes; other times, she will give it the "New England treatment" of adding peas.

Lamb Loin with Hudson Valley Stuffing

Here is a recipe for lamb from Mohonk Mountain House. This National Historic Landmark has been owned and operated by the Smiley family for 120 years; Albert K. Smiley, great-grandnephew of founder Albert Smiley, is now in charge. Construction of the sprawling Victorian castle spanned thirty years, from 1879 to 1910. The hotel sits at the top of the Shawangunk Ridge, overlooking 64-feet-deep Lake Mohonk, and is known for its beautiful setting as well as its kitchen. In the following recipe, executive chef Stephe Gerike stuffs a lamb loin with a fruit mixture and roasts the loin in a slow oven for succulent results. Slice the lamb and serve with a hot apple-cider sauce.

SERVES *4 per pound of meat*

PREPARATION TIME: *about 20 minutes*

ROASTING TIME: *about 20 minutes per pound of lamb*

4   pounds deboned lamb loin
3   tablespoons olive oil
4   McIntosh apples, peeled, cored, and chopped
2   Bartlett pears, peeled, cored, and chopped
1   large sweet onion, diced fine
4   cloves garlic, minced
1   sprig fresh thyme, chopped and with
       stems removed
1   sprig fresh mint, chopped and with stems
       removed
1   sprig fresh rosemary, chopped and with
       hard stems removed
8   dried prunes, pitted and diced fine
    Salt to taste
    Freshly ground pepper to taste

Ask the butcher to cut a pocket through the length of the lamb loin, large enough to fit stuffing. Preheat the oven to 325° F. In a large frying pan, heat the olive oil and sauté the apples, pears, onion, garlic, and fresh herbs. Cook until onion is translucent. Remove from heat and add the prunes; season to taste with salt and freshly ground pepper. Let the mixture cool enough so that you can handle it and stuff the loin. Season the stuffed loin all around with salt and pepper. Leftover stuffing can be spooned on or around the roast. Place in the oven and roast for about 20 minutes per pound, or until the meat reaches an internal temperature of 145° F. Remove and cover. Let the roast stand for 10 minutes before carving. Carve in thick slices and serve with warm cider sauce.

WARM CIDER SAUCE

2   cups apple cider
1   teaspoon arrowroot, or more
¼   teaspoon pumpkin pie spice

In a small saucepan, heat the cider and whisk in the arrowroot and spice, until thickened to your liking. Pass separately.

MAPLE SYRUP

Maple Baked Beans

Jane Smith of Smith's Maple Products in Napanoch, New York, shares a few suggestions for quick recipes using maple syrup: A tablespoon of maple syrup in hot milk makes a delicious drink for cold weather. Try a tablespoon of maple syrup on a grapefruit half, and broil the fruit until the syrup is bubbly. It's a lovely start of the day and also makes a nice dessert. Scrub an apple and cut it in half. Take out the core, place a spoonful of syrup in the hollow, and bake until done to your liking. In the following recipe two native American products, beans and maple syrup, are combined.

SERVES *4–8, depending on the accompaniments*

PREPARATION TIME: *about 15 minutes*

SOAKING TIME: *1 hour*

BAKING TIME: *about 4 hours*

1	**pound navy beans**
1	**onion, cut in half**
5	**whole cloves**
1	**whole onion**
6	**slices bacon, cut in half**
⅓	**cup dark brown sugar**
½	**cup maple syrup, dark amber grade, plus some extra**
1	**teaspoon dry mustard, preferably Colman's**
1	**teaspoon salt or less**
¼	**teaspoon freshly ground pepper**

Wash and pick over the beans to remove small stones. In a large saucepan, place the beans with the onion halves and pour in enough water to cover them by 2 inches. Bring to a boil; boil 2 minutes. Remove from heat, cover, and let stand for 1 hour.

Drain and discard the onion. Fill the pan with an equal amount of fresh hot water and bring to a boil. Simmer the beans for about 20 to 30 minutes, or until partially done. Drain, but reserve cooking water.

In the meantime, preheat the oven to 250° F.

Stick the cloves in the whole onion and place it in a bean pot. Place a layer of beans on top. Add three bacon slices, then more beans, then the rest of the bacon slices, and top with a layer of beans.

In a small bowl, combine sugar, maple syrup, dry mustard, salt, and pepper, and stir in ½ cup of bean cooking water. Pour this mixture over the beans, cover the pot, and place in the middle of the oven. Bake for about 3½–4 hours. Uncover the pot in the last half hour to brown the top. Check that the beans do not cook dry. If you like, pour a little extra syrup on the beans before serving.

Maple Syrup Cake with Maple Butter Frosting

When the Westchester Exceptional Children's School in Purdys, New York, needed funds for air conditioning because the school is now open year-round, the staff put together a charming little cookbook as a fundraiser. The following recipe was contributed by Suzannne Della Corte, associate director of the school. This delicious cake uses one of the darker grades of maple syrup to best advantage.

SERVES *8 or more*

PREPARATION TIME: *5–10 minutes*

BAKING TIME: *35–40 minutes*

---

   2   *cups all-purpose flour*
   1   *tablespoon baking powder*
   ¾   *teaspoon salt*
   1   *cup maple syrup (preferably the darker
          grade B, or grade A amber syrup)*
   1   *cup heavy cream*
   2   *eggs, lightly beaten*
   ½   *stick (4 tablespoons) butter, melted*

Preheat oven to 350° F. Sift together flour, baking powder, and salt; set aside.

Mix together the syrup, cream, and eggs and add to the flour mixture. Beat well and stir in the butter. Turn into a 9-by-13-inch pan that has been greased and lined with wax paper. Bake 35–40 minutes. Cool on a rack. Serve with or without the following frosting.

MAPLE BUTTER FROSTING

½   stick (4 tablespoons) butter, softened
2   cups confectioners' sugar, or more
⅓   cup maple syrup

Cream the butter with two cups of sugar. Add the syrup and beat until creamy. Add more sugar if necessary to make a spreading consistency.

VEGETABLES, HERBS, AND EDIBLE FLOWERS

Asparagus, Ham, and Egg Platter

The Dutch make much of the ''primeurs'' of each season. My mother who, with the indomitable spirit that I so admire, always found something to celebrate, even on the drabbest, grayest day, would treat us in very early spring to the following dish. The object is to use only the finest and freshest ingredients. Use the best ham you can afford for this dish—Westphalian, if you can find it.

Hot asparagus, steamed or boiled
Cold ham, sliced as for sandwiches and
  rolled into cigar shapes
Hot hard-boiled eggs, peeled and sliced
  lengthwise
Melted butter
Small red-skinned potatoes, boiled in their
  skins

Chopped parsley
Fresh whole nutmeg

For each person use about ½ pound asparagus, ¼ pound ham and 1 egg. Arrange the asparagus, rolled ham slices, and hard-boiled egg halves attractively on a large platter. Sprinkle the potatoes with the parsley and serve separately. Set out a bowl of melted butter and pass a nutmeg grater for the asparagus and eggs.

Asparagus Marinara Sauce for Fettuccine

Ellen Todd is manager of the Greig Farm Market in Red Hook, New York, the only farm in the region that I know of where you can pick your own asparagus. Ellen puts together recipes as the farm's produce becomes available. In her asparagus marinara sauce, she combines a very light tomato sauce with crisp, sweet asparagus pieces. She warns that freshly picked asparagus are very tender, so cooking time should be ''drastically reduced.''

SERVES 2–3

PREPARATION TIME: *about 5 minutes*

COOKING TIME: *9–15 minutes, depending on the freshness of the asparagus*

2–3	tablespoons olive oil
2	cloves garlic, minced
2	cups canned crushed tomatoes
2	tablespoons fresh basil, chopped, or 1½ teaspoons dried basil
1	pound asparagus, cut into 1-inch pieces, tips separated
¼–½	cup dry white wine
	Sugar to taste
	Salt to taste
	Freshly ground pepper to taste

Freshly cooked fettuccine or other
pasta of your choice

Heat olive oil in a large skillet, add garlic, sauté for just a minute, then add crushed tomatoes and basil. Bring to a boil and simmer for about 5 minutes. Add cut asparagus but not tips. Steam the asparagus in the sauce until almost done to your liking, then add the tips. Cook a few minutes more. Do not overcook. Stir in white wine. Taste and add a touch of sugar if desired and salt and freshly ground pepper. Serve over hot pasta.

Asparagus Vinaigrette with Violets

When violets are blooming, use them to make a pretty spring asparagus dish. Flowers that are to be eaten should be picked carefully. Avoid flowers that grow on chemically treated lawns, and never pick those that grow on the sides of roads because they may be contaminated with lead deposits. Pick the violets, swish them through soapy water, then rinse them and remove all stems. Use them as follows.

PREPARATION TIME: *15 minutes; marinade: 1 hour*

COOKING TIME: *5 minutes for the asparagus and 9 minutes for the egg(s)*

    Steamed asparagus
    Vinaigrette dressing
1 *hard-boiled egg (if you have a large*
      quantity of asparagus, use two eggs)
    Handful of violets, cleaned as
      described above

Marinate the steamed asparagus for at least an hour in the vinaigrette dressing. Place in a bundle on a pretty platter. Peel the egg and separate yolk from white. Mash each separately. Carefully sprinkle them over the bundle of asparagus to create a yellow and white ribbon. Where they meet in the middle, carefully dot with violets. The purple ones are prettiest for this presentation.

Baked Fish with Yogurt and Chives

The little green sprouts of chives coming up in early March mean to me that it is time to make one of my favorite fish dishes. I cut off as many tops as possible. Chives like to be cut; after all, the Germans call them schnittlauch, *or cutting herb. Moreover, if I don't cut them, the deer will do the work for me. Chives have their own distinct onion flavor, but if you must substitute, use 3 scallions with their greens.*

SERVES 3–4

PREPARATION TIME: *3 minutes; marinade: 30 minutes*

COOKING TIME: *20 minutes*

---

1   **pound flounder, scrod, or similar fish fillets, rinsed**
    Salt to taste
    Freshly ground pepper to taste
1   **tablespoon butter, for greasing baking dish**
1   **tablespoon flour**
8   **ounces plain yogurt**
3   **tablespoons chives, or more, finely chopped**

Preheat the oven to 350° F.

Sprinkle the rinsed fillets with salt and pepper and place them in a buttered, ovenproof dish. Combine the flour, yogurt, and chives, reserving one teaspoon of chives for garnish. Pour the mixture over the fish. Allow dish to stand for 30 minutes for the flavors to marry.

Bake fish for 20 minutes, or until it flakes easily and the sauce is bubbly. Sprinkle with the reserved chives and serve. Boiled potatoes and cooked carrots, liberally sprinkled with chopped parsley, are a traditional accompaniment.

Blamensier (Chicken with Rice, Almonds and Violets)

Another dish with edible flowers is the recipe I created years ago for a medieval feast at the Harvey School in Katonah, New York. The classic forerunner of blancmange was not a sweet, creamy custard, as we know the dish now, but an almond porridge with pieces of chicken. My version of the yellow saffron-colored rice with chicken pieces, topped with whole toasted brown almonds and sprinkled with purple violets, is a delicious and handsome side dish for any spring meal. Later in the season other edible flowers may be used, such as chive blossoms or nasturtiums. This is a perfect dish for a buffet table. Warning: Not all flowers are edible; some, such as lilies of the valley, are toxic, so be sure to check edibility.

Flowers that are to be eaten should be picked carefully. Avoid flowers that grow on chemically treated lawns, and never pick those that grow on the sides of roads, because they may be contaminated with lead deposits. Pick the violets, swish them through soapy water, then rinse them and remove all stems. Use them as follows.

SERVES 4

PREPARATION TIME: *15–20 minutes*

COOKING TIME: *about 45 minutes*

One 2½–3-pound chicken
1 celery rib, cut into 3 pieces
1 carrot, scraped and cut in half lengthwise
1 medium onion, halved
1 cup brown rice
⅛ teaspoon powdered saffron, or saffron threads pulverized with a mortar and pestle
½ cup whole almonds
2 tablespoons butter or margarine

Salt to taste
Handful of purple violets

Place chicken in a large pot and pour in water to cover. Slowly bring to a boil and boil 2–3 minutes. Discard the water and rinse the chicken with cool water to remove any scum. Cover the chicken with fresh water. Add the celery, carrot, and onion and simmer until tender, about 40 minutes.

Remove the chicken, strain the broth through several layers of cheesecloth, and set aside. Skin the chicken and remove the meat from the bones. Cut the meat into small pieces and set aside.

Cook the rice according to package directions, substituting the chicken broth for water and adding saffron.

In the meantime, preheat the oven to 300° F. Spread the almonds on a baking sheet and toast them for 5–7 minutes, until light brown, and set them aside. When the rice is done, combine it with the chicken pieces and the butter; season to taste with salt. Reheat to warm the chicken pieces. Add the almonds, but reserve a few, and toss lightly. Strew violets and reserved almonds on top.

Broccoli di Rabe Sandwiches

Broccoli di rabe is an early vegetable. It is excellent quickly sautéed with garlic in oil and mixed with pasta and grated cheese. Or use it in the following sandwich.

SERVES 2

PREPARATION TIME: *5 minutes*

COOKING TIME: *about 12 minutes*

---

2   *tablespoons olive oil*
6-8   *ounces sweet Italian sausage*
2   *cloves sliced garlic*
1   *bunch broccoli di rabe, washed, most of the stems removed, and coarsely chopped*
2   *hero-style hard rolls*

Heat the oil and fry the sausage until cooked through. Remove to a plate and keep warm. Add the garlic, fry for a minute or so, then add the broccoli di rabe and cook until wilted. Slice the sausage and mix with the vegetable. Open up the rolls and divide the mixture between the two rolls.

Candying of Violets and Other Flowers

One of the joys of spring is to pick fragrant small bouquets of multihued violets. No wonder that, for centuries, people have also used these lovely little flowers, fresh or preserved, to enhance their foods.

King Louis XIV is said to have eaten salads strewn with violets. The Dutch, more interested in hearty foods, mixed violets with bacon drippings and spread the mixture on their bread for a colorful open-faced sandwich. Violets are not the only edible flowers: squash blossoms, chive blossoms, pansies, calendula, and nasturtiums are only a few of those that can be eaten. But others, such as lilies of the valley, are toxic, so be sure to check edibility. Some farms in the Hudson region—for example, Breezy Hill Orchard, in Staatsburg, New York—sell edible flowers.

Besides using flowers immediately in cookery, they can be preserved for later use by candying. Here are two ways of preserving violets. (Primroses, rose petals, and mint leaves are among other blooms and herbs that can be treated in this manner.)

Flowers that are to be eaten should be picked carefully. Avoid flowers that grow on chemically treated lawns, and never pick those that grow on the sides of roads because they may be contaminated with lead deposits. Pick the violets, swish them through soapy water, then rinse them and remove all stems. Use them as follows:

To candy violets with egg white and confectioners' sugar:

PREPARATION TIME: *20–30 minutes for 10 violets*

   Handful of violets, washed as indicated above
1 *egg white beaten with a teaspoon of water Confectioners' sugar*
1 *small paintbrush, such as those used for painting watercolors*

One at a time, dip the flowers into the beaten egg white and gently press them into confectioners' sugar to cover them completely. Brush off any excess sugar. Dry on a cake rack covered with a piece of wire mesh. Turn the flowers a few times as they are drying. For best results, dry them for at least 8 hours. Pack them between layers of tissue paper in an airtight box. Will keep several weeks.

To candy violets with gum arabic and superfine sugar:

PREPARATION TIME: *20–30 minutes for 10 violets*

---

1   *small paintbrush, such as those used for*
      painting watercolors
    Gum arabic (see note)
    Handful of violets
    Superfine sugar

Dip your paintbrush in the gum arabic and thoroughly coat all parts of the flower. Gently sprinkle fine sugar onto the coated flower. Shake off excess sugar and dry as described above. Pack them between layers of tissue paper in an air-tight box. Will keep 6-8 months.

NOTE: Gum arabic is sold in some pharmacies or can be obtained from pharmaceutical mail-order houses. If necessary, ask your pharmacist for help. It should be diluted with water until it is of the consistency of a medium-thick glue.

Peter's Beer Soup with Spinach, Cheese, and Sausage

Beer is my drink of choice, and I also like to cook with it. You can experiment with different beers for this soup; each will impart its own flavor. A bowl of this soup and some crusty bread make a light spring meal.

The Raccoon Saloon in Marlboro, New York, is an excellent place to try different beers. It boasts a beer menu with close to a hundred varieties. To the left of the cozy bar hang some photos that explain its name. Until twelve years ago, there was a hole in the wall of the barroom and raccoons would come to beg for their favorite handout: peanuts. Even now the raccoons come to visit. One of the regular customers saw two raccoons on the back porch, together with a woodchuck and a fox.

SERVES 4

PREPARATION TIME: *about 15–20 minutes*

COOKING TIME: *15 minutes*

---

   8   *ounces breakfast sausage*
1–2   *tablespoons vegetable oil*
   4   *scallions, finely chopped*
   1   *pound fresh spinach, washed, tough*
          stems removed, and coarsely chopped
  ¼   *cup flour*
   2   *cups skim milk*
   1   *cup or more full-bodied beer (see note)*
   8   *ounces grated cheddar cheese*
      Salt and freshly ground pepper to taste

Cut the sausage into small pieces and brown in a pan that is large enough to hold the soup. Drain and set the sausage aside.

Heat the oil in the same pan. Add the scallions and cook for 3 minutes, then add the chopped spinach. Cook and stir until the spinach is wilted. Add the sausage. Sprinkle the mixture with the flour. Slowly add the skim milk, stirring continuously.

If you need to hold the soup, prepare it up to this point. When ready to serve, add the beer. Bring the soup to a boil. Add the cheese and cook until it has melted. Taste and season with salt and pepper. Serve immediately.

NOTE: Try Molson Gold—or the local Albany Amber, for a different flavor.

Radish Salad

•.

The pepperiness of radish disappears when it is marinated in the following honey mixture. You will see, they will taste like water chestnuts and add a lovely crunch and pink color to a salad.

SERVES 4

PREPARATION TIME: *5–10 minutes; marinade: 30 minutes*

---

  2 **bunches red radishes**
  ¼ **cup herb vinegar, preferably basil vinegar**
  2 **tablespoons honey**
  ½ **teaspoon dried ground ginger**
  2 **tablespoons minced parsley**

Wash and thinly slice the radishes; place in a small bowl. Combine the other ingredients, except the parsley, add 1 tablespoon water, and pour over the radishes. Stir to combine. Marinate for half an hour, then add the parsley. Serve on lettuce leaves, torn into bite-sized pieces.

Reuben Soup

•.

Arleen and Samuel Harkins of the Village Diner in Red Hook, New York, gave me the next recipe. The diner is on the National Register of Historic Places as an intact example of the type of streamlined, stainless-steel diner—modeled after railroad cars—introduced in the 1920s and manufactured until 1950. The inside is more that of a luncheonette than a plush railroad car. It has retained most of its original decor, such as tile floors and wainscoting, in the then popular color scheme of turquoise and black. Arleen Harkins told me that her Reuben Soup, based on the ingredients for the sandwich of pumpernickel bread spread with mustard and filled with corned beef, sauerkraut, and melted Swiss cheese, is one of their most popular winter dishes. It is a perfect recipe, of course, for the leftovers from a St. Patrick's day dinner, which is why it is included in this chapter on the early spring. I adapted it to family size.

•.•.•.•.•.•.•.•.

SERVES 4–6

PREPARATION TIME: *about 10 minutes*

COOKING TIME: *15–20 minutes*

½ stick (4 tablespoons) butter or margarine
½ cup chopped onions
⅓ cup chopped green pepper
1½ tablespoons Dijon mustard
⅓ pound cooked corned beef, shredded
¼ pound sauerkraut, rinsed, drained,
    and chopped
½ teaspoon freshly ground black pepper
½ teaspoon caraway seed (optional)
6 tablespoons flour
5 cups canned beef broth, or the equivalent
    amount of homemade broth, or the
    broth from cooking the corned beef
1 cup shredded Swiss cheese, or more
    Croutons (optional)
    Pumpernickel bread and butter

In a large saucepan or Dutch oven, melt the butter and fry the onion and pepper until tender. Add the mustard, corned beef, sauerkraut, pepper and caraway seeds, if used, and the flour. Stir to combine thoroughly, then slowly stir in the broth to make a smooth sauce. Simmer for about 10 minutes, stirring occasionally. Stir in Swiss cheese and heat until the cheese melts. Serve hot, topped with croutons if desired or accompanied by pumpernickel bread and butter.

Sorrel Soup

It is March; there is a stack of seed catalogues on the side of my desk and I have spring fever. I am anxious to eat something green and fresh from the garden. When I go out to check if perchance the sorrel has come up, I find that, in spite of a dusting of snow, some small green blades are hiding under a covering of last year's dry leaves. There are enough little leaves to give me the two handfuls I need for the following soup. Later in the summer I will add sorrel to our salads and use it in other ways. Sorrel is available from farms in the region in the summertime. To everyone in my household, however, that first small bowl of sorrel soup is the sign that spring is coming.

SERVES 4

PREPARATION AND COOKING TIME: *about 8 minutes*

½ stick *(4 tablespoons) butter*
¼ *cup flour*
1 *quart (4 cups) milk*
2 *large handfuls sorrel (about 4 ounces)*
   Salt to taste
   Freshly ground pepper to taste

Melt the butter in a saucepan; add the flour. Stir with a whisk. Add the milk a little at a time while stirring. Bring to a boil and cook for 2 minutes to remove the raw flour taste. Add the sorrel and cook for 30 seconds more, just enough to wilt the leaves. Sorrel turns a grayish color when cooked too long. Taste and season with salt and pepper.

VARIATION

If you do not like flour in soups, try this alternative: peel and dice two large potatoes. Fry the pieces lightly in butter (this is done to give the soup rich flavor, but this step can be omitted). Cook the potato pieces in the 4 cups of milk until they are very tender. Purée the mixture in a blender or food processor. Return to the pan, heat through, then add the sorrel and cook for 30 seconds more, just enough to wilt the leaves. Serve with a warm loaf of French bread and butter.

2. Late Spring

 The subjects of the late spring chapter are fish, fruits, and vegetables.

Fish

This is the season when river fishermen cast their nets for female sturgeon, whose bellies are heavy with "Hudson caviar." In June 1991, 14 ounces of caviar sold for $87.50 wholesale, and retailed in some stores, including Neiman Marcus in White Plains, New York, for $119 per 7-ounce container. At 140 calories an ounce, these are expensive calories. Male sturgeon (bulls) are sold for their meat, as are the females (cows) once the caviar is removed.

Two kinds of sturgeon can be found in the Hudson. The short-nose, which is on the endangered species list, and the longnose, or Atlantic, sturgeon, which may not be kept if it is under 4 feet long. Sturgeon was once so popular and so abundant that it was called "Albany beef."

Fruits

Rhubarb, strawberries, gooseberries, and currants are some of the fruits of this season. While pick-your-own farms and farm stands are wonderful sources for berries, the most romantic and exciting way to obtain them is to find them in the wild. Have you ever picked enough juicy wild berries for a pie? You'll probably be scratched and a bit dirty by the time you come home with your bounty, but you won't forget that pie for a while.

Vegetables

Peas, broccoli, and greens make up the vegetable harvest of the late spring. We all know what peas and broccoli look like, but many of the greens grown in the Hudson region are not quite so familiar. Furthermore, because people eat less meat now, the salad, anointed with a flavored vinegar and virgin olive oil, has become an even more important component of the meal. In New York City restaurants, you will be served salads made with a large variety of greens and sometimes edible flowers, delivered to them washed and ready to be put on the plate by Hudson region growers. Vince D'Attolico, the "lettuce king," grows forty different varieties of lettuce, plus sixty or so other vegetables, in the black dirt of Pine Island, New York. He tells his customers to use them in salads or to sauté briefly chopped greens, such as broccoli di rabe or Swiss chard, in olive oil and garlic and mix them into pasta.

Native American Customs

For Native Americans, June is "strawberry month." In one of his classes, He Who Stands Firm stressed the importance of berries, particularly strawberries, to the Native Americans. Berries were preserved by drying over fire: straw-covered racks were placed over a small fire, high enough so that the straw would not burn. Berries were placed on top of the straw and dried. Blueberries and elderberries were especially popular for drying. Dried berries were mixed with other ingredients and baked into breads and used in other ways to augment the diet.

He Who Stands Firm explained that strawberries were also eaten fresh or made into a drink. Important and complex ceremonies were held at strawberry time in the context of the longhouse. They were essentially rites of thanksgiving for Mother Earth's bounty. In a prayer to Grandfather (the Creator) medicine man Little Tree reveals how June is a time for rejoicing:

This is strawberry time; berry-picking time. This brings a lot of happiness into our homes. Our children pick the berries and they get all excited and they start laughing and giggling and that brings a warmth to our heart, a warmth that we forgot and we thank the Creator for this.

RECIPES FEATURING:

Fish
Baked Sturgeon
Fried Sturgeon
Smoked Sturgeon with Horseradish Cream

Fruits
Berries
Cherry Bounce
Currant Syrup
Gooseberry Fool
Rhubarb-Pear Chutney
Rhubarb Bread
Rhubarb-Strawberry Pie
Rice Balls with Fruit
Sour Cherry Dessert
Strawberry Cream Pie
Strawberry Daiquiris
Mother's Strawberry Punch
Shortcake Biscuits

Vegetables
Beef and Beer Stew with Fresh Peas
Broccoli Slaw
Pea and Peapod Quiche

FISH

Baked Sturgeon

▪▪▪

I like sturgeon best baked whole, or in large pieces, with the skin on. When the fish is cooked, the crocodile-like skin can easily be cut away and the firm pieces of fish cut off the bone and into serving-sized pieces. It is a very dense fish and therefore takes a long time to cook through. Leftover baked sturgeon is delicious in a fish salad, flavored with curry powder.

SERVES *at least 6*

PREPARATION TIME: *5–10 minutes*

BAKING TIME: *45–60 minutes*

---

 1 *teaspoon freshly grated nutmeg*
 ½ *teaspoon cinnamon*
1½ *teaspoons salt*
 ½ *teaspoon freshly ground pepper*
 1 *piece sturgeon, about 5 pounds, with the*
       skin on and split open lengthwise,
       bone-in
 5 *tablespoons butter*

Preheat the oven to 375° F.

In a small dish, combine the nutmeg, cinnamon, salt, and pepper. Rub the mixture onto the exposed flesh (but not the skin). Place pats of butter all along the middle of the split fish and place the fish in a baking dish. Bake uncovered for about 45–60 minutes, or until opaque all the way through. It might be necessary to cut into the fish to check doneness. Cut away the skin and cut into serving pieces.

Fried Sturgeon

The most common way to prepare sturgeon, it seems, is to prepare it like fried breaded veal cutlets, although I far prefer it baked. But because it is a Hudson region classic, I have created my own directions for fried sturgeon, which I put together by trying the methods of various fishermen.

SERVES 3–4

PREPARATION TIME: *about 10 minutes*

FRYING TIME: *about 5–10 minutes, depending on the thickness of the slice*

> 1 **pound sliced sturgeon**
>   **Milk**
> ½ **cup flour**
> 1 **egg, lightly beaten with 1 tablespoon**
>   **water**
> ½ **cup toasted bread crumbs**
>   **Salt to taste**
>   **Freshly ground pepper to taste**
>   **Freshly grated nutmeg, to taste**
> ¼ **cup minced parsley**
>   **Oil for frying**

In a shallow container, place the sturgeon slices in one layer and pour on milk to cover. Soak for 30 minutes. Remove and let the slices drip-dry for a moment, then lightly pat dry with a paper towel. Place the flour in a pie plate or other flat dish. Dip the slices in the flour and shake off the excess. Place the egg and water in another flat dish and dip the slices in the mixture. In a third flat dish, mix the bread crumbs, salt, pepper, nutmeg, and parsley. Dip the sturgeon slices in the mixture and shake off the excess. You want a light coating. Heat oil in a frying pan and fry the slices quickly, about 2–3 minutes on each side, or until the fish is lightly browned and its flesh opaque. Serve with lemon wedges.

Smoked Sturgeon with Horseradish Cream

•:•.•

Sturgeon is smoked by some of the people who fish for it and by the region's smokehouses, and the result, served with horseradish cream, makes a perfect spring appetizer.

Add 1 tablespoon prepared horseradish sauce to ½ cup cream, whipped with a touch of salt.

FRUITS

Berries

Joe and Beth Gilbert are the dedicated owners of the Berry Farm in Chatham, New York. They not only have strawberry fields where you can pick your own, but also grow blueberries, blackberries, fall raspberries, grapes, and lesser-known berry varieties such as black, purple, yellow, and red raspberries; red, white, and black currants; and red and green gooseberries.

All berries are delicious by themselves. Some might need a little sugar; others are fine without. They can be baked in a flaky crust, topped with crème fraîche or yogurt, ladled over ice cream or around pudding, or heaped on top of your favorite chocolate torte—to mention just a few possibilities. Furthermore, they can be used in cold fruit soups, muffins, quick breads, and grunts, and when there are too many of them at once, preserved in jams, jellies, syrups, and brandies.

Berries keep better if left unwashed and not hulled until needed. Keep them in the refrigerator, uncovered. When ready to use, float them in small batches in cold water. Very gently rinse off the dust and remove them carefully from the water. Then hull them or stem them gently so that as little juice as possible is lost. To freeze berries, put them on trays in the freezer and when they are hard, pack them in resealable bags. If they are clean, berries such as blueberries or currants can be frozen dry in rigid freezer containers; that way you can easily take out what you need. I prefer to freeze strawberries sprinkled with a little sugar.

•:•.•:•.•:•.•:•.•:•.•

Cherry Bounce

From the files of Alice Delafield Livingston, of Clermont, in Germantown, New York, a descendant of the Robert R. Livingston who was one of the five drafters of the Declaration of Independence comes the following recipe for cherries in rum. It is a nice way to preserve some of that short cherry season for a later date. The drink is easy to make and adds bounce to your step!

MAKES: *about 1½ quarts*

PREPARATION TIME: *30 minutes*

STANDING TIME: *1 week plus another 6 weeks after the Bounce has been prepared*

---

5 *pounds sweet cherries*
1 *quart rum*
  Brown sugar

Wash and stem cherries. The original recipe says to place them in a basin and crush them with a rolling pin; I found it was easier to crush them between my fingers. Pour the rum over them and let them stand 1 week. Stir them every day. After 1 week, strain them into a bottle or screw-top jar that has been rinsed with boiling water. Measure the juice, and add sugar in proportion; for every gallon of juice add ¾ pound brown sugar. Allow the Bounce to stand 6 weeks before serving. I keep it in the refrigerator—it is very nice cold or poured over ice cubes.

Currant Syrup

Red currants are an old-fashioned fruit, vastly popular at one time, when Ulster County was the leading currant grower. When we have eaten our fill of fresh currants, sprinkled with some sugar, I pick the rest of them and make currant syrup to freeze or to use during the summer months. Currants are removed from their stem by putting a fork at the top and pulling downward, pushing the berries off the little side stems. It is a bit of a job, so invite a friend over; the work will go much quicker when you have someone to talk to! When I serve them for dessert, I let my guests destem their own.

Currant Syrup is delicious poured over custard, vanilla ice cream, or a fresh fruit salad. You can also use it as a drink: Put a small amount of syrup in a glass, add a couple of ice cubes, and fill the glass with soda water. Or add a little syrup to a glass of lemonade.

PREPARATION TIME: *depends on the amount of currants you are using*

COOKING TIME: *10–15 minutes*

> **Currants, washed and stemmed**
> **Water**
> **Sugar**

Weigh the stemmed currants and use one-quarter of their weight in sugar. In a large saucepan, add the currants, the sugar, and enough water to come halfway up the currants in the pan. Bring to a boil and boil gently for about 10–15 minutes, until the currants are very tender. Place a large sieve in a bowl and pour the currants into the sieve. Press down on the fruit with a wooden spoon to extract every bit of juice. Cool and taste; add more sugar if necessary.

Gooseberry Fool

▪▪

Gooseberries are another old-fashioned fruit. I like them best cooked and made into a fool. Trust me, there is nothing foolish about this dessert. It is utterly delicious. An added advantage is that you can avoid the chore of tipping and toeing (taking the tips and the little stems off) the berries, since the berries are sieved after they have been cooked. The gooseberry purée freezes well for later use. You can make a fool out of any berry.

SERVES *4–6*

PREPARATION TIME: *2 minutes*

COOKING TIME: *about 15 minutes*

> **About 4 cups gooseberries, washed**
> **About 1 cup sugar, depending on the**
>   **ripeness of the berries**
> **1** **cup heavy cream, whipped**

In a medium saucepan combine the gooseberries, sugar, and ¼ cup water. Bring to a boil and gently boil for about 15 minutes, until the berries are very soft. Place a sieve in a bowl and pour in the berries. Press down very hard with a wooden spoon to extract every bit of the juice and pulp. Chill the purée. Just before serving, fold the purée into the whipped cream. Serve in old-fashioned flat champagne glasses with a plain butter cookie as accompaniment.

Rhubarb-Pear Chutney

Ken Migliorelli has a 50-acre farm in Tivoli, New York, where he grows arugula, Swiss chard, kale, collard greens, mustard greens, and a variety of other greens, as well as herbs and rhubarb. He sells his produce at the Greenmarket farmers markets in New York City. Here is a recipe for a tangy chutney made with rhubarb and firm pears. Warning: Rhubarb leaves, full of oxalic acid, are toxic and should not be eaten.

MAKES   *about 1 pint*

PREPARATION TIME: *about 15 minutes*

COOKING TIME: *about 45 minutes*

1	*pound rhubarb, cut into 1-inch pieces*
4	*firm pears, peeled, cored, and chopped*
1	*cup dried currants or raisins*
1	*cup chopped onion*
1	*cup chopped red sweet pepper*
1	*cup firmly packed dark brown sugar*
1	*cup cider vinegar*
1	*tablespoon cinnamon*
1½	*tablespoons finely minced or grated fresh ginger*
1	*teaspoon salt*
1	*teaspoon dried red pepper flakes*

Combine all ingredients in a heavy saucepan. Bring to a boil over moderate heat; lower heat and simmer, stirring often, for about 45 minutes, until the chutney thickens. Cool. Rinse container with boiling water. Spoon into container and refrigerate, or freeze for later use.

Rhubarb Bread

This recipe comes from Mary Film of Buskirk, New York. Mary is an inveterate baker, but for not herself. She bakes for a cause: the restoration of the old Knickerbocker Mansion in Schatigcoke. The Mansion, located in a valley known for centuries as the ''vale of peace,'' is listed on the National Register of Historic Places. Started in 1709 and not completed until 1770, it stands near the spot where the Witenagemot Oak was planted in 1676 as a symbol of peace between local Indian tribes, the Dutch, the English, and the French. Washington Irving transformed the Knickerbocker name into a household word with the writing of his Knickerbocker History of New York.

So far, the small restoration committee has managed to save the mansion from destruction and has restored it to the point where it is structurally sound, an impressive accomplishment for an organization run entirely by volunteers. No doubt they will go on with their bake sales—such as the one last Christmas, for which they baked hundreds of pies—until the mansion is restored to its eighteenth-century splendor. Mary Film's rhubarb bread, with its contrasting tastes of tart and sweet, is always a popular item at the bake table.

MAKES *two 9-inch loaves*

PREPARATION TIME: *about 12–15 minutes*

BAKING TIME: *1 hour*

1½	cups light brown sugar
1	egg
⅔	cup oil
1	cup buttermilk
1	teaspoon vanilla extract
2½	cups flour
1	teaspoon salt
1	teaspoon baking soda
2	cups thin rhubarb stalks, cut into ½-inch pieces; if stalks are thick, cut in half lengthwise
½	cup chopped nuts

TOPPING

½ cup sugar
1 tablespoon butter or margarine
½ teaspoon cinnamon

Preheat the oven to 350° F. Stir together brown sugar, egg, oil, buttermilk, and vanilla. Add flour, salt, and baking soda and stir until completely combined. Gently stir in the rhubarb and nuts. Spoon into two greased 9-inch loaf pans. Combine the topping ingredients and sprinkle the topping on the loaves. Bake for 1 hour, or until a toothpick inserted in the center comes out clean. Remove and cool on a rack.

Rhubarb-Strawberry Pie

Rhubarb was long known as the "pie plant," and the classic rhubarb strawberry pie captures the essence of spring. Warning: Rhubarb leaves, full of oxalic acid, are toxic and should not be eaten.

SERVES 6

PREPARATION TIME: *about 15 minutes*

BAKING TIME: *about 55 minutes*

---

1 pound rhubarb, cut into ½-inch pieces
1 pound strawberries, washed, hulled, and
    cut in half
¼ cup flour
¾ cup sugar
1 egg, lightly beaten
1 unbaked 9-inch pie shell

Preheat the oven to 425° F.
In a large bowl combine the rhubarb, strawberries, flour, sugar,

and egg. Line a 9-inch pie plate with the pastry and flute it in such a way that it stands up about ½ inch above the rim. Spoon in the fruit mixture. Place the pie plate on a baking sheet to catch possible spills. Bake for 10 minutes, then reduce the heat to 350° F and bake for about 45 minutes longer, or until the crust is browned and the filling is bubbly. Cool.

Rice Balls with Fruit

I found this recipe in the handwritten cookbook of Eliza Cruger, dated January 1829, in the archives of Boscobel Restoration, Inc. The mansion, an outstanding example of New York Federal domestic architecture, stands high above the river in Garrison-on-Hudson, New York. It was moved to this location when the house was threatened with destruction during the 1950s. Although the title of the recipe is a bit offputting, the actual recipe is quite charming. Round, molded individual little rice puddings, made in teacups, are stuck with sliced almonds to resemble little hedgehogs. The puddings are surrounded with lightly sugared berries. Do try to find rosewater, widely used before vanilla became in fashion. It can be purchased in some gourmet stores and pharmacies.

SERVES 6

PREPARATION TIME: *10–15 minutes*

COOKING TIME: *about 20 minutes*

---

   1   *cup short-grain rice*
1½ *cups whole milk*
   1   *stick cinnamon, about 2 inches long*
 ⅓ *cup sugar*
   3   *egg yolks, beaten*
 ¾ *teaspoon rosewater (substitute: vanilla*
       extract)
      Sliced toasted almonds
      Sugared strawberries, raspberries, or
        other berries, for garnish

In a small saucepan bring the rice, the milk, ½ cup water, the cinnamon stick, and the sugar to a boil. Reduce the heat and gently cook for about 15 minutes, or until the rice is done and very thick. Stir in the egg yolks and cook for a few minutes more while stirring. Be sure to keep the heat low. Remove from the heat and stir in the rosewater. Divide the mixture among 6 round rinsed teacups. Chill in the refrigerator. When ready to serve, unmold the little puddings and stick them all over with the sliced almonds to make them resemble hedgehogs. Surround the base of each pudding with the sugared berries.

Sour Cherry Dessert

From the farm kitchen of Helen Kent in Milton, New York, comes the following recipe for a sour cherry dessert. On their 60 acres, the Kents grow apples, quince, cherries, raspberries, plums, peaches, and pears, and sell them on the Greenmarket farmers markets in New York City. This is a nice, homey family dessert and a good way to use up canned or frozen sour cherries. If you want to use fresh cherries, briefly cook them; then incorporate them in the recipe.

SERVES *8*

PREPARATION TIME: *5 minutes*

BAKING TIME: *35 minutes*

---

   1   **cup sugar**
   1   **egg**
   2   **tablespoons butter, melted**
   1   **cup drained sour cherries**
   1   **cup flour**
   1   **teaspoon baking soda**
  ½   **cup chopped walnuts**
       About 1 cup cherry juice
   1   **teaspoon cornstarch mixed with 1 tablespoon water**
  ½   **pint heavy cream, whipped with a little sugar to taste**

Preheat the oven to 350° F.

Mix together the sugar, egg, and melted butter. Add the cherries and stir in the flour, baking soda, and nuts. Spoon into a greased 8-inch-square pan and bake for 35 minutes, or until a knife inserted comes out clean. Let cool.

In a small saucepan, heat the cherry juice until boiling. Stir in the cornstarch mixture and stir until lightly thickened. Remove. When the cake is cooled, spread the top with whipped cream and drizzle with the cherry juice. Serve the dessert cut into 2-by-4-inch pieces.

Strawberry Cream Pie

If you want to do just a little more than serve strawberries and cream, serve them together in the following pie. Give everyone a fork and spoon. The cream sets lightly, but not quite as much as a custard.

SERVES *6–8*

PREPARATION TIME: *about 15 minutes*

BAKING TIME: *about 55 minutes*

---

1 *quart fresh strawberries, washed and hulled*
½ *cup sugar, or more*
¼ *cup flour*
1 *unbaked 9-inch pie shell, fitted into a 10-inch pie plate*
1 *cup heavy cream*

Preheat the oven to 425° F.

Combine the strawberries, sugar, and flour. Put them into the pie shell; pour the cream over them. Bake for 10 minutes, then reduce to 350° F and bake for 45 minutes, until lightly set.

Strawberry Daiquiris

When we go strawberry picking at Greig Farm in Red Hook each year, we time it in such a way that we can pick sugar snap peas as well. The day after picking, we call our friends to come for an impromptu party, at which we serve daiquiris, fresh peas with a good dip, and two or three different Hudson region goat cheeses with bread and crackers. It's easy and everybody loves to get our ''strawberry call!'' Frozen strawberries may also be used, without thawing, for the daiquiris.

MAKES *at least 6 good strong drinks*

PREPARATION TIME: *5–10 minutes*

- 3 *cups ice cubes*
- 2 *ample cups strawberries, washed and hulled*
- ¼ *cup sugar*
   Juice of 1 lemon
- 6 *ounces light rum*

Combine all ingredients in a blender and blend until slushy. They can be thinned by adding more crushed ice. Serve in champagne glasses.

Mother's Strawberry Punch

Use very nice, ripe strawberries for the following punch. Add a plain cake and some good chocolates to the menu, polish your prettiest crystal glasses, sweep the patio and place candles everywhere, invite your best friends, and have a dessert party on one of those flower-scented, moonlit evenings in June. You can cut the ingredients in half for a smaller group.

MAKES *32–36 four-ounce glasses*

PREPARATION TIME: *about 20 minutes*

COOLING AND MACERATING TIME: *all day*

---

2 quarts small strawberries, washed
    and hulled
  About 2 cups sugar, or less, depending on
    the sweetness of the berries
4 750 ml bottles Mosel wine
2 750 ml bottles slightly sweet Champagne
2 ounces cognac (optional)

In the morning, clean the strawberries and put them in a large punch bowl; layer them with the sugar as you go along. Pour one bottle of Mosel wine over the mixture. Let it rest in the refrigerator for the entire day. Put the other bottles in the refrigerator to cool. When ready to serve, add the other bottles of wine and Champagne and, if you like a potent drink, the cognac. Stir carefully so you don't crush the berries.

Shortcake Biscuits

Strawberry shortcake, freshly made, spells spring. This biscuit recipe comes from Eleanor Smith of Tuthilltown Grist Mill and County Store in Gardiner, New York. The mill is on the National Register of Historic Places and has been in constant operation for nearly two centuries. Except for some minor modifications, it stands today as it was built in 1788 in a romantic spot on the Shawangunk River.

The Tuthilltown Mill is the only mill in the United States that makes the Ultra Holy Flour for Passover matzohs, which must be made on stones, as in the days of Moses. The flour is shipped all over the world. The adjacent country store sells all kinds of flour, including their own milled all-purpose flour, cracked wheat, cornmeal and flour, pastry flour, and other products, such as a large variety of spices, fruits, and nuts, and baked products.

MAKES 12 2-inch biscuits (a 1¾-inch cutter will make 16 biscuits; a 1½-inch cutter will make 24 biscuits)

PREPARATION TIME: *about 15 minutes*

BAKING TIME: *12 to 15 minutes*

2   *cups sifted all-purpose flour*
2   *teaspoons baking powder*
½   *teaspoon salt*
4   *tablespoons butter or oil*
1   *egg*
¾   *cup milk*

Preheat oven to 450° F.

Combine flour, baking powder, and salt and sift together. With two knives or a pastry blender, cut in the butter, or stir in the oil.

Combine the egg with the milk and slowly stir the mixture into the dry ingredients until a soft dough is formed.

Turn out onto a lightly floured board and knead 30 seconds, or enough to shape. Roll or pat out the dough to a thickness of ½-inch and cut with a 2-inch floured biscuit cutter. Bake on an ungreased baking sheet for 12 to 15 minutes.

VEGETABLES

Beef and Beer Stew with Fresh Peas

Use a New Amsterdam ale or amber, Albany Amber, a Brooklyn Lager, or another beer of your liking for the following beer stew. Each beer will impart its own taste. Fresh peas are essential for the success of the dish. It has a flavor reminiscent of sauerbraten but uses less expensive stew beef cubes rather than pot roast. If the sauce becomes too thick after the bread with mustard is added, just pour in a little more beer and allow the stew to cook a little longer. Serve it with new potatoes, dressed with plenty of chopped parsley, and a medley of spring greens for a salad.

SERVES 6

PREPARATION TIME: *15–20 minutes*

COOKING TIME: *about 1 hour and 45 minutes*

---

2 pounds very lean beef stew meat, cut
      into cubes
   Shortening
   Salt to taste
   Freshly ground black pepper to taste
1 large onion, chopped
1 tablespoon flour
12 ounces beer
2 tablespoons brown sugar, dissolved in
      2 tablespoons vinegar
½ teaspoon dried thyme
2 bay leaves
1 thick slice pumpernickel bread, thickly
      spread with a prepared mustard
2 cups fresh peas, cooked just until tender

Brown the meat in the shortening. Season with the salt and pepper and remove from the pan. Add the onion to the pan and brown lightly, then sprinkle it with the flour. Stir to combine. Add the beer. Add the sugar-and-vinegar mixture, thyme, and bay leaves and return the meat to the pan. Simmer for 1½ hours or until the beef is very tender.

Add the bread slice. Cook until the bread is dissolved in the liquid and the sauce is thick. If the sauce seems too thick, add more beer and cook a few minutes longer. Just before serving, stir in the fresh peas.

Broccoli Slaw

The Cornell Cooperative Extension of Westchester created this broccoli slaw recipe with a low-calorie yogurt dressing some years ago. It is an excellent example of the kind of good common-sense recipes extension offices in the region distribute.

SERVES 6

PREPARATION TIME: *about 10–15 minutes*

COOKING TIME: *3–5 minutes*

2   cups broccoli florets, steamed for
       3–5 minutes
½   cup grated carrot
¼   cup finely chopped onion
½   cup plain yogurt
2   teaspoons sugar
2   teaspoons lemon juice
2   tablespoons prepared oil-and-vinegar
       dressing
2   tablespoons finely minced celery leaves

In a large bowl, combine the broccoli, carrot, and onion. In a small bowl, combine the yogurt, sugar, lemon juice, salad dressing, and celery leaves. Mix well. Pour the yogurt dressing over the vegetables and toss to coat.

Pea and Peapod Quiche

Peas and snow peas naturally mix well, as the following tart or quiche recipe proves. Served by itself, or with a fried or grilled pork chop, it makes a simple, seasonal dinner

SERVES 4

PREPARATION TIME: *about 15 minutes*

BAKING TIME: *about 50 minutes*

1   unbaked 9-inch pie shell
1½ cups coarsely grated young
        Gouda cheese
6   ounces peapods, tipped, strings
        removed
10 ounces shelled fresh peas, briefly
        cooked to almost tender (or the
        equivalent amount of frozen
        tiny peas)

½   cup chopped flat-leaf parsley
2   tablespoons cornstarch
½–1   teaspoon salt
    Freshly ground pepper to taste
1½   cups half-and-half
3   eggs, lightly beaten
    Handful of grated Parmesan cheese

Preheat the oven to 450° F.

Line a 10-inch deep-dish pie plate with the pastry. Prick all over with a fork and bake for 10 minutes until lightly browned. Remove from the oven and reduce the heat to 375° F.

Line the pastry shell with the Gouda cheese. In a small bowl, combine peapods, peas, and parsley. Top the cheese with this mixture. In the same bowl, combine the cornstarch, salt, and pepper; gradually stir in the half-and-half until smooth; then add the eggs and stir until well blended. Carefully pour onto the peas-and-cheese mixture. Top with the grated Parmesan. Bake for 35–40 minutes, until the filling has set. Serve as suggested above.

3. Summer

The subjects of the summer chapter are crab, foods for warm-weather occasions, and menus for a picnic along the Hudson, a sail on the Hudson, and a moonlight dinner on the patio.

Crab

Summer is the season for crabs. According to Christopher Letts on a most informative poster he created for the Hudson River Foundation, "the shallow and slightly salty waters of the tidal wetlands in the lower fifty miles of the river provide the essential sheltering and feeding grounds that make the Hudson River crabs the stuff of legend." Crabs are caught on baited lines and in traps in 6 to 25 feet of water. Fresh fish or chicken parts are commonly used for bait. You can catch up to fifty crabs a day for your own use without a permit. If you catch more, you are considered a commercial crabber and will need a permit.

Keep the captured crabs out of the sun, wrap them in burlap and hold them on ice until you are ready to cook them. This will also numb them and make them easier to handle. Hardshell crabs should be cooked alive. If you do not have a seafood steamer, use any appropriately sized pot and place a colander or trivet inside it. Fill the bottom of the pot with about 2 inches of water. Add vinegar and salt if you wish. Bring the water to a boil. Add the live crabs in layers. Sprinkle seafood seasoning between the layers. Cover tightly and steam about 30 minutes. Serve them hot, or chill in the refrigerator for later use.

For safe crab cooking and eating, make sure that the cooked crabs do not come into contact with live crabs or with the surfaces with which live crabs have been in contact. Be sure to discard the water in which you have cooked the crabs; use fresh water for each batch. The New York Department of Health recommends that the viscera (the yellowish part that constitutes the liver and pancreas) of Hudson River crabs not be eaten. They further recommend that no more than six Hudson River blue crabs be eaten per week.

Christopher Letts gives the following step-by-step instructions on how to dismantle a cooked crab:

1. Break off the claws and set aside.
2. Pull off the top shell. To do this, hold the backfin with one hand. Using the index finger of your other hand or a knife, pry the shell off.
3. Once the shell is off, scrape away the "devil's fingers," or gills (the grayish-white feathery material), from both sides of the crab.
4. Cut out the face, using a sharp knife. Dislodge viscera (yellowish matter) and discard.
5. Slice laterally across the top of the remaining shell. Using the knife, lift out the compartmental lumps of white crabmeat.
6. Now take the claws. With a knife or mallet, crack their shell all the way around. Using two hands, pull away the shell by tugging at either end.

Foods for Warm-Weather Occasions

In summer, the living is indeed easy in the Hudson region. Swimming, sailing, boating, fishing, canoeing, rafting, tubing, hiking, camping, horseback riding, kite flying, hang-gliding—there are too many activities to choose from to mention them all! In case you wondered whether the Hudson is safe enough to swim in, let me tell you the story of Skip Storch. In August 1991, this marathon swimmer swam the length of the Hudson and became the first swimmer to cover the 153 miles from Albany to the Statue of Liberty in New York Harbor. It took him 54 hours and 50 minutes, divided among seven days. Other than the waters immediately adjacent to the City, he found the Hudson safe for swimming; judging from the big grin he shows in the picture taken by a regional paper, he seems to have enjoyed his trip.

Native American Customs

Native Americans gathered plants, roots, and berries as well as great quantities of fish and shellfish throughout the summer and fall. Late July was the Green Corn Time, according to Peggy Turco, who studied with He Who Stands Firm. She notes in her article on ''Indian Life on the Hudson River'' that at that time ''the gardens began to be harvested and the Corn Mother was celebrated with thankfulness.''

RECIPES FEATURING:

Crab
Martha Washington's Crab Soup
Phyllis Lake's Hudson River Crab Cakes
Tom Lake's Hudson River Crab Salad

Warm-Weather Foods
Basil Rotini Salad
Barley with Peppers and Tomatoes
Cadet Mess Pasta Salad
Corn, Cheese, and Potato Skillet
Gail's Granola
Grilled Vegetables
Herb-Flavored Oil for Grilling Vegetables
Pasta Supreme
Soldiers' Salad

A Picnic Along the Hudson
Curried Turkey and Water Chestnut Salad Sandwiches
Shaker Gingerbread

A Sail on the Hudson
Cucumber Basil Salad
Seashells with Vegetables
Applesauce Cakes

A Moonlight Dinner on the Patio
Cold Melon Soup
Beef Ribbons with Ginger and Lime
Rice and Black Bean Salad
Salad of Hudson Region Lettuces, Greens, and Edible Flowers
Caledonia Ice with Chocolate Sauce

Summer Drinks
Lemonade
Lemon Balm Lemonade
Norman's Dream

CRAB

Martha Washington's Crab Soup

In The Presidential Cookbook, *Henrietta Nesbitt, the White House house-keeper during the twelve years of the Roosevelt administration, recalls that Franklin Roosevelt was extremely fond of fish as well as of soups. Martha Washington's crab soup was a particular favorite because of its tradition. Here is an adaptation of the recipe as served by Mrs. Nesbitt at the White House. Use Hudson River steamed crab meat when in season for the soup. For directions on how to cook and clean crab, see the introduction to this chapter. The soup is quickly made; serve it when ready. It does not reheat well.*

SERVES *8–10*

PREPARATION TIME: *10–15 minutes*

COOKING TIME: *about 10–12 minutes*

½   *stick (4 tablespoons) butter*
¼   *cup flour*
2   *hard-boiled eggs, mashed*
     Grated zest of 1 lemon
2   *teaspoons minced onion*
1   *quart (4 cups) milk*
1½ *pounds crab meat, picked over to*
         remove cartilage and cut into large pieces

½   teaspoon salt
¼   teaspoon freshly ground pepper
½   cup dry sherry

In a double boiler or in a saucepan set over a low flame, blend the butter and flour; add the mashed eggs, lemon zest, and minced onion. Stir to combine thoroughly. Whisk in the milk a little at a time. Stir in the crab meat and season the soup. Simmer for about 5 minutes, then stir in the sherry. Taste and adjust seasonings, if necessary. Serve hot.

Phyllis Lake's Hudson River Crab Cakes

•••

Phyllis Lake, wife of Hudson river fisherman Tom Lake, is known for her crab cakes. For the cakes she uses Old Bay, from the Baltimore Spice Company, a seafood seasoning favored by all the crabbers on the Hudson I have interviewed. For directions on how to cook and clean crab, see the introduction to this chapter.

MAKES *1 dozen cakes*

PREPARATION TIME: *5–10 minutes*

COOKING TIME: *about 6 minutes*

---

1   pound Hudson River blue crab meat
1   teaspoon Old Bay seasoning
¼   teaspoon salt
1   tablespoon mayonnaise
1   tablespoon Worcestershire sauce
1   tablespoon chopped parsley
1   tablespoon baking powder
1   egg, lightly beaten
2   slices of crustless white or whole-wheat
      bread, torn into small pieces and moist-
      ened with a little milk
      Vegetable oil, for frying

•••••••••••••

Mix all ingredients but oil and shape into 2-inch flat cakes. In a frying pan, heat about ¼ inch of oil and fry the cakes on both sides until golden.

Tom Lake's Hudson River Crab Salad

Tom Lake of Wappingers Falls, New York, has been fishing the Hudson for the last twenty-two years or so. He is very pleased with the abundance of crabs in the river these last few years. He catches great quantities of them, steams them, uses what he needs, and freezes the rest of the sweet crab meat for later use. His crab salad is so superb that not long ago a friend even asked for a bowlful as a wedding present! For directions on how to cook and clean crab, see the introduction to this chapter.

SERVES *6–8*

PREPARATION TIME: *about 10 minutes*

---

3 *medium-sized green peppers, diced*
3 *ribs celery, diced*
4 *large carrots, diced*
8 *radishes, diced*
1 *red onion, diced*
1 *cup mayonnaise*
1 *tablespoon prepared mustard*
1 *teaspoon freshly ground black pepper*
  Salt to taste
2 *pounds Hudson River blue crab meat, cleaned and picked over to remove cartilage*

Combine the vegetables in a large mixing bowl. Add the mayonnaise, mustard, black pepper, salt, and blue crab. Mix thoroughly. Serve on a hard roll, or on lettuce leaves.

WARM-WEATHER FOODS

Basil Rotini Salad

With plenty of basil available at farm stands in the Hudson region in the summer months, use it to best advantage in the following pasta salad. The recipe comes from the late Herbert Graefe, of the Willow Inn, in Armonk, New York. This is not only an excellent side dish for a back yard barbecue but also a tasty picnic salad that can safely be taken along.

SERVES 4

PREPARATION TIME: *10 minutes*

COOKING TIME: *about 8–10 minutes*

---

    8   ounces uncooked rotini pasta
    ⅓   cup fresh basil, sliced
    3   ounces Romano cheese, cut into pieces
    ¼   cup red wine vinegar
    ¼   cup olive oil
    3   scallions, including green parts, minced
        Salt to taste
        Freshly ground pepper to taste

Cook the pasta according to package directions or to your taste. Pasta for salads should always be slightly undercooked because the dressing will soften it further. Drain and cool under running water. Drain again. Put all the other ingredients in a blender and blend to make a dressing. Combine the dressing with the pasta and allow the salad to stand for a few hours to marry the flavors.

Barley with
Peppers and Tomatoes

Potlucks are easy get-togethers. Nobody has to carry the whole burden of meal preparation when everyone brings a dish. Potlucks are favorites with supporters of the Clearwater, *the flagship of the Hudson River environmental movement.*

With its "Classroom of the Waves" programs and waterfront festivals, the Clearwater *brings its message of concern for the river to thousands of children and adults each year as it sails from docks along the Hudson River, in New York Harbor, and Long Island Sound. Back in 1966, folk singer Pete Seeger had the idea that by learning to care for one boat and one river, people would come to care for all threatened waterways. He inspired a dedicated group to make the dream become a reality.* Clearwater's *story is a history of people who have given of themselves as members, supporters, and volunteers—a community that holds the unwavering belief that each individual can make a difference in bringing about a cleaner, safer environment.*

Groups of river lovers meet in different locations as members of a dozen different sloop clubs up and down the river. They start their monthly meeting with a potluck supper. At a recent meeting of the Beacon Sloop Club, a groaning board contained several pasta dishes, salads, stews, breads, and desserts.

Here is a great potluck recipe. It uses barley, a grain grown in the Hudson region by the early Dutch settlers, as is demonstrated by the only record of the original purchase of Manhattan. This is a letter of November 5, 1626, written in Amsterdam, the Netherlands, by Pieter Jansen Schagen, deputy to the States General. He writes:

> *High Mighty Sirs: here arrived yesterday the ship The Arms of Amsterdam which sailed from New Netherland out of the Mauritius [Hudson] River on September 23; they report that . . . they have bought the island Manhattes from the wild men for the value of sixty guilders, is 11,000 morgens in extent. They sowed all their grain in the middle of May, and harvested it the middle of August. Thereof being samples of summer grain such as wheat, rye,* barley, *[emphasis mine], oats, buckwheat . . .*

Barley, with its chewy texture and nutty flavor, makes an excellent substitute for rice or potatoes. It takes an hour to cook but can be made ahead and reheated. It can also be frozen. This wholesome and pretty dish travels well, so bring it to your next potluck party or picnic. At home, serve it as a vegetarian meal with a salad, or use it as a side dish for grilled fish or meats.

SERVES 6

PREPARATION TIME: *about 10 minutes*

COOKING TIME: *1 hour*

> 1   cup pearl barley, washed and picked over
> 3   tablespoons vegetable oil
> 1   small onion, finely chopped
> 1   each red, yellow, and green pepper, finely
>   chopped, about ¾–1 cup in total
> 2   ripe tomatoes, finely chopped
> ½   cup flat-leaf parsley, finely chopped
>   Salt to taste
>   Freshly ground pepper to taste

Boil the barley in 6 cups water for about an hour, or until done to your taste. Drain. In the meantime, heat the oil in a large skillet and cook the onion and peppers until limp and light brown. Add the tomatoes and parsley. Cook together for a few minutes. Add the barley to the vegetables and combine. Heat through and taste for seasoning. Add salt and pepper. Cook a few minutes more on low heat to combine the flavors.

Cadet Mess Pasta Salad

What is it like to feed 4,400 cadets every day? Manuel Mendes, who is the cook and general foreman of the Food Prep Unit at the United States Military Academy in West Point, New York, seems to take this enormous task in stride and has done so for thirty-five years. He sent me a batch of the cadets' favorite recipes, among them the one that follows. This pasta salad was served to former President Ronald Reagan, when he visited West Point on October 28, 1987. For the next occasion when you need to prepare 4,500 portions, here is the recipe!

> 200   pounds pasta (corkscrew type)
> 60   pounds peas, green
>   6   cans red pepper, diced, #10 cans

```
60  pounds ham, julienned
 4  gallons creamy Italian dressing
 4  gallons creamy garlic dressing
20  pounds almonds, sliced, toasted
```

Cook pasta until tender. Drain and cool. Cook peas. Drain and cool. Mix all ingredients except almonds together and garnish with almonds.

For days when you have fewer guests, here is an adapted recipe.

SERVES *6–8, depending on the accompaniments*

PREPARATION TIME: *10–15 minutes*

COOKING TIME FOR THE PASTA: *10–12 minutes*

```
  12  ounces rotini pasta, cooked
   2  cups small peas, cooked
   1  small red pepper, cored, seeded, and diced
  ½  pound cooked ham, diced, about 1–1½ cups
   4  scallions, chopped fine (optional)
      Creamy italian or creamy garlic dres-
         sing, bottled or homemade
½–¾  cup sliced toasted almonds
```

Prepare the salad as indicated above.

Corn, Cheese, and Potato Skillet

Phyllis Milliken of Hurley, New York, now eighty-eight, told me how in days past she and her friends would go horseback riding in the Catskills and would camp overnight. For such occasions they would make a skillet dinner. They would simply bring a skillet and a can opener. "[We would also] pack some cooked potatoes, a couple of cans of corn, a hunk of cheese, and some butter in our saddlebags," she said. Mrs. Milliken gleefully recalled that when a friend gave out this recipe on her radio show at that time, a listener "liked it so well he wanted to marry her." No one could wish for a better recommendation! From Mrs. Milliken's story I put the following recipe together.

SERVES 4

PREPARATION TIME: *3 minutes*

COOKING TIME: *8–10 minutes*

½   **stick (4 tablespoons) butter**
2   **cans of whole-kernel corn**
½–1   **pound sharp cheddar cheese, cut into**
        small pieces
4   **cooked potatoes, sliced**

Melt the butter in the skillet. Add the corn with its liquid and the cheese and cook until the cheese is melted. Then stir in the sliced potatoes and cook until they are heated through.

VARIATION

If you would like to make this simple dish at home with fresh ingredients, lightly brown the butter, or heat some vegetable oil, and fry thinly sliced raw potatoes—one per person—with finely chopped onion, until the potatoes are done, about 10 minutes. Then stir in leftover cooked corn, cut from the cob, and the cheese. Cook until cheese is melted. Sprinkle the dish with parsley, if available, and serve straight from the skillet. It is good, hearty fare.

Gail's Granola

G.O.R.P., the acronym that stands for "Good Old Raisins and Peanuts," is a traditional snack for hikers. Here is a much fancier but much more delicious version, named for my friend Gail Daigle of South Salem, New York, who gave me

*the recipe. She makes jars of this granola as edible Christmas presents. It is a de-
licious snack for a strenuous hike in winter or summer. The trick to making it
lies in watching the baking time carefully. Do not overbake, to ensure that the
granola stays chewy.*

MAKES *about 6 cups*

PREPARATION TIME: *about 5–10 minutes*

BAKING TIME: *about 12 minutes*

2	*cups rolled oats*
½	*cup wheat germ*
½	*cup sunflower seed*
½	*cup raisins*
½	*cup chopped walnuts*
½	*cup slivered almonds*
½	*cup pumpkin seed*
½	*cup grated coconut*
2	*tablespoons sesame seed*
⅓	*cup vegetable oil*
¼	*cup concentrated orange juice*
½	*teaspoon salt*
½	*teaspoon vanilla*
½	*cup dark brown sugar, firmly packed*

Preheat the oven to 350° F.

In a large bowl, toss all ingredients together. Spread on a baking
sheet with a rim and bake for about 12 minutes, stirring very gently
several times during baking, until the mixture sticks together in
chunks. Do not overbake.

Grilled Vegetables

*Vegetables get a nice smoky taste when barbecued, and most need little more
preparation than cleaning. Grilled vegetables are a perfect way of showing off the
bounty of the Hudson region.*

Start cooking the food at about 5 inches above the coals and move the grate up or down as needed. Spreading out the coals is another way of controlling the heat during the cooking process. The coals should burn until they are a greyish-white with no black points showing. A squirt bottle with water is handy for flare-ups, but might deposit ashes on the vegetables. Moving the food itself for a moment while the fire burns out is the safer way. Never use gasoline or other flammable liquids; they not only are dangerous but also impart a nasty flavor to the foods on the grill.

Brush the vegetables with oil, preferably an oil infused with herbs (see next recipe), and cook as indicated. Here are a few of the many vegetables that can be grilled.

Mushrooms: Brush whole mushrooms of 1½ to 2 inches in diameter lightly with oil. Grill 5 inches above the coals, turning occasionally until tender, 8 to 12 minutes.

Onions: Peel the onions and slice them ½ inch thick. Brush lightly with oil. Grill 5 inches above the coals, turning occasionally until tender, about 15 to 20 minutes.

Potatoes: Cook well-scrubbed red potatoes until barely tender. Rinse in cold water to stop the cooking; drain. Thread the potatoes (or chunks of potatoes, if necessary) on skewers. Brush lightly with oil. Grill 5 inches above the coals, turning occasionally, until tender, 10 to 15 minutes.

Scallions: Cut off their ends and brush them lightly with oil. Grill 5 inches above the coals, turning occasionally, until tender, about 5 minutes.

Sweet potatoes: Peel the potatoes and slice them ½ inch thick. Brush lightly with oil. Grill 5 inches above the coals, turning occasionally, until tender, 14 to 16 minutes.

Tomatoes: Cut the tomatoes in half, or slice them ¾ inch thick. Brush lightly with oil. Grill 5 inches above the coals, turning once, about 3 to 5 minutes.

Zucchini or yellow squash: Cut small squash in half lengthwise. Brush them lightly with oil. Grill 5 inches above the coals, turning occasionally until tender, 8 to 12 minutes.

•.•.•.•.•.•.•.•.

Herb-Flavored Oil for Grilling Vegetables

••

PREPARATION TIME: *about 5 minutes*

STEEPING TIME: *2–3 weeks in a sunny place*

Handful of fresh marjoram, washed,
*   picked over, and large stems removed*
Handful of fresh basil, washed, and
*   picked over*
1 *clove garlic*
1 *large bay leaf*

Pack herbs, garlic, and bay leaf in a bottle and fill it with a good olive oil. Let the flavored oil steep in a sunny place for 2 weeks or so. Strain and use when grilling vegetables. Store the oil in a dark cupboard, where it will keep for months.

Pasta Supreme

••

When I do not have time to cook, or feel that I deserve a break, I head for Healy's in Katonah, New York, to buy some of Art Hanley's great pasta salads.

It is always fun to watch someone do a job well, and Art Hanley is a good cook who loves his work. His creativity is most apparent in the pasta salads. He uses every imaginable shape and size of pasta and combines them inventively with fresh and cooked ingredients. Aside from their eye appeal, the different shapes hold the dressings differently, he told me, so there are practical reasons for using one over the other. My family loves this Pasta Supreme, with its interesting combination of spinach fusilli and cheese tortellini. Hanley also has a real knack for dressings. This one has just the right mixture of herbs without being over-powering. We found that the salad is good with or without the artichoke hearts. It is another excellent side dish for a barbecue.

SERVES *6–8*

••••••••••••••

PREPARATION TIME: *10 minutes*

COOKING TIME: *10–12 minutes; marinade: 2–3 hours*

---

1   *pound fresh, frozen, or dried spinach
      fusilli*
1   *pound fresh or frozen cheese tortellini*
1   *pound carrots, scrubbed or scraped
      and diced*
2   *packages (10 ounces each) frozen artichoke
      hearts (optional)*

DRESSING

---

1   *cup mayonnaise*
2   *tablespoons lemon juice*
¼   *cup milk*
⅓   *cup grated Parmesan cheese*
½   *cup chopped fresh parsley*
¼   *cup chopped fresh basil, or 2 teaspoons
      dried basil*
1   *teaspoon dried marjoram*

Red leaf lettuce, for garnish
Ripe olives, for garnish

Cook both pastas al dente. Let cool.

Place diced carrots and artichoke hearts in boiling water and cook until the water returns to a boil, or steam the vegetables until barely tender. Let cool. Cut the artichoke hearts into bite-sized pieces.

In a small bowl, combine the dressing ingredients. Thoroughly mix the dressing with the salad ingredients. Allow 2 or 3 hours for the salad to marinate before serving. Art Hanley suggests serving the salad in a bowl lined with red leaf lettuce and garnishing it with sliced ripe olives.

•.•.•.•.•.•.•.•.

Soldiers' Salad

My father's specialty, which he would make for festive occasions, was a main course salad that is called ''Huzarensla'' in Dutch, or hussar salad. But when my daughter was little she could not pronounce the word, so we have come to call it Soldiers' Salad. According to the most popular story about its origin, it was created during World War I, when the Dutch hussars were in garrison along the Netherlands' borders. The soldiers would date the kitchen maids in town, who would fix them a salad from the family's leftovers. It is a rather grim story, but gets the point across that Soldiers' Salad is made from cooked ingredients.

My parents would make the salad from scratch. Their salad making was one of our most treasured family traditions. My mother would cook everything; my father would put the ingredients together. He would mound the salad on a very large oval platter, then smooth the top of the salad and press it into a perfect oval shape. The yolks of hard-boiled eggs would be mashed separately from the whites and ''ribbons'' of white and yellow would go across the top of the salad with little sprigs of parsley at equal distance in between. He would place Boston lettuce leaves around the base of the salad and further decorate with sweet-and-sour gherkins. These were cut in a fan shape by slicing them in three parts from the top but not all the way through and spreading slices into a fan. Deviled eggs and tomato halves filled with tuna salad would be alternated on the long sides. At one end he would place steamed asparagus rolled in ham, and at the other he would place cooked crab meat, shrimp, sardines, or sliced chicken breast. Served with hot French, whole-wheat, and pumpernickel breads and butter, the salad makes an appetizing meal that is as pretty as a picture. Here is his recipe for the salad. Make it a day ahead so that all the flavors have time to blend. The decoration and accompaniments are only limited by your imagination! The salad can be a meal in itself, or you can serve it together with grilled meats from the barbecue.

SERVES *at least 8, depending on accompaniments*

PREPARATION TIME: *about 1 hour for salad and presentation*

COOKING TIME: *about 15 minutes*

STANDING TIME: *best when made the night before serving, so the flavors have a chance to marry*

About 4   cups boiled potatoes, cut into
            small cubes (see note)
About 4   cups all together of cooked peas,
            and carrots and green beans, cut
            into small cubes
     3   medium sweet-and-sour apples
            such as Golden Delicious or
            Granny Smith, peeled, cored, and
            cut into small cubes
     1   large cucumber, peeled
     2   cups cooked beef, cut into small
            cubes (for this you may use left-
            over roast) (optional)

DRESSING

   ¾   cup mayonnaise
   2   hard-boiled eggs, mashed
   2   tablespoons vinegar, or more
       Salt to taste
       Freshly ground pepper to taste

In a large bowl combine the cubed potatoes, vegetables, and apples. Cut the cucumber in half lengthwise and remove the seeds with a spoon. Cut into long strips and then across into small cubes. Add, together with the cubed beef (although the salad is very good without it), and combine with the other ingredients.

In a small bowl, stir together the dressing ingredients and stir the dressing into the salad ingredients. Taste and adjust seasonings. You might need a little more mayonnaise to hold the salad nicely together. Refrigerate overnight. Taste; it may need a bit more vinegar. Mound the salad on the platter and create an appealing presentation as described above.

NOTE: You can use small red or yellow potatoes, well scrubbed and boiled in their skins.

A PICNIC ALONG THE HUDSON

Curried Turkey and Water Chestnut Salad Sandwiches

There are many wonderful parks, gardens, and special little spots along the Hudson where you can go for a picnic. I like to keep picnics simple. I start by almost freezing cans of soft drinks; these will serve to keep the rest of the food cold when carried. Then I make curried turkey salad and pack it in a plastic container and refrigerate. I put some Romaine lettuce leaves together with a good handful of alfalfa sprouts in a sandwich bag and put four pitas in another. I cut two generous squares of Shaker gingerbread and they go in yet another sandwich bag. When it is time to go, I pack everything in a six-pack holder, tuck in some napkins, a spoon, two apples, and a small tablecloth—and a compact, delicious picnic for two is ready! Here is the recipe for the salad.

No measurements are necessary; just keep in mind that you need three times as much turkey as water chestnuts. Cube the cooked turkey. Mince a scallion or two. Slice the canned water chestnuts. In a small bowl, combine the ingredients and add curry powder to taste. Then add enough mayonnaise to bind the ingredients. Taste and adjust seasonings. To serve, open a pita bread. Line with lettuce leaves and spoon in some of the salad. Top with alfalfa sprouts.

Shaker Gingerbread

Soft gingerbread is a homey, year-round dessert that Americans liked early on. Food historian Karen Hess notes that perhaps the recipes for gingerbread in Amelia Simmons' American Cookery *of 1796 were the first ones printed for this cake in America.*

The recipe that follows comes from Two Hundred Years of Lebanon Valley Cookery, *by the Ladies Guild of the Church of Our Saviour in Lebanon Springs, New York. At the suggestion of the Shaker Museum in Old Chatham, New York, I included it to represent the Shaker community of the Hudson region. I give you the full text of the recipe first and then a modern, smaller version, which neatly fills a nine-inch-square baking dish. It is a full-flavored gingerbread that is even better a day or so after it is baked and travels very well.*

SISTER AMELIA'S RULE FOR SOFT GINGERBREAD

6 cups molasses, 4 cups sugar, 4 cups butter, scant, 6 cups buttermilk, 7 eggs, 4 tablespoons ginger, 1 large nutmeg, 6 teaspoons soda, scant. Stir butter and sugar together; add molasses, ginger and spice. Stir. Then add eggs well beaten, and flour until the right consistency for soft gingerbread. At the last dissolve soda in hot water, stir in quickly, bake in shallow tins. This amount will fill ten of our baked apple tins, which is an abundant meal for Family, with margin. For nice finish, immediately when taking out of oven, touch surface with molasses and dredge lightly with granulated sugar. This will keep it moist.

SERVES *6–8*

PREPARATION TIME: *about 10 minutes*

BAKING TIME: *about 1 hour*

2	**sticks (½ pound) butter**
1	**cup sugar**
1½	**cups molasses**
1	**tablespoon ground ginger**
½	**teaspoon freshly grated nutmeg**
1	**whole egg and half of 1 beaten egg**
1½	**cups buttermilk**
4	**cups all-purpose flour**
1½	**teaspoons baking soda, dissolved in**
	1 tablespoon water
	Molasses, for topping
	Sugar, for topping

Preheat the oven to 350° F.

Cream together butter and sugar. Add molasses, ginger, and nutmeg. Stir to combine, and add eggs and buttermilk. Slowly stir in the flour, a cup at a time. When all is combined, stir in the baking soda. Spoon the batter into a buttered 9-inch-square baking dish. Bake for about 1 hour (but start checking after 45 minutes), until dark brown and firm. Remove from the oven and brush with molasses and sprinkle lightly with sugar.

•.•.•.•.•.•.•.

A SAIL ON THE HUDSON

It's very exciting to get an invitation to go sailing or boating in general, especially when you only occasionally get a chance to explore the Hudson River that way. In my experience, some captains are so adept at having landlubbers along that they have a ready-made list in mind of things for you to bring; others assume that you know. In either case, inquire if additional life vests are necessary: the law requires that there is one on board for everyone. Bring a sweater and a jacket, wear soft-soled shoes or tennis shoes, and tuck in a tube of sun screen. Carry your things in a soft bag that can be easily stored in any corner, for space on board is always at a premium.

If, in return for the trip, you offer to bring the food for a boating trip, always discuss your menu beforehand with the captain, not only to check on preferences but especially to verify what storage and cooking facilities are on board. Some boats have full galleys; others just manage with a camping stove and an ice box which is literally that, a box filled with bags of ice. For this reason I chose a menu that is completely safe, even if the foods are not refrigerated. Bring the food along in large resealable bags—double-bag if necessary—to avoid having to take containers home.

Below follow suggestions for safe, convenient, home-made fare, just the kind of sustenance for which captain and crew might be hankering. The menu was tested and found to be extremely workable when five of us sailed to New York Harbor for the Statue of Liberty celebrations some years ago. The 23-foot *Stonehorse* of Mary Brown, then director of the Rye Library, in Rye, New York, got quite a workout with so many people on board. Our menu consisted of cucumber salad, seashells with vegetables, and applesauce cakes.

Cucumber Basil Salad

SERVES 4

PREPARATION TIME: *5–7 minutes*

---

  1 *large cucumber, peeled and thinly sliced*
  ¼ *cup distilled vinegar or tarragon vinegar*
  2 *tablespoons vegetable oil*
  ½ *teaspoon salt*
  ¼ *teaspoon freshly ground black pepper*
2½ *teaspoons sugar*
  1 *tablespoon minced fresh basil leaves*
  ½ *medium onion, chopped*

Combine all ingredients and toss. Set aside, stirring now and then to make sure the sugar dissolves. The salad is best made the day before or in the morning of the day you plan to serve it. The waiting period gives the flavors a chance to marry. Store and serve at room temperature. The recipe may be doubled or quadrupled.

Seashells with Vegetables

This comforting, nutritious dish is the main course of our menu for a sailing or boating trip on the Hudson.

SERVES 4–6

PREPARATION TIME: *about 20 minutes*

COOKING TIME: *about 15 minutes*

---

  3 *tablespoons vegetable oil*
  3 *cups broccoli, broken into small*
      florets
  1 *green pepper, cored, seeded, and cut*
      into thin strips

    3   large carrots, peeled and diced
    4   scallions, minced, white and
          green parts
    2   celery ribs, cut into strips
    1   8-ounce can water chestnuts,
          drained and sliced, or sliced
          radishes
    2   large ripe tomatoes, diced
    ¼   teaspoon each dried marjoram and
          basil, or 1 teaspoon each fresh,
          chopped
    1   pound seashell pasta, cooked
          according to package directions
2 or 3 tablespoons tomato purée
          (optional)
        Salt to taste
        Freshly ground pepper to taste
About 2 cups grated Parmesan cheese, for
          serving

Heat the oil in a wok or large frying pan. Add the broccoli, green pepper, and carrots; toss to combine, cover, and cook for 5 minutes. Add the scallions, celery, water chestnuts, tomatoes, and herbs. Stir to combine, cover, and cook for an additional 4 or 5 minutes, until the vegetables are done to your liking.

Combine with the cooked seashells and heat through. Taste, adding some tomato purée if it seems necessary, and season with salt and pepper. Cool. Reheat or serve at room temperature with plenty of freshly grated Parmesan cheese.

Applesauce Cakes
•.

Homemade baked goods are always welcome, especially if your hosts have been on the water for a while. That's why I included them in our menu for a sailing or boating trip on the Hudson. Applesauce cakes are particularly practical because they can do triple duty. The cakes make a delicious easy-to-eat dessert, they are great for breakfast with a steaming cup of coffee, and small wedges can be munched on for a snack. They are also an easy-to-carry addition to a picnic.

•.•.•.•.•.•.•.•.

The recipe comes from Linda and David Rooke of Fort Edward, New York, the owners of Rooke's bakery, "home of the finger roll." These slender, finger-size, buttery rolls, five inches long and one inch in diameter, are so popular in Warren and Washington counties that Rooke's sells 5,000 dozen at Christmastime. Naturally they would not part with the trade secrets for such a favored baked good, but Linda Rooke did send me the following excellent recipe. Bake the cakes in two aluminum foil pans, which can be washed and left on board to be reused.

MAKES *two 9-inch cakes*

PREPARATION TIME: *about 10–15 minutes*

BAKING TIME: *about 40–45 minutes*

2	**cups sugar, or less if the applesauce is very sweet**
½	**cup shortening**
2	**eggs**
1½	**cups applesauce**
½	**teaspoon salt**
½	**teaspoon cinnamon**
½	**teaspoon cloves**
½	**teaspoon allspice**
2½	**cups sifted all-purpose flour**
1	**cup raisins**
1	**cup chopped walnuts**
	Confectioners' sugar

Preheat the oven to 350° F.

In an electric mixer, cream the sugar with the shortening. Add the eggs and incorporate thoroughly. Stir in applesauce.

In a separate bowl sift the salt, cinnamon, cloves, allspice, and flour. Stir the dry ingredients into the sugar-egg mixture and add the raisins and walnuts. When everything is completely combined, spoon the mixture into two greased 9-inch round cake pans. Bake for about 40 minutes, or until a knife inserted in the center comes out clean. Cool. Dust with confectioners' sugar.

A MOONLIGHT DINNER ON THE PATIO

A menu of light, flavorful dishes makes dinner by moonlight on the patio on one of those warm, flower-scented evenings we know in the Hudson region an even more memorable occasion. Add some candles, flowers for the table, and colorful china, and invite your best friends. Cold melon soup is the first course; it is followed by grilled beef ribbons with ginger and lime, rice and black bean salad, as well as a salad of Hudson region lettuces, greens and edible flowers as the main dishes. Caledonia ice with chocolate sauce is served for dessert.

Cold Melon Soup

▪:▪.

From Saving Grace: A Collection of Recipes and Graces, *from St. Matthew's Church, in historic Bedford, New York, comes the first recipe for our menu. It was contributed by Joy Luke.*

Several Hudson Valley wineries now make champagne, so choose your favorite kind, or use any one of the many dry white wines the valley's wineries are known for, to stir into the soup.

SERVES *8*

PREPARATION TIME: *10–15 minutes*

CHILLING TIME: *at least 2 or 3 hours*

---

  3 *cups chopped cantaloupe*
  3 *cups chopped honeydew*
  2 *cups* **fresh** *orange juice*
  ⅓ *cup* **fresh** *lime juice*
  3 *tablespoons honey*
     Chilled dry white Hudson Valley wine
       or champagne

Place melon, juices, and honey in the blender and purée. Pour in a bowl and chill very well. Serve in small bowls and pass the champagne or wine bottle to add a dash or more to the soup as desired.

▪:▪.▪:▪.▪:▪.▪:▪.▪:▪.

Beef Ribbons with Ginger and Lime

▪•

Summer is a good time to experiment with New York wines. Wineries in the Hudson region are open and ready to give you a taste of many different varieties, made from hybrids as well as vinifera grapes. The different vineyards and wineries can be visited by traveling along the Hudson. Many of them have picnic areas and are close to other spots worth seeing. Exploring the region, stopping at the wineries, visiting the historic houses and museums, and buying or picking some fresh produce or fruit to take home as a souvenir are perfect ways of spending a summer weekend in the Hudson region.

The following recipe, part of our menu for a moonlight dinner on the patio, comes from the New York Wine & Grape Foundation in Penn Yan, New York, established for the purpose of promoting New York wine, juices, and grapes. These grilled ribbons are lean and light. Leftovers, if there are any, are good cold for lunch the next day. The Foundation suggests a medium-bodied, buttery Chardonnay, a fruity blush wine, or a light red wine as an accompaniment.

SERVES *6–8*

PREPARATION TIME: *15–20 minutes; marinade: at least 4 hours*

GRILLING TIME: *about 3 minutes*

---

3   *pounds beef tenderloin*
1   *cup beef broth*
½   *cup lime juice*
2   *tablespoons grated fresh ginger*
2   *tablespoons sugar*
    Salt to taste
    Freshly ground pepper to taste
1   *tablespoon grated lime zest*
    Bamboo skewers
    Lime slices, for garnish

Partially freeze the beef for ease in slicing. Cut in thin slices (about ⅛ inch thick). Cut the slices in half lengthwise. In a shallow noncorrosive baking pan, mix the remaining ingredients. Stir in the beef strips until completely covered with the marinade. Cover

▪•▪•▪•▪•▪•▪•▪•

the pan and refrigerate for at least 4 hours. Turn the beef occasionally. While the beef is marinating, soak the bamboo skewers in
cold water. Thirty minutes before serving, heat the grill. Drain the
marinade and reserve. Skewer the beef strips on bamboo skewers.
Heat the marinade and reduce until slightly thickened. Broil the
skewers 1 to 1½ minutes per side. Remove to a heated platter. Pour
the sauce over the skewered beef and garnish with lime slices.

Rice and Black Bean Salad

*The next recipe is also part of our menu for a moonlight dinner on the patio, but
it will be a hit at other times as well.*

SERVES *6–8*

PREPARATION TIME: *5–10 minutes*

---

3   *cups cooked rice (1 cup raw)*
1   *can (1 pound) black beans, drained
        and rinsed*
1   *cup finely chopped celery*
½   *cup finely chopped parsley*
1   *small red pepper, seeded, finely chopped*
4   *scallions, white and green parts
        finely chopped*
     Vinaigrette dressing

Combine all ingredients. Chill, or serve at room temperature.

Salad of Hudson Region Lettuces, Greens, and Edible Flowers

A salad of assorted greens is an appropriate component of a menu for a moonlight dinner on the patio, not only because so many varieties of greens and lettuces are grown in the Hudson region but also because the first settlers, the Dutch, were very fond of salads. While we might think that our present-day mixtures of different greens, lettuces, and edible flowers are the height of innovation, let me prove to you that this is not so. Here follows a salad recipe from the 1683 edition of De Verstandige Kock, *or* The Sensible Cook, *the definitive Dutch cookbook of the seventeenth century:*

> *To prepare raw salads.*
> *Take head lettuce, leaf lettuce, curly lettuce, lamb's lettuce, also the shoots of the dandelions or wild chicory, also the shoots of chicory roots [what we now call Belgian endive], endive, or red and white cabbage or cucumbers, whatever one has on hand that is best or that is in season and all well cleaned is eaten with a good oil of olives, vinegar and salt. On some [vegetables] additional herbs are used according to everyone's desire, but the usual are cress, catnip, purslane, burnet, rocket, tarragon, buttercup, one may also add the flowers of bugloss, borage, rose and calendula. This salad is also eaten with melted butter and vinegar gently heated together instead of oil and vinegar, according to everyone's desire.*

With the above instructions in mind, you can create a beautiful salad of mixed greens. Make a vinaigrette of herb vinegar and olive oil. Strew the salad with edible flowers. Some farms in the region— for example, Breezy Hill Orchards in Staatsburg—now sell them. Pick your own flowers carefully. Avoid flowers that grow on chemically treated lawns, and never pick those that grow on the sides of roads, because they may be contaminated with lead deposits. Warning: Not all flowers are edible; lilies of the valley, for instance, are toxic, so be sure to check edibility.

Caledonia Ice with Chocolate Sauce

▪•

The late Elizabeth Remsen Van Brunt, of Ossining, New York, gave me the following recipe years ago. She was known as a lecturer, teacher, and author on herbs and herb gardening. She also had a longtime association with the Brooklyn Botanic Garden, its former Kitchawan Research Station, and the Herb Society of America. Her recipes always have an unexpected twist, as in this adult dessert of sophisticated refinement. The barely discernible oatmeal gives body to the cream. The anise and orange combine in a digestive, fragrant blend of tastes. The smooth chocolate sauce enhances and rounds out the flavors.

SERVES 6

PREPARATION TIME: *about 10 minutes*

FREEZING TIME: *overnight*

1　*tablespoon sugar*
1　*cup heavy cream*
5　*tablespoons uncooked quick-cooking oatmeal*
1　*teaspoon crushed anise seed*
1　*tablespoon grated orange zest*

In the bowl of an electric mixer, add the sugar to the cream and whip until stiff. Fold in the oatmeal, anise seed, and orange zest. Spoon into a shallow dish or into ice cube trays without the dividers. Cover with foil or plastic wrap. Freeze overnight. Remove one half hour before serving and refrigerate. Serve with chocolate sauce.

CHOCOLATE SAUCE　　PREPARATION TIME: *about 10 minutes*

1　*tablespoon butter*
2　*squares unsweetened chocolate*
¾　*cup sugar*
¾　*cup milk*
¼　*teaspoon salt*
½　*teaspoon vanilla*

▪•▪•▪•▪•▪•▪•▪•▪•▪•

Place a small bowl or pie plate with the butter and the chocolate pieces on a heating tray set on high. Stir occasionally until melted. Or, if you prefer, melt the chocolate and butter in the microwave according to manufacturer's instructions. When melted, alternately stir in the sugar and milk, a little at a time. When all is combined, stir in the salt and vanilla. This makes a glossy, thick sauce. Serve at room temperature in a small pitcher to accompany the Caledonia Ice.

SUMMER DRINKS

Lemonade

What is better than a cooling glass of lemonade after a tennis match or an afternoon of pulling weeds in the summer's sun? With a lemon syrup ready in the refrigerator you can supply soothing drinks for thirsty people at the spur of the moment. It is made with the zest, the shiny, yellow, bumpy exterior of the lemon that contains the rich lemon oil, as well as with the juice of the lemon. The syrup can also be used with gin. Chill the gin as well as the syrup and mix them to taste, about two parts syrup to one part gin. Serve over ice.

MAKES *5–5½ cups syrup, enough for 20–22 glasses lemonade*

PREPARATION TIME: *15–20 minutes*

COOKING TIME: *about 5 minutes*

---

  7   *lemons*
3½ *cups sugar*

With a sharp vegetable peeler, strip the yellow zest from the lemons, avoiding the bitter white pith. Squeeze and strain the juice. In a saucepan, combine the sugar and 2 cups water and bring to a boil over medium heat, stirring constantly until sugar is dissolved. When it is completely dissolved and the syrup is clear, lower the heat and simmer 2 or 3 minutes. Combine with the lemon juice and zest, and let stand, covered, at room temperature for several hours. Refrigerate. To serve, pour about ¼ cup syrup over ice cubes and fill the glass with plain water or soda water.

Lemon Balm Lemonade

Lemon balm is easy to grow, almost too easy. One little plant becomes a veritable bush in the course of the summer. You will have an endless supply of big bunches of the herb to add to large pitchers of lemonade.

PREPARATION TIME: *5–10 minutes, depending on whether you use frozen juice or freshly squeezed*

The rule of thumb is to use the juice of 1 lemon for every two cups of water. Make a pitcher full, add sugar to taste. Add ice. Pick a bunch of about 8 sprigs of lemon balm. Remove any dead leaves and rinse carefully. Add the entire bunch to the pitcher of lemonade. Refrigerate for an hour or so.

Norman's Dream

The next recipe for an ice-cold summery after-dinner drink is so simple and so good, I like to serve it as dessert with a plate of cookies and chocolates on the side. I named it for Norman Larson, who is known among his friends for his home-made curaçao.

PREPARATION TIME: *2 minutes*

FOR EACH DRINK:

1½ ounces curaçao
1 generous scoop chocolate ice cream
  Whipped cream, chocolate shavings, and
    grated orange zest, for garnish (optional)

Place curaçao and ice cream in the blender and blend until just smooth. Pour into a champagne glass. Top with whipped cream, chocolate shavings, and grated orange zest, if desired. It is quite good without these trimmings.

4. Fruit Harvest

The subjects of this chapter are the fruits of summer and fall only. Early fruits have already been discussed in the preceding chapters.

Blueberries, wild strawberries, and grapes are native to the Hudson region; other fruits, such as apples and pears, have been brought here over the centuries by settlers. From Adriaen van der Donck's *A Description of the New Netherlands*, written in 1655 to entice his fellow Dutchmen to settle in the New World, we learn that the imports "thrive well" in this country. In addition to apples and pears, colonists brought cherries, apricots, plums, currants, gooseberries, and quince, to mention only a few. Van der Donck was especially pleased with the way peaches grew here:

> If a stone is put into the earth, it will spring in the same season, and grow so rapidly as to bear fruit in the fourth year, and the limbs are frequently broken by the weight of the peaches, which usually are very fine.

Almost a century later, the Swedish botanist Peter Kalm remarked on the abundant growth of peaches and reported that roaming pigs gorge themselves on the ones that have fallen. And Jasper Danckaaerts, in his journal of 1679–1680, says that nowhere else had he seen such fine apples as in New Netherland. He notes specifically the Double Paradise, the Newtown Pippin, the Kingston Spitzenburgh, the Poughkeepsie "Swaar-apple," the Redstreak, and the "Guelderleng." Today, when supermarkets sell only about half a dozen apple varieties, which are chosen mostly for their durability rather than their taste, these old varieties barely survive. There is a large glimmer of hope, however; some Hudson region growers are making an effort to continue to produce these "antiques," and buyers at the Greenmarket farmers markets in New York City delight in rediscovering the amazing variety of taste and texture of the older kinds of apples.

With a history of fruit growing that spans almost four centuries, the region's main agricultural activity deserved to be documented and recorded. In 1986, Elizabeth Ryan, of Breezy Hill Orchard in Staatsburg, New York, started on this mammoth task with a planning grant from the New York State Council for the Arts (NYSCA). Although her aim was first to record oral histories from present-day growers—more than eighty have been collected so far—she finds her project reaching further and further back in time. Many important historical materials such as posters, nursery catalogues, promotional literature, photographs, and equipment have been located. A multimedia exhibition is being planned for the Albany Institute of History and Art in the near future.

For some of the recipes in this and later chapters it is advisable to use sterilized containers. To sterilize jars place them on a rack in a large pot filled with water. Bring to a boil and boil for 10 minutes. Place flat lids in a saucepan with water. Bring to a boil; remove from heat. Let them stand in hot water until ready to use. Drain well.

RECIPES FEATURING:

Apples:
Apple Cobbler with Hot Raisin Sauce
Marlboro Pudding

Apricots
Apricots in Brandy

Blueberries
Blueberry Muffins

Grapes
New York Sparkler
Sparkling Virgin Sangría

Melons
Melon Compote

Nectarines
Nectarine Compote

Nuts
Hazel Adams's Nut Loaf
Walnut Macaroons

Peaches
Peach Chutney
Peach Chutney Dip

Pears
Pear Tart
Poached Devoe Pears in White Wine and Honey

Plums
Prune Plum Pie

Pumpkins
Waldy Malouf's Pumpkin-Apple Soup
Pumpkin Cornmeal Pancakes

Quince
Baked Quince

Raspberries
Mother's Raspberry Tart
Raspberry Mountain Pie

APPLES

Apple Cobbler with Hot Raisin Sauce

Here is a lovely old-fashioned cobbler recipe. It comes from Helen Bartholomew of Stanfordville, New York, who makes it just as her mother and grandmother prepared it. The raisin sauce makes it special. It is so good that you'd better make a double batch of sauce —people will come back for more, I assure you!

SERVES *6–8*

PREPARATION TIME: *about 20 minutes*

BAKING TIME: *about 30 minutes*

> 8   *pie apples, peeled, cored, and sliced*
> ½   *cup sugar*
> 2   *tablespoons fresh lemon juice*
> 1   *tablespoon cinnamon*
> ¼   *teaspoon freshly grated nutmeg*
> ½   *stick (4 tablespoons) butter*
> 2   *cups biscuit mix*
> ½   *stick (4 tablespoons) butter, melted*
> ¼   *cup sugar*
> ½   *cup milk*

Preheat the oven to 450° F.

In a large bowl, combine the apples, ½ cup sugar, lemon juice, cinnamon, and nutmeg. Turn the mixture into a 13- by 9-inch ovenproof dish and dot with the 4 tablespoons of butter.

In a small bowl, mix the biscuit mix with the melted butter, ¼ cup sugar, and milk to make a very soft dough. Place it on a heavily floured board and pat it out with your hands into a rectangle to top the apples. Transfer the dough, entire or in pieces, as is convenient, to the surface of the apples.

Bake for 10 minutes at 450° F. Lower the temperature to 350° F and cook for about 20 minutes longer, or until topping is done and the apples are tender. In the meantime, make the sauce.

HOT RAISIN SAUCE

> 1   *cup raisins*
> 2   *tablespoons lemon juice*
> 1   *tablespoon cinnamon*
> ½   *cup dark brown sugar*
> 1   *tablespoon cornstarch*

In a small saucepan, bring 2 cups water to a boil with the raisins, lemon juice, cinnamon, and brown sugar. Mix the cornstarch with a little cold water and add to the sauce. Stir and cook the sauce for a few more minutes to remove any raw taste from the cornstarch and to thicken the sauce. Ladle the hot sauce on each serving of apple cobbler.

Marlboro Pudding

The recipe for Marlboro pudding comes from the first chapter of Recipes from Locust Grove, *published by the Young-Morse Historic Site in Poughkeepsie, New York. The book was compiled and edited by Alice J. Hasbrouck to commemorate the two hundredth anniversary of the birth of Samuel Finley Breese Morse, inventor of the telegraph, on April 27, 1791. Its first chapter contains the transcription of handwritten recipes by the mother of the inventor, Elizabeth Ann Breese. She calls it ''A Common Place Book'' and dates it April 10, 1805. After Samuel Morse had become famous for inventing the telegraph in 1847, he acquired Locust Grove as his country estate. He is believed to have brought his mother's recipe book there with him.*

Marlboro pudding is a very delicate and rich apple pie. The instructions are simple:

> *Take 12 spoons of stewed apples, 12 of wine, 12 of sugar, 12 of melted butter, and 12 of beaten eggs, a little cream, spice to your taste, lay in paste. Bake one hour and a quarter.*

I adapted the recipe to modern measurements as follows:

SERVES *6–8*

PREPARATION TIME: *about 10 minutes*

BAKING TIME: *1 hour and 25 minutes*

¾ **cup homemade unsweetened applesauce**
¾ **cup Rhine wine**
1 **cup sugar less 1 tablespoon**
1½ **sticks (¾ cup) butter, melted**
3 **eggs, beaten very well with a whisk**
¼ **cup heavy cream**
   Scant ¼ teaspoon freshly grated nutmeg

½   teaspoon cinnamon
1   unbaked 9-inch pie shell, fluted with
     ½-inch upstanding rim

Preheat the oven to 450° F.

Stir together all filling ingredients and pour them into the pie shell. Bake for 10 minutes; then lower the oven temperature to 325° F and bake for an hour and 15 minutes, until a knife inserted in the center comes out clean. Let cool.

APRICOTS

Apricots in Brandy

Putting fruits in brandy is an age-old method of preserving. I am giving you my mother's method, which is to flavor the following drink with vanilla. Others prefer lemon peel. The drink is served in small, pretty crystal glasses accompanied by little silver spoons. I have served it that way as dessert with a plate of simple butter cookies on the side.

MAKES   *about 3 pints*

PREPARATION TIME: *about 30 minutes*

STANDING TIME: *about 3 months*

---

1   *pound dried apricots, washed thoroughly*
1   *cup sugar*
1   *vanilla bean*
1   *quart brandy*

Sprinkle the apricots with ¼ cup sugar and soak in 2 cups of water for 48 hours. Drain, reserving the soaking liquid. Measure the liquid and add additional water to make a total of 4 cups. Bring the liquid to a boil with the remaining sugar and boil until the sugar is completely dissolved. Let cool. If the apricots seem too large, cut them into smaller pieces. Score the vanilla bean gently lengthwise (do not cut all the way through). Add to the cooled syrup together with the apricots. Add the brandy and stir to combine. Rinse out a large screw-top jar and lid with boiling water or use a sterilized jar. Pour the mixture into the jar. Cover and let rest for about 3 months in a cool place.

BLUEBERRIES

Blueberry Muffins

•.

The next recipe comes from Carol and Pete Ferrante, of Walkill View Farm in New Paltz, New York. They sell these delicious muffins, baked without oil or butter, at their roadside stand, along with pies, their home-grown vegetables, and a full line of fruits in season.

MAKES *5 dozen*

PREPARATION TIME: *about 10 minutes*

BAKING TIME: *15–20 minutes*

---

    4 *cups flour*
    1 *cup sugar*
    2 *tablespoons baking powder*
    1 *teaspoon salt*
    2 *cups milk*
    2 *eggs*
    4 *cups blueberries*
       Confectioners' sugar

Preheat the oven to 350° F.

Mix together the flour, sugar, baking powder, and salt. In a separate bowl or measuring cup, beat together the milk and the eggs. Stir into the dry ingredients until thoroughly combined. Then gently stir in the blueberries. Line muffin tins with paper liners and fill them three-quarters full. Bake for 15–20 minutes, until a toothpick inserted in the middle of a muffin comes out clean. These muffins do not brown very much, so be careful not to overbake. When cool, sieve a little confectioners' sugar over tops.

•.•.•.•.•.•.•.•.

GRAPES

New York Sparkler

Not only is New York the nation's oldest producer of grape juice, it is also the largest. In the Hudson region, the Royal Kedem Wine Company of Milton, New York, makes a variety of grape juices as well as kosher wines. Cut your caffeine intake by combining cold tea with grape juice for a refreshing change.

SERVES *1*

PREPARATION TIME: *1 minute*

½ *cup cold tea*
½ *cup sparkling New York white grape juice*
Lemon wedge

Pour both liquids into a tall glass filled with ice. Top with a wedge of lemon.

Sparkling Virgin Sangría

The New York State Wine & Grape Foundation, who brought us the New York Sparkler, offers yet another recipe using the region's grape juice. At harvest time in September, most wineries will make grape juice for a brief time, while others sell juice all year round. This is a recipe you can play with and adjust to your own taste or to what you have on hand. I like to add table grapes, washed and cut in half, to the mixture instead of or in addition to the traditional citrus fruit slices.

MAKES *1 quart*

PREPARATION TIME: *10 minutes*

---

1 *bottle (750 ml) sparkling white grape juice*
Juice of 1 orange, 1 lemon, and 1 lime
Thin strips of zest from lemon and orange

Citrus slices and/or washed table grapes,
cut in half

In a large pitcher or bowl, combine juices and zest. Add ice cubes and citrus slices and/or cut grapes.

MELONS

Melon Compote

A compote is served in a dish by the same name, preferably footed and crystal. It is not always that easy to choose a melon that is perfectly ripe. Here is a remedy for those occasions when you are disappointed with your choice.

Cut the flesh in cubes. Do not cut it too close to the rind where it has a lighter color, because that part is usually sour or tasteless. Place the fruit in a container, sprinkle with a little sugar, and stir to combine. Refrigerate until ice-cold. Spoon into a pretty compote dish. Serve as is or, better yet, pour on some ice-cold champagne or sparkling wine and serve immediately. This compote makes for a refreshing late-summer dessert.

NECTARINES

Nectarine Compote

Nectarines are grown mostly in the southern part of the region. Bruce Salinger, of Salinger's Orchards, in Brewster, New York, has been growing them for the last thirty years. They have a short season—from about August 15 to September 20—but freeze beautifully. Nectarines, members of the rosaceae and amygdalus families, are a fruit in their own right rather than a fuzzless peach, or an apricot-peach cross-breed, as some have asserted. Like the melon pieces in the previous recipe, the fruits also look very pretty served in a crystal compote dish. I like to poach them, cut in half, and fill the hollow with a teaspoonful of raspberry preserves.

PREPARATION TIME: *5–10 minutes*

COOKING TIME: *8–10 minutes*

Nectarines, washed
Sugar
Fresh lemon juice
Raspberry preserves

Cut the nectarines in half and place them in a saucepan. Pour in water until it is about one-quarter of the way up the side of the fruit. Taste one of the fruits to determine how much sugar they need; add the sugar and a dash of fresh lemon juice. Bring to a boil, reduce the heat, and simmer for about 5 minutes, until the fruit is tender but not disintegrating. Let cool. Remove the nectarine halves and fill each hollow with a teaspoonful of raspberry preserves. Layer them in the compote dish and pour the juice over them. Refrigerate to cool further.

NUTS

Hazel Adams's Nut Loaf

Every year in the fall, Hazel Adams of South Salem, New York, would wait until her husband Joseph had cracked enough hickory nuts in his vise—hickory nuts are hard—to make one cup, and then she would bake a nut loaf. Sometimes they would gather black walnuts, or butternuts, that had fallen from the old trees surrounding their house and use those in the recipe. Each kind of nut imparts its own delicious flavor. You can use store-bought walnuts as well.

MAKES *one 8- by 4- by 3-inch loaf*

PREPARATION TIME: *about 15 minutes*

BAKING TIME: *1 hour and 15 minutes*

2 *cups sifted cake flour*
2½ *teaspoons baking powder*
½ *teaspoon salt*
⅔ *cup shortening*
1 *cup sugar*
1 *teaspoon vanilla*

> 3 *eggs*
> 1 *cup finely chopped nuts (see above)*
> 6 *tablespoons milk*

Preheat the oven to 350° F.

In a medium bowl, sift flour, baking powder, and salt.

In another bowl, cream the shortening, and add the sugar and the vanilla. Add one egg at a time and incorporate, then stir in the nuts. Finally add the flour mixture, alternating with the milk.

Spoon into a loaf pan, 8 by 4 by 3 inches. Bake for 1¼ hours, or until golden brown and a toothpick inserted in the center comes out clean. Let cool on a rack.

Walnut Macaroons

The following recipe comes from the archives of the Chapman House in Glens Falls, New York. It is part of a unique local cookbook, the Glens Falls Cookery Book. *This book was apparently so popular that five editions appeared, spanning the four decades between 1880 and 1923. The recipe was contributed by Frances T. E. Boyd. She says: "These [macaroons] are better if kept over one day in a cool place," but do not refrigerate them, or they will become moist and sticky. This is a nice, chewy walnut confection.*

MAKES *15–18 macaroons*

PREPARATION TIME: *5 minutes*

BAKING TIME: *20 minutes*

> 1 *egg*
> 1 *cup confectioners' sugar*
> 1 *cup chopped walnut meats*
> 3 *tablespoons flour*

Preheat the oven to 300° F.

Beat the egg until light and foamy; add sugar, nuts, and flour.

Grease a baking sheet. Drop by the scant teaspoon onto the baking sheet, about 2 inches apart. Bake for 20 minutes, until light brown and firm. Remove immediately.

PEACHES

Peach Chutney

The following recipe is one of my most prized possessions. It was given to me years ago by Ruth Sansone, formerly of Mount Kisco, New York. It has never failed me and has always brought enthusiastic praise. Ruth set out to imitate chutney in the style of Major Grey's, but I think she has far surpassed the original. Get together with a friend and make a double batch. The work goes so much faster when you have company. The chutney makes a welcome edible gift anytime.

MAKES *3–4 pints*

PREPARATION TIME: *about 45 minutes*

COOKING TIME: *3–4 hours*

4–5 pounds peaches, scrubbed thoroughly
     but not peeled
2 large green peppers, cored, seeded,
     and quartered
2 large onions, quartered
1 can (3 ounces) green chili peppers
4 large cloves garlic
½ cup chopped fresh ginger
2 teaspoons salt
1 teaspoon dried red pepper flakes
3½ cups brown sugar
2½ cups cider vinegar
1½ cups raisins

Slice the peaches very thin, discarding the pits as you go along, and place in a heavy large pan. Chop the green peppers, onions, chilies, garlic, and ginger very fine. Add the salt and pepper flakes. Add the chopped ingredients to the sliced fruit; then add the brown sugar, vinegar, and raisins. Stir to combine.

Cook uncovered on low heat for 3–4 hours, allowing the mixture to boil slightly. Stir frequently. The juice should be syrupy.

Rinse out clean jars and their lids with boiling water or use sterilized jars. Fill and place in the refrigerator. Or divide the chutney over small containers and freeze.

Peach Chutney Dip

With this chutney you can make a very appealing dip for fresh vegetables or bread sticks.

MAKES *2–2½ cups*

PREPARATION TIME: *5 minutes*

1½ **cups peach chutney, or an equal amount of commercial chutney**
1 **cup mayonnaise**
1½ **tablespoons lemon juice**
2 **cloves garlic**
1 **teaspoon Worcestershire sauce**

Place all ingredients in the container of a blender and blend until smooth. Serve as suggested above.

PEARS

Pear Tart

.•.

In the following tart, the currants are a tangy accent for the sweet pears in a buttery crust. Serve with a dollop of sweetened whipped cream, if you like to gild the lily.

SERVES *8*

PREPARATION TIME: *15–20 minutes*

BAKING TIME: *30–40 minutes*

½	cup currants
2	cups flour
⅓	cup light brown sugar, firmly packed
11	tablespoons cold butter (do not use margarine)
2	egg yolks, lightly beaten
10–12	small pears, peeled, cored, cut into quarters and then into 2 or 3 lengthwise slices
⅓–½	cup sugar, depending on the sweetness of the pears
½	teaspoon dried ground ginger
1	teaspoon cinnamon

Place the currants in a small saucepan. Cover with water and bring to a boil. Allow them to boil for 1 minute, then turn off the heat. Let the currants soak for about 5 minutes. Drain thoroughly and set aside.

Preheat the oven to 375° F.

Combine flour, salt, and brown sugar, and cut in the butter with a pastry blender or two knives until it resembles coarse meal. Stir in the egg yolks. Knead this mixture until smooth. This takes time!

Press the dough out onto the bottom and sides of a 9-inch springform pan. Neatly finish the rim. In a large bowl, gently combine the pear slices, sugar and the spices. Stir the currants into

•.•.•.•.•.•.•.•.

the mixture. Carefully arrange the fruits in the crust. Bake for about 30 to 40 minutes, until the crust is golden. Cool and serve.

Poached Devoe Pears in White Wine and Honey

Elizabeth Ryan and her husband Peter Zimmerman, of Breezy Hill Orchards, in Staatsburg, New York, grow many "antique" varieties of fruit, including the Devoe pear, a native to the Hudson region. Elizabeth explains:

> *The Devoe pear originated on the farm of Charles Greiner in Marlboro, N.Y., in the late 1920's. It was noticed as a chance seedling growing behind the packing house near an orchard of Bosc and Worden seckels. Mr. Greiner's attention was attracted by the unusual shape of the first few pears, very long with a beautiful red blush. They almost looked like red bananas on the tree. The pears themselves were extremely smooth, almost lacking the gritty stone cells of other varieties. Additionally, they had a wonderful, elusive, almost perfumed flavor. He began grafting them onto other trees and eventually patented the variety, naming it Devoe after his mother Josephine Devoe. Mr. Greiner sold the patent to Bountiful Ridge Nursery, who sold trees all over the country for 20 years. Today the Devoe pear has almost disappeared from production, but continues to be cherished and cultivated on 10 or 12 Hudson Valley farms.*

She adds that they were especially pleased to find "a row of Devoe pears at Breezy Hill Orchard" when they purchased the farm in 1984. The Devoe pear is picked in late August and is wonderful in fruit salads or for eating out of hand, but it is also perfect for poaching.

SERVES 4–6

PREPARATION TIME: *about 10–15 minutes*

COOKING TIME: *about 35 minutes*

---

2 *pounds Devoe pears, peeled but stem left on*
½ *bottle good white wine (not too dry)*
½ *cup honey*

Prepare the pears and set aside. In a medium saucepan, bring to a boil the wine, 1½ cups water, and the honey. Drop each pear into the simmering liquid and cover. Simmer lightly until the pears are cooked but not too soft, about 30 minutes. Remove the pears carefully and continue reducing the syrup to about three-quarters of its original volume. Chill pears and syrup separately and then combine.

PLUMS

Prune Plum Pie

▪▪▪

My readers tell me this is one of their favorite recipes from my column. This flavorful summer pie is very juicy, so serve it with a spoon and a fork. For juicy pies like this, I like to place the pie shell in a larger pie plate and, just to be sure I do not get any messy oven spills, place the plate on a baking sheet.

SERVES *6–8*

PREPARATION TIME: *about 15–20 minutes*

BAKING TIME: *about 40 minutes*

3½ **cups prune plums, cut in half and pitted**
½ **cup sugar**
¼ **cup flour**
1 **tablespoon lemon juice**
1 **tablespoon butter, melted**
1 **unbaked 9-inch pie shell, placed in a**
    10-inch pie dish

TOPPING

¾ **cup flour**
¼ **cup sugar**
⅔ **stick (5⅓ tablespoons) butter**

Preheat the oven to 425° F.

In a large bowl, combine the plums, sugar, flour, lemon juice, and melted butter. Spoon into the unbaked shell.

Make the topping:

Sift the flour and sugar together, and cut the butter into this mixture. Use a pastry blender or two knives to make fine crumbs. Sprinkle the crumb mixture over the pie. Bake for 10 minutes; reduce the heat to 350° F and continue to bake for another 30 minutes, until the crust is brown and the filling bubbles through the crumbs here and there.

PUMPKINS

Waldy Malouf's Pumpkin-Apple Soup

It is natural that the Hudson River Club in New York City, a restaurant situated on the river with a sweeping view of New York Harbor and the Statue of Liberty, would use products from the Hudson region. Executive Chef Waldy Malouf, of Pound Ridge, New York, makes a sincere effort to incorporate in his menus the fine seasonal produce, meats, and fish of the area. Here is one of his best-known recipes—pumpkin-apple soup. His guests keep coming back for more! What a perfect soup for a Halloween party, or any other chilly fall night.

SERVES *20 or more*

PREPARATION TIME: *45 minutes*

COOKING TIME: *about 2 hours*

¼	*pound bacon, diced*
10	*Granny Smith apples, cored and chopped (unpeeled)*
2	*carrots, scraped and chopped*
2	*large onions, chopped*
2	*celery ribs, chopped*
1	*leek, white part only, chopped*
2	*cloves garlic, chopped*
1	*tablespoon cinnamon*
1	*tablespoon freshly grated nutmeg*
1	*tablespoon ground allspice*

4   ounces apple brandy or Calvados, or more
4   ounces dry white wine
1   gallon chicken stock, fresh or canned
1   smoked ham hock
2   cups pumpkin purée, fresh or canned
    Bouquet garni, wrapped in cheesecloth
        1 tablespoon black peppercorns
        3 bay leaves
        1 teaspoon dried thyme
        8 parsley stems
        4 whole cloves
    Salt to taste
    Freshly ground pepper to taste
    Chopped parsley, for garnish
    Crisp bacon bits, for garnish
    Cinnamon croutons, for garnish
    (recipe follows)

In a heavy pot large enough to hold all ingredients, render and brown the bacon. Add the apples, carrots, onions, celery, leek, and garlic and brown lightly. Add the cinnamon, nutmeg, and allspice, and allow them to heat through and develop their flavor. Deglaze the pan with the brandy and wine, and reduce until dry; watch for burning. Pour in the chicken stock and add the ham hock, pumpkin purée, and bouquet garni. Bring to a boil; then lower to a gentle simmer and cook for 2 hours uncovered. Remove bouquet garni and ham hock. Take the meat off the bone, chop it, and return it to the soup. Discard bones and bouquet garni. In a blender, purée the soup in batches until smooth. Taste and season with salt and freshly ground pepper. Add more apple brandy to taste.

To serve, bring soup back to a boil and ladle into bowls or a tureen. Top each serving with chopped parsley, crisp bacon bits, and cinnamon croutons.

CINNAMON CROUTONS

6   ¼-inch-thick bread slices, cut into small cubes
6   tablespoons butter, melted
¼   cup sugar mixed with 1 teaspoon cinnamon

Preheat the oven to 350° F.

Toss the bread cubes with just enough melted butter to moisten the cubes. Spread them on a baking sheet and sprinkle them with the cinnamon sugar. Bake for 10–15 minutes or until light-brown and crisp.

Pumpkin Cornmeal Pancakes

Peter Kalm, the Swedish botanist, found pumpkin cornmeal pancakes pleasing to his taste. In his 1749 diary he explains how a thick pancake was made "by taking the mashed pumpkin and mixing it with corn-meal after which it was . . . fried." With those instructions in mind, I created the following recipe.

MAKES   *at least 18 seven-inch pancakes*

PREPARATION TIME: *about 5–8 minutes*

FRYING TIME: *about 3 minutes on each side*

---

  1   **cup all-purpose flour**
  1   **cup yellow cornmeal**
  1   **cup confectioners' sugar**
  ½   **teaspoon ground ginger**
  ½   **teaspoon cinnamon**
  1   **cup mashed cooked pumpkin, or**
         use canned
  2   **eggs, lightly beaten**
  3½ **cups milk, or less**
       Vanilla or butternut ice cream, for
         serving (optional)
       Maple syrup, for serving (optional)
       Confectioners' sugar, for serving (optional)

In a large bowl, combine dry ingredients.

In a medium bowl, combine pumpkin and eggs. Beat into dry ingredients. Add milk slowly to make a smooth, thin pancake batter, but not too thin, or you will not be able to turn the pancakes. Heat some butter in a crêpe pan and pour in the batter to make a 7-inch pancake. Fry each pancake on both sides until golden, about 3 minutes on each side.

To serve, place 2 tablespoons ice cream on each and drizzle with a little maple syrup. Or serve the pancakes simply with a heavy dusting of confectioners' sugar.

QUINCE

Baked Quince

How I like to sing the praises of quince to you. It is a forgotten fruit, yet so full of flavor that once you taste it, you will make it part of your cooking repertoire. Fortunately, quince is still grown in the Hudson region, and in its season, October/November, you can find it even in some supermarkets. Although quince might look like pears, they cannot be eaten like them. Our modern palate, accustomed as it is to sugar, will not tolerate their tartness when eaten fresh, so nowadays quince are for cooking. Centuries ago, however, they supposedly were enjoyed for precisely that sour taste and eaten like an apple or pear.

A bonus of cooking quince is the lovely smell that will permeate the whole house. Fresh quince have a more subdued but equally haunting fragrance.

If you never have had a quince, the following easy recipe is a simple way to try its mouth-filling flavor. The baked quince without any further flavoring will taste like a chutney. If the quince is ripe, it will turn pink in baking. Serve as an accompaniment to meat.

YIELD: *Serves 2 as a condiment*

PREPARATION TIME: *5–10 minutes*

BAKING TIME: *about 25 minutes*

---

1 *golden-yellow quince*
¼ *cup sugar*

Preheat the oven to 375° F.

With a sharp knife, quarter the quince then peel and core each quarter. Remove every hard part, especially the white seed pods. Slice each quarter into four slices and place them in a small ovenproof dish. Sprinkle the sugar over the fruit and pour in ¼ cup water. Cover. Bake for about 25 minutes, until the slices are very tender. Let cool.

RASPBERRIES

Mother's Raspberry Tart

The raspberry tart that follows was the first recipe my mother taught me how to bake. The buttery crust offsets the slightly tart berries perfectly. Naturally we always serve it with a large dollop of whipped cream.

SERVES *8*

PREPARATION TIME: *10–15 minutes*

BAKING TIME: *about 30 minutes*

---

    2   cups flour
        Pinch salt
    ⅓   cup light brown sugar, firmly packed
   11   tablespoons butter (do not use margarine)
    2   egg yolks, lightly beaten
   12   ounces frozen raspberries, thawed
        Sugar to taste
    1   tablespoon cornstarch

Preheat the oven to 350° F.

Combine flour, salt, and sugar, and cut in the butter with a pastry blender or two knives until it resembles coarse meal. Stir in egg yolks. Knead this mixture until smooth. This takes quite a bit of time.

Press the dough out into a buttered 9-inch pie plate or tart plate to make a flat cake. Bake for 30 minutes or until light brown. Do not overbake. Let cool. Remove from the pan.

In the meantime, prepare the topping. Select 10 or so pretty raspberries and set aside. Place the rest with the juice in a saucepan; add sugar to taste and bring to a boil while stirring. Mix the cornstarch with some water and add to the boiling fruit. Keep stirring until it thickens and then cook for 1 minute more to remove the starchy taste. Remove from the heat. Turn the cooled tart *right side up* and place on a serving plate. Carefully pour the cooked raspberries onto the tart. There is just enough for an even layer without the fruit sauce dripping over the sides. Add the reserved berries in a decorative pattern. Cool and serve with or without whipped cream.

Raspberry Mountain Pie

Marion Greig and her husband Robert have been growing fruits for over forty years on their farm in Red Hook, New York—a favorite place to pick your own asparagus, peas, strawberries, blueberries, blackberries, raspberries, and pumpkins. You can even finish the year's harvest by cutting your own Christmas tree at Greig Farm. From Marion's charming little book of family recipes comes her mother's recipe for raspberry pie. It has a cakelike crust that will envelop the fruit which is poured into the batter. It's fun to bake, and everyone will love it.

SERVES 6

PREPARATION TIME: *about 10 minutes*

BAKING TIME: *40–45 minutes*

---

3   *tablespoons butter*
1   *cup flour*
1   *cup sugar*
1½   *teaspoons baking powder*
½   *teaspoon salt*
¾   *cup milk*
2½   *cups raspberries, sweetened with*
      ⅓ cup sugar
   Whipped cream, for serving (optional)
   Ice cream, for serving (optional)

Preheat oven to 375° F.

Melt the butter in a 9-inch deep pie plate. (Just place the pie plate in the oven while it is heating up.) In a large bowl, mix the dry ingredients. Add the milk, stir until smooth, and pour the batter onto the melted butter. Pour fruit into middle of the batter, juice and all. Do not stir. Bake for about 40 to 45 minutes, until the crust is firm. Serve warm or cold, with or without whipped cream or ice cream.

5. Vegetable Harvest

The subjects of this chapter are the vegetables of summer and fall only. Early vegetables have already been discussed in the preceding chapters. Mid-July through mid-September is the height of the vegetable harvest season in the Hudson region, and farm stands are filled with a mouth-watering display of mixed greens, dark-red beets, snowy white cauliflowers, bright-yellow squash, and deep-purple eggplant, with centerpieces of juicy, sun-ripened tomatoes.

Many of the farmers not only sell at their farm but also bring their produce and products to the Greenmarket farmers markets in Manhattan, the Bronx, or Brooklyn. Most markets are open one day a week, but the largest—Union Square Market—is open three days a week. These open-air markets were organized in 1976 to support farmers and preserve farmland by providing growers with an opportunity to sell their produce and farm products directly to the consumer. Only growers, family members, or their employees may sell at Greenmarket. No middlemen or brokers are allowed. Greenmarket is a program of the Council on the Environment of New York City, a privately funded, not-for-profit organization operating out of the mayor's office.

In addition to fruits and vegetables, the farmers markets sell meats, fish, cider and fruit juices, honey, jams and preserves, cheese, butter, eggs, baked goods, plants and flowers, maple syrup, and grains. They also provide a wonderful way for the city dweller to have direct contact and dialogue with the grower, which creates better understanding of problems encountered by both the customer and the supplier. Questions on the ingredients, on the use and preparation of the products, and on the advantages and disadvantages of certain fertilizers and pesticides arise constantly and are patiently answered over and over again.

The early settlers already gave high praise to the fertility of the Hudson region. Dutch-American poet Jacob Steendam called New Netherland "a land of milk and honey." In 1650, Attorney-General Cornelis Van Tienhoven describes how a garden was started as soon as a house was built:

> After the house is built . . . gardens are made, and planted in season with all sorts of pot herbs, principally parsnips, carrots, and cabbage, which bring great plenty into the husbandsman's dwelling.

In 1653, Van der Donck further elaborates, and indicates that both imported and native plants were cultivated:

> The garden products in the New Netherlands are very numerous: some of them have been known to the natives from the earliest times, and others introduced from different parts of the world, but chiefly from the Netherlands.

Native American Customs

The main crops for Native Americans were the "three sisters": corn, beans, and squash. One-sided wars, one-sided battles with European diseases, and played-out crop lands led to the reduction of these people from the region. In 1976 and 1977, He Who Stands Firm, at the time curator of the Ward Pound Ridge Reservation Museum in Cross River, New York, led a group of researchers to Oklahoma, Wisconsin, and Ontario (Canada), to track down descendants of Native Americans from the Hudson region, who belonged to a Delaware people referred to as Munsee. They found elders in Oklahoma who spoke the Unami dialect of the Delaware language and, in Ontario, people who spoke Munsee. The expeditions' field notes, tape recordings, and photographs are housed in the museum.

The notes contain a description of a meal served to He Who Stands Firm and his group. He believes that it was probably little different from what Native Americans were eating several hundred years ago. The meal included a stew of meat and corn, and dumplings in grape juice. These dumplings were cooked for a long time in order to soak up the juice and become completely purple and gelatinous. He Who Stands Firm told me he thought Native Americans might have learned this dish from the settlers. He also asked if, in spite of the migration, the custom of eating early shoots—discussed in Chapter 1—still prevailed today with descendants of the Hudson region's Native Americans. In response to that question he was shown well-stocked freezers filled with venison, trout, *and* parboiled milkweed shoots. His experience proves, once again, that foodways die out very slowly.

RECIPES FEATURING:

Beans
Daka Chili
Pole Bean Soup

Beets
Beets and Beet Greens

Cabbage
Coleslaw (Cabbage Salad)
Red Cabbage with Apples

Carrots
Carrot and Parsnip Quiche

Corn
Corn Bread from the *Isaac Newton*
Corn Pot Pie

Cucumbers
Cucumber Sandwiches
Grandma's Bread and Butter Pickles
King's Pickles (1841)

•.•.•.•.•.•.•.

Eggplant
Eggplant and Mushroom Appetizer

Fennel
Grilled Fennel

Jerusalem Artichokes
Jerusalem Artichoke Salad

Kohlrabi
Grated Kohlrabi with Cream or Milk

Lovage
New York Unit Lovage Soup

Mixed Vegetables and Herbs
Homemade Herb Vinegar
Mother's Piccalilli
Shane Newell's Summer Vegetable Soup
Vegetable Pancakes

Mushrooms
Wild Mushroom Clam Chowder

Onions
Pickled Onions

Sorrel
Pasta with Chicken-Sorrel Sauce

Squash
Mini-Pattypan Squash with Shrimp, Tomatoes, and Feta
Spaghetti Squash with Vegetable Topping
Zucchini-Chive Fritters

Swiss Chard
Swiss Chard Pie

Tomatoes
Tomato Corn Relish
Tomato, Cucumber, and Chickpea Spread

Turnips
Turnip Soup

BEANS

Daka Chili

▪•

In 1987, a chili cook-off was inaugurated at the annual "Day-in-the-Country" at the Ward Pound Ridge Reservation in Cross River, New York, a major fundraising event for the Westchester Lighthouse for the Blind, with an attendance of thousands of visitors. Although the recipe that follows did not win, it certainly had my vote and I have had more requests for it than for any other recipe I have printed in my column.

The recipe was created by Daniel Fedro, then executive chef of General Foods' World Headquarters in Rye Brook, New York, but I made some changes in it. One change has to do with the amount of beans. Fedro's mixture was mostly meat with a few beans, whereas I prefer the mix to be the other way around, particularly with these two delicious bean varieties, which make this recipe so special. This is also why I included the chili in the vegetable chapter rather than in the meat category, where chili normally would be placed. You can adjust the recipe to your preference. The second change has to do with cooking times. I like foods with texture and therefore did not sauté the vegetables until completely done, as Fedro had suggested. Again, suit your own taste. This recipe can be doubled or tripled and freezes well.

SERVES *4–8, depending on the amount of beans used*

PREPARATION TIME: *about 45 minutes*

COOKING TIME: *about 3½ hours*

½–2	**cups dry Great Northern beans, cooked separately, or canned cannellini beans with liquid**
½–2	**cups dry black beans, cooked separately, or canned black beans with liquid**
2	**pounds ground beef**
½	**pound tasso, diced, see note**
1½	**cups peeled fresh tomatoes, diced**
4	**cloves garlic, minced**
1	**medium red onion, minced**
1	**small white onion, diced**
1	**yellow pepper (about ½ pound), cored, seeded, and diced fine**

▪•▪•▪•▪•▪•▪•▪•▪•▪•▪•▪•

1   red pepper (about ½ pound), cored,
        seeded, and diced fine
1   (long) light green Italian pepper with
        seeds, minced
1   can (16 ounces) tomato purée
½   teaspoon oregano
1   teaspoon thyme
1   teaspoon cumin
3   tablespoons mild chili powder, or less
½   teaspoon cayenne pepper, or less
    Pinch of black pepper
    Pinch of white pepper
1   ounce dark molasses or a little more

Cook the white and the black beans separately. Wash and pick them over and place them in a saucepan with water about 1 inch above the beans. Bring to a boil and boil vigorously for 1 minute. Turn off the heat and let the beans soak for 1 hour. Drain and bring them to a boil again, in fresh water, reduce the heat, and cook them gently until done to your liking (about 40 minutes). Drain and set aside. This can be done a day ahead; store the cooled beans in a tightly covered container in the refrigerator.

Brown the ground beef and tasso or its substitute; drain and set aside. Discard the grease. Heat the oil and sauté the tomatoes, garlic, both onions, and the three peppers until done to your liking (see the above comments). Add tomato purée and cook 5 minutes more.

To this mixture add the oregano, thyme, cumin, chili powder, cayenne, black pepper, white pepper, and molasses. Simmer 8 to 10 minutes. In a large pot, stir together meats and vegetables. Cook covered on low heat for 1 hour. Simmer uncovered for ½ hour, if necessary, to reduce the liquids. Stir frequently. Gently stir in the beans and cook for another few minutes to blend flavors. Serve hot.

NOTE: Tasso is cured smoked ham. If not available, substitute as follows: Slowly fry 8 slices of bacon until crisp. Drain. Combine the bacon slices, cut into small pieces, with ½ cup diced regular ham.

Pole Bean Soup

The following main-course soup has an intense, fresh bean flavor.

SERVES 4–6

PREPARATION TIME: *about 20 minutes*

COOKING TIME: *about 2 hours*

---

   2 *pounds chuck steak with bone, or 1 pound*
        boneless meat and several soup bones
   1 *pound pole beans or 2 packages (10 ounces*
        each) frozen french-cut beans (do not
        defrost)
   5 *potatoes*
        Sugar
        Salt
        Freshly ground pepper
        Maggi (see below) to taste

In a soup pot, bring meat, bones, and 3 quarts of water to a boil over high heat and skim the surface carefully to remove the foam and other impurities. Reduce heat and simmer for 1–1½ hours. Let cool and refrigerate overnight.

The next day remove the hardened fat and discard. Cut all usable meat off the bones and into small pieces. Discard the bones. Pour the broth through a sieve back into the rinsed soup pot. Reheat the broth.

In the meantime, clean the pole beans and cut them on a slant, in the so-called "French cut." Peel the potatoes and cut them into chunks. Add the beans and the potatoes to the broth and cook until the potatoes are soft enough to be mashed into the broth with the back of a spoon. Add the meat pieces. Taste the soup; then season with a little sugar to accent the beans' sweetness, and add salt and freshly ground pepper. Soups in Europe are seasoned with Maggi, a liquid seasoning made from water, hydrolyzed plant protein, and salt, which some find indispensable for the right flavor. Add some drops of Maggi to taste, if desired.

BEETS

Beets and Beet Greens
•.

When you buy beets at a farm stand or farmer's market, you usually get them with their greens. Make sure the greens look fresh. They can be cooked like spinach and mixed with the sliced beets—it's a natural combination.

SERVES 4

PREPARATION TIME: *about 10 minutes*

COOKING TIME: *20–30 minutes, depending on the size of the beets*

---

1 **bunch beets with beet greens attached**
2 **tablespoons butter or margarine**
  Sugar to taste
  Salt to taste
  Freshly ground pepper to taste

Cut off the greens and place in a bowl with water. Scrub the beets and boil them with water to cover until they can easily be pierced with a fork.

In the meantime, wash the beet tops and stems thoroughly and cut into ½-inch pieces. When the beets are done, remove them from the pan and place them in cold water until cool enough to handle. Slip off the skins and cut each beet in half and then into thin slices. Rinse out the pan and add the butter. Melt the butter, add the cut beet greens, and cook them for just a few minutes to wilt; then add the sliced beets. Cook just long enough to heat through. Season with sugar, salt, and freshly ground pepper.

•.•.•.•.•.•.•.•.

CABBAGE

Coleslaw (Cabbage Salad)

In Swedish botanist Peter Kalm's remarkably complete diary of 1749, I found a description of an "unusual salad" he was served by his Dutch landlady, Mrs. Visscher, in Albany. He says it "tastes better than one can imagine," and goes on to describe how it is prepared:

> She took the inner leaves of a head of cabbage, namely, the leaves which usually remain when the outermost leaves have been removed, and cut them in long, thin strips about ½ to ⅙ of an inch wide, seldom more. When she had cut up as much as she thought necessary, she put them upon a platter, poured oil and vinegar upon them, added salt and some pepper while mixing the shredded cabbage, so that the oil etc. might be evenly distributed, as is the custom when making salads. Then it was ready. In place of oil, melted butter is frequently used: This is kept in a warm pot or crock and poured over the salad after it has been served.

Even inexperienced cooks will recognize Mrs. Visscher's salad as our omnipresent coleslaw, derived from the Dutch koolsla, *or cabbage salad. I used the above description to create this recipe. The combination of red and green cabbage gives it extra flavor.*

SERVES 4–6

PREPARATION TIME: *about 10 minutes*

2　cups green cabbage, cut into thin strips
2　cups red cabbage, cut into thin strips
⅓　cup herb or wine vinegar
¼　cup vegetable oil, or ½ stick (4 tablespoons) butter, melted and hot
　Salt to taste
　Freshly ground pepper to taste

Mix all the ingredients well ahead of dinnertime so that the flavors can marry. If you use butter, keep the salad in a warm place so that the butter does not harden, or serve the hot butter dressing separately.

Red Cabbage with Apples

Red cabbage lends itself very well to be cooked with fruit. This recipe is my mother's way of cooking the vegetable. At times, I have added a cup or so of wild grapes to the recipe. They give a unique flavor and lovely deep color. Dried currants or raisins are also a tasty addition, and a glassful of raisin brandy does not hurt either! I serve it with venison or beef stew, lots of fluffy mashed potatoes, and applesauce on the side.

SERVE 4–6

PREPARATION TIME: *10 minutes*

COOKING TIME: *about 35 minutes*

1½	pounds red cabbage, washed and chopped
6	whole cloves
3	bay leaves
3	large tart apples, such as Granny Smith or Northern Spy, peeled, cored, and sliced
½	stick (4 tablespoons) butter or margarine
1	teaspoon salt
3	tablespoons red wine vinegar
1–2	tablespoons sugar, according to taste
1	tablespoon cornstarch mixed with 2 tablespoons water

In a large, heavy pot place the cabbage, the cloves, the bay leaves, and 1 cup water and place the apple slices on top. Cover and bring to a boil. Reduce heat and simmer for about ½ hour. Check occasionally to make sure the mixture does not boil dry. Add water if necessary.

When the cabbage is very tender, mash the apples into the cabbage and stir. Discard the bay leaves and cloves. Add the butter and allow it to melt. Then add the salt, vinegar, and sugar. Stir thoroughly. Thicken with cornstarch mixture. Cook for a few minutes more while stirring to remove the starch taste.

CARROTS

Carrot and Parsnip Quiche

▪▫

When George Morrison of Briarcliff Manor, New York, taught a class on winter gardens and late fall harvesting at the former Kitchawan Research Station of the Brooklyn Botanic Garden in Ossining, New York, it quickly became clear that he also knew how to cook his harvest. After class he gave me the following recipe for a vegetable pie or quiche that is the most beautiful shade of orange. It makes a fine vegetarian meal, together with a salad of mixed greens, or it could be an excellent side dish for Thanksgiving dinner.

SERVES 4–6

PREPARATION TIME: *about 10 minutes*

COOKING TIME: *10–15 minutes for the carrots and parsnips*

BAKING TIME: *40–50 minutes*

> **10** *ounces carrots (about 4 medium)*
> **10** *ounces parsnips (about 3), peeled and cut into chunks*
> **1½–1¾** *teaspoons salt, or less*
> **2** *tablespoons toasted bread crumbs*
> **3** *eggs*
> **3** *tablespoons butter, melted*
> **1** *tablespoon lemon juice*
> **1** *tablespoon sugar*
> **1** *unbaked 9-inch pie shell*

Preheat the oven to 375° F. Boil the carrots and parsnips until tender, about 15–20 minutes. Drain if necessary. Combine all ingredients in a blender or food processor and blend until fairly smooth. Taste and adjust seasonings. Pour into the pastry shell and bake for 30–40 minutes.

▪▫▪▫▪▫▪▫▪▫▪▫

CORN

Corn Bread from the *Isaac Newton*

Several years ago I transcribed a handwritten cookbook entitled, "Mrs. Lefferts Book," from the archives at Lefferts Homestead, part of Prospect Park Alliance in Brooklyn. Tucked in the back of the book, written on blue paper, was a recipe that reads as follows:

RECEIPT FOR CORN BREAD, FROM THE BLACK COOK ON BOARD STEAMER "ISAAC NEWTON."

2 Eggs to 1 lb Indian [corn meal]
1 oz Butter
½ teaspoon Salaeratus [Saleratus, an early form of baking powder] to 4 lbs Indian
Dissolve the Salaeratus in hot water: mix the bread with sour milk; mix the bread and milk, the butter before you put in the Salaeratus; put the butter in last; beat Eggs well Stir all very well; put the loaf into hot oven. 2 lbs of Indian will make enough for 10 or 12 persons.

The Isaac Newton was one of many steamers on the Hudson. From 1846 to 1863 it was a nightboat from New York to Albany. It was probably named for an Albany businessman, as was the fashion, rather than for the scientist of that name. According to Allynne Lange, Education Director at the Maritime Museum in Rondout, New York, such boats were the equivalent of a fine hotel. Any dignitary coming to this area would take a trip on the Hudson. Boats almost always had a band or orchestra and were known for their elegant dining rooms. I adapted the above recipe as follows. It is particularly good made with fresh, stone-ground cornmeal from the mill at Philipsburg Manor in Tarrytown, New York.

MAKES *one 8-inch loaf*

PREPARATION TIME: *10–15 minutes*

BAKING TIME: *about 30 minutes*

1½   cups yellow cornmeal
½   teaspoon baking soda
1½   teaspoons baking powder
1   teaspoon salt

1   *cup buttermilk*
1   *egg, lightly beaten*
1   *tablespoon butter, melted and cooled*

Preheat the oven to 425° F.

In a large bowl combine the cornmeal, baking soda, baking powder, and salt. In a 2-cup measuring cup combine the buttermilk, egg, and melted butter and slowly pour into the dry ingredients, stirring well to combine thoroughly. Pour into an 8-inch loaf pan. Bake for 30 minutes, or until a knife inserted in the center comes out clean.

Corn Pot Pie

The major commercial crop of the ''Hurley Flats'' is corn. This prompted the Hurley Heritage Society to put together a cookbook named Hurley's Corny Cookbook, *to which many townspeople contributed. I chose the following recipe by Virginia Murphy for a pot pie that will make a simple, inexpensive, yet tasty family meal and is a good way to use up leftover cooked corn or leftover hard-boiled Easter eggs.*

SERVES 4

PREPARATION TIME: *about 10–15 minutes*

COOKING TIME: *for the potatoes and eggs about 10 minutes*

BAKING TIME: *about 30 minutes*

---

2   *cups fresh-cut corn from the cob (or*
      leftover cooked corn)
4   *medium potatoes, diced and parboiled*
2 or 3 *hard-boiled eggs, chopped*
1   *tablespoon flour*
      Salt to taste
      Freshly ground pepper to taste
2   *tablespoons butter*
1   *cup milk*
1   *unbaked pie crust, large enough to*
      cover a 9-inch square pan.

Preheat the oven to 350° F.

In a buttered 9-inch square baking dish, layer the corn, potatoes, and eggs. Sprinkle with flour. Season with salt and freshly ground pepper. Add pats of butter. Pour milk over everything.

Cover the dish with pie crust. Cut a few small slits in the crust to let the steam escape. Bake for about 30 minutes, until the crust is nicely browned.

CUCUMBERS

Cucumber Sandwiches

Every time I serve cucumber sandwiches, I am asked how they are made, so here is the recipe. Cucumber sandwiches not only are appropriate for tea but also make nice hors d'oeuvres. Use the best bread and butter you can find.

MAKES *12–24 sandwiches, depending on cut*

PREPARATION TIME: *about 10 minutes ; marinade: 30 minutes*

---

  1 *cucumber, peeled*
     Salt
 12 *thin slices white bread, crusts removed*
     Butter, softened (do not use margarine)
     Parsley sprigs, for garnish

Thinly slice the cucumber, place in a bowl, and sprinkle with salt. Set aside for ½ hour. Drain and press dry in paper towels. Butter the bread slices, top with cucumber slices, and cover with another buttered slice of bread. Cut into halves or quarters. Serve on a pretty platter, garnished with parsley.

Grandma's Bread and Butter Pickles

Yvonne Lawrence of Lawrence Farms Orchard, located near the Beacon/ Newburgh bridge in Newburgh, New York, gave me the wonderful pickle recipe that follows. It comes from her grandmother on her father's side, Viola Flemming, of Newburgh.

MAKES *5 quarts (see note)*

PREPARATION TIME: *30–40 minutes*

STANDING TIME: *overnight*

COOKING TIME: *about 15 minutes*

25–30	*young skinny cucumbers, with few seeds*
8	*medium onions, chopped*
½	*cup kosher salt*
5	*cups distilled vinegar*
5	*cups sugar*
2	*tablespoons mustard seed*
1	*tablespoon turmeric*
1	*tablespoon celery seed*

Scrub the cucumbers thoroughly. Cut them in ¾-inch slices. Combine them with the onions in a large bowl. Sprinkle them with the salt and let them stand overnight.

The next morning, drain them and rinse them with cold water. In a large kettle, bring the vinegar, sugar, and spices to a boil and simmer for 5 minutes. Add the cucumbers and onions, and gently boil together for about 10 minutes, or until barely tender. Pack into hot sterilized jars.

Mrs. Lawrence says these pickles need no processing. If you prefer to process them in a hot-water bath, follow manufacturer's instructions.

NOTE: I like to make them in a little batch of about one-fifth of the recipe, which neatly fills a quart jar, and keep them in the refrigerator.

King's Pickles (1841)

As a curiosity, I include here a recipe for pickles from King's Pickle Works, King Street, Ardsley, New York, which operated from 1841 to 1878. Captain John King had been captain of the sloop Eliza Ann, *which sailed from Dobbs Ferry to Snedens Landing to New York City on a regular schedule from 1827 to 1841. Captain King was the grandfather of the late Mrs. Walter J. Travis of Pough-keepsie, New York, who submitted the recipe for the Dutchess County Historical Society's book* A Taste of History. *For the purpose of that book, the quantities in the recipe were reduced to household size.*

---

1   *peck pickle cucumbers (50)*
½   *cup salt*
¼   *cup dry mustard*
    Alum (size of a grape)
4   *cups pure cider vinegar*

Wash the cucumbers and pack them lightly in a medium-sized crock. Add the above pickling ingredients along with 2 quarts water. Use an old plate to hold the pickles down. Swish around daily. The pickles will be ready in about 2 weeks.

EGGPLANT

Eggplant and Mushroom Appetizer

Eggplant slices are used as a base for sautéed mushrooms and cheese. It makes a delicious first course for a summer meal.

SERVES *4–6*

PREPARATION TIME: *10 minutes*

COOKING TIME *3–5 minutes for the eggplant; 5 minutes for the mushrooms*

BROILING TIME: *3 minutes*

2   small eggplants
2   tablespoons vegetable oil
½   pound small mushrooms, sliced
2   tablespoons minced scallions
1   tablespoon minced parsley
¼   teaspoon dried marjoram
    Salt to taste
    Freshly ground pepper to taste
    Swiss cheese slices

Cut the eggplants into 2-inch chunks; parboil or steam them briefly until barely done. Set aside.

Heat the oil and fry the mushrooms, scallions, parsley, and marjoram until light brown, about 3–5 minutes. Season with salt and pepper to taste. Remove with a slotted spoon and heap onto each eggplant chunk. Cover with a slice of Swiss cheese. Place on a baking sheet and broil until the cheese has melted.

FENNEL

Grilled Fennel

Fennel, with its licorice taste, is a deliciously crisp addition to a salad, but it also tastes very good when cooked. I like to boil fennel and then grill it with cheese. The broth in which it was cooked is a wonderful bonus: it will add full-bodied flavor to soups or fish dishes. A few stalks of fennel greatly enhance a court bouillon and the feathery leaves make an artistic garnish to a plate.

SERVES 2–4

PREPARATION TIME: *about 5 minutes*

COOKING TIME: *12–15 minutes*

BROILING TIME: *2–3 minutes*

1   fennel bulb, about 1¼ pounds
1½ cups well-seasoned beef broth

1   tablespoon butter or margarine
¼   cup grated cheese, such as Hawthorne
      Valley Farm's Alpine cheese

Wash fennel thoroughly. Trim to 1 inch below the greens. Set the greens aside for garnish. Cut the bulb in half lengthwise. Now treat the fennel as you would celery. Trim the ribs and peel where necessary, but keep each half intact as much as possible. Wash again. Place the halves side by side in a large saucepan and pour in the broth. Gently braise the vegetable for 12 to 15 minutes, or until barely tender. Remove with a slotted spoon. Place in the broiler pan and top with the butter, cut into small pieces, and the grated cheese. Broil until the cheese is melted. Serve at once, garnished with a few sprigs of the pretty green tops.

JERUSALEM ARTICHOKES

Jerusalem Artichoke Salad

If you use your own home-grown Jerusalem artichokes, be sure to scrub them very well. They tend to keep the dirt between all their little nubby nooks and crannies. Jerusalem artichokes are so named for their taste of artichoke hearts, but they belong to the sunflower family and are a native American plant. I confess that I prefer to buy nice, clean ones from the supermarket, where they are sold under the name of sunchokes. They do make an interesting, crunchy salad.

SERVES 4–6

PREPARATION TIME: *about 10 minutes*

---

1   pound Jerusalem artichokes, scrubbed
1   cucumber, peeled and seeded
1   large carrot, scraped
½   cup red wine vinegar
¼   cup sugar
¼   teaspoon ground ginger
¼   teaspoon salt

Dice the vegetables, making them all about the same size.

In a medium bowl, combine ⅓ cup water and the vinegar, sugar, ginger, and salt. Stir until the sugar is dissolved. Add the diced vegetables. Stir to combine thoroughly. Allow to stand several hours for flavors to marry.

KOHLRABI

Grated Kohlrabi with Cream or Milk

Kohlrabi gets its German name from its taste: Kohl *is cabbage and* Rabi *is tur-nip, and the flavor of kohlrabi is indeed reminiscent of both vegetables. The recipe is adapted from* The Victory Garden Cookbook, *by Marian Morash, whom I greatly admire, and whose book is a marvelous source for vegetable recipes.*

SERVES 4

PREPARATION TIME: *5–10 minutes*

COOKING TIME: *about 5 minutes*

2–3 **tablespoons butter**
1 **bunch of 3 kohlrabis**
¼ **cup heavy cream, half-and-half, or milk**
   Salt to taste
   Freshly ground pepper to taste
2 **tablespoons minced parsley**

Cut off the tops and stems of the kohlrabis and peel them as you would peel a potato. Grate them. In a frying pan, heat the butter, add the kohlrabi, and cook 2–3 minutes, until barely tender. Add the cream and heat through until bubbly. Cook for 1 minute more. Season with salt and pepper and stir in the parsley. Serve at once.

LOVAGE

New York Unit Lovage Soup

•▪•

A highlight on the calendar every fall is the annual Herb Fair, presented by the New York Unit of the Herb Society of America. The fair features plants, potpourri, sachets, dried flowers and herbs, herbal wreaths, crafts, books and magazines, herbal tote bags, aprons, stationery, and napkins, as well as elegant box lunches. A traditional part of the box lunch is lovage soup, which is so popular that servers "race through 14 gallons and it is not enough." The recipe was published in the New York Unit's very own cookbook, Come to the Fair.

Lovage, a perennial, grows all summer long and until frost and can be harvested as needed. I purchased my plant years ago at the Herb Fair and it has grown to a veritable bush, providing gallons of tasty soup. Lovage, referred to in the seventeenth century as "meat herb," enhances meat stews and gravies.

SERVE 4–6

PREPARATION TIME: *about 15 minutes*

COOKING TIME: *about 15 minutes*

---

2 *leeks (white part only), washed thoroughly and minced*
2 *white onions, chopped*
2 *tablespoons butter, divided*
4 *Eastern potatoes, peeled and sliced*
3 *cups chicken broth*
½ *teaspoon salt*
1 *cup shredded lovage leaves*
3 *cups half-and-half*

Put the leeks and onions in a heavy saucepan with 1 tablespoon of the butter. Simmer until soft but not brown. Add the potatoes, salt, and broth and cook until the potatoes are very soft. In a small, covered skillet, cook the lovage in the other tablespoon of butter until tender. Press the potato mixture through a fine sieve or process in a blender. Pour this back into the saucepan, add the lovage and half-and-half, and heat through.

•▪•▪•▪•▪•▪•▪•▪•▪•▪•

MIXED VEGETABLES AND HERBS

Homemade Herb Vinegar

•▪•

You no longer have to pay a fortune for flavored vinegars! Make them yourself; it is very easy to do and fun too! Even if you do not grow herbs, you can make good-tasting vinegar with herbs from a farmer's market, or from the super-market. I grow opal basil especially to make a lovely rose-colored basil vinegar, but such niceties are not required for the taste. Try the following directions, and you will soon be making up your own formulas. Homemade vinegar also makes a great gift.

YIELD: *1 gallon*

PREPARATION TIME: *15 minutes*

---

1 *gallon distilled vinegar*
2 **heaping** *cups of herbs, a good handful*
     each of marjoram, chives, basil leaves,
     thyme, and flat-leaf parsley

In a large pan, heat the vinegar until hot but not boiling. Wash and pick over the herbs, but leave them whole. Pack them in a clean glass gallon jug, or divide them over two large glass jars. Fill with vinegar to 1 inch from the top. Set outside in the sun. Shake once every day for at least 3 weeks. Taste for flavor and add more vinegar if it is too strong. Filter into clean small bottles with twist tops. I always rinse my bottles with boiling water.

Mother's Piccalilli

•▪•

My mother was known for her piccalilli. Late in the fall, friends and family would inquire if "it" was ready yet. I would beg and beg for an early taste to sa-vor with a cheese sandwich. Most of the time she would eventually break down and allow us to take out a dollop or so to test if it was mellow, with flavors in bal-ance, just right to be eaten. Other years she was steadfast and saved this wonderful crock full of crisp vegetables in their spicy mustard sauce until the

•▪•▪•▪•▪•▪•▪•

Christmas holidays. She taught me to rinse all the utensils, including the jar or crock and its lid, with boiling water. She also felt strongly that only Colman's mustard should be used for her piccalilli.

YIELD: *2–3 quarts*

PREPARATION TIME: *about 45 minutes*

COOKING TIME: *12–15 minutes*

---

2 pounds small pearl onions, peeled and left whole
2 pounds small gherkin/cucumbers, finger-size, unpeeled and left whole
2 teaspoons salt
12 ounces dry Colman's mustard
3 quarts distilled vinegar
3 cups sugar
1 teaspoon ground ginger
1 large cauliflower, broken into small florets
1½ pounds green beans, cleaned and cut into 1-inch pieces
1½ pound carrots, cleaned and cut into strips, and then into 1-inch pieces
12 small dried red hot peppers, whole, or fewer
3–6 tablespoons cornstarch
Turmeric

Put the onions and cucumbers in a large bowl and shake them with the salt. Set aside.

Mix the mustard with some of the vinegar to make a smooth paste. Put the rest of the vinegar, the sugar, and the ginger in a large pan and bring to a boil. Gradually add the mustard mixture. When this has returned to a boil, add the cauliflower, green beans, and carrots. Drain the onions and cucumbers and add them to the saucepan, together with the peppers. Gently boil everything for about 10 minutes, stirring occasionally. The vegetables should be crisp.

Mix 3 tablespoons of cornstarch with some water and add this to the boiling mixture while stirring constantly. How much cornstarch you will need depends on the amount of moisture the vegetables have. The final products should have the consistency of a commercial mustard. Add the turmeric, a tablespoon at a time, to color the mixture nicely yellow.

Let cool and store in glass jars or in a crock with a cover. Store in a cool place, or in the refrigerator. This relish should mellow for at least 6 weeks before eating. Restrain yourself, even though I never could; the wait will be worth it.

Shane Newell's Summer Vegetable Soup

The Grist Mill restaurant in Warrensburg, New York, is the most romantic restaurant I know in the Hudson region. The original mill equipment has been preserved and provides a stunning ambiance. The dining room literally overhangs the rapids of the Schroon River, which only 2 miles north from there rushes into the Hudson. Ask for a window table so you can watch the rippling water below while you enjoy chef-owner Shane Newell's fresh regional cuisine, for which he uses local products as much as possible.

Newell is more interested in the techniques of cooking than in recipe making. He therefore gave general directions, which I incorporated into this recipe for his outstanding summer vegetable soup, ever popular with his customers.

SERVES *8–10*

PREPARATION TIME: *about 20 minutes*

COOKING TIME: *about 15 minutes*

---

1 *can (1 pound) Great Northern beans, or substitute small white beans or cannellini*
1 *can (1 pound) kidney beans*
1 *can (1 pound) tomato sauce*
6 *cups freshly made chicken stock, or use canned broth*
4 *cups vegetables, such as carrots, zucchini, yellow squash, peeled broccoli stems, chopped chicory, fresh corn, and Spanish onion*

3–4 tablespoons vegetable oil
  2 cloves garlic, crushed
1½ tablespoons minced fresh oregano
1½ tablespoons minced fresh basil
    Salt to taste
    Freshly ground pepper to taste
  3 tablespoons scallions, minced, green
      part included
    Freshly grated Romano cheese

Into a soup pot drain the juice from the cans of beans and add the tomato sauce and chicken stock. Set the beans aside. Bring the liquids to a boil and simmer for 10 minutes.

In the meantime, julienne the vegetables where appropriate. In a skillet or wok, heat the vegetable oil, add the garlic, cook for 2 minutes, then add the vegetables. Stir-fry for just a few minutes to lightly cook them, but keep them crisp. In the last minute of cooking add the oregano and basil.

Remove the garlic cloves and add the vegetable mixture to the simmering broth. Stir in the beans. Cook the soup for 2 or 3 more minutes and remove from the heat. Taste and season with salt and pepper.

Garnish each serving with a sprinkling of minced scallion and Romano cheese; this garnish is essential to the taste.

Vegetable Pancakes

You can vary the combination of vegetables for the following recipe according to what you have on hand. It has been a favorite with readers of my column.

MAKES *twelve 4-inch pancakes*

PREPARATION TIME: *about 20 minutes*

COOKING TIME: *3–4 minutes on each side*

---

2 cups peeled potatoes, coarsely grated or
    finely julienned
½ cup carrots, coarsely grated or finely
    julienned
½ cup zucchini, coarsely grated or finely
    julienned
2 eggs, beaten lightly
2 tablespoons all-purpose flour
1 tablespoon chopped chives or minced
    scallions
2 tablespoons vegetable or olive oil
    Ketchup, for serving (optional)

Wrap the grated vegetables in a clean kitchen towel and squeeze the towel to remove excess moisture. In a large bowl, thoroughly combine the vegetables with the eggs, flour, and chives.

Heat the oil in a large skillet. Fry 4 little pancakes at one time, using ¼ cup of vegetable mixture for each pancake. With a pancake turner, flatten each pancake to a 4-inch round. Cook until golden brown, turn to brown the other side. Drain on paper towels and keep warm in preheated oven. Repeat with remaining vegetable mixture, adding more oil to the skillet as needed.

Serve hot, with or without ketchup.

MUSHROOMS

Wild Mushroom Clam Chowder

Maryellen and Steve Stofelano, owners of the Mansion Hill Inn, in Albany, also believe strongly in using local products. Since its inception, their restaurant has served New York State wines and beers. The small inn is located just around the corner from the governor's executive mansion. Built in 1861 for Daniel D. Brown, an Albany brush maker, the house is a focal point in a neighborhood of restored buildings of the same vintage.

Chef David Martin, a Culinary Institute of America graduate, uses local mushrooms, harvested by a mycologist in the Adirondacks, in his signature dish, a pungent mushroom clam chowder. You can use any combination of edible wild mushrooms for this dish.

SERVES *12*

PREPARATION TIME: *about 30 minutes*

COOKING TIME: *about 30 minutes*

STANDING TIME: *overnight for the dried mushrooms*

1	*ounce dried shiitaki mushrooms, or*
	1 cup fresh
½	*ounce dried morel mushrooms, or ½ cup fresh*
½	*ounce dried chanterelle mushrooms, or ½*
	cup fresh
1	*dozen clams for chowder*
1	*stick (8 tablespoons) butter*
½	*cup Spanish onions, diced*
⅛	*teaspoon dried red pepper*
1	*teaspoon freshly ground pepper*
1	*cup white mushrooms, sliced*
1¼	*cups flour*
1	*ounce clam base bouillon (see note)*
3	*tablespoons fresh parsley, chopped*
1	*teaspoon dried oregano*
¼	*teaspoon dried thyme*
4	*drops Tabasco*
2	*cups diced peeled potatoes*
2	*cups half-and-half*
	Pink peppercorns, for garnish (optional)
	Minced parsley, for garnish (optional)

Hydrate overnight the three kinds of dried mushrooms in 2 cups water. Drain, saving the water, and dice the mushrooms. Set aside. If using fresh mushrooms, wipe them clean, and dice. Set aside.

Bring 4 cups water to boil, add the clams, cover, and remove from heat. Allow to stand until all clams are opened (see note). Remove the clams from the water, save the water, and strain it through a paper coffee filter to remove grit and shell particles. Set aside. Take the clams out of the shells and dice. Set aside.

In a 4-quart pan, melt the butter, add the onions, and cook until translucent and tender. Add the red and black pepper, as well as all mushrooms, and sauté until tender. Sprinkle on the flour; cook and stir for 4 to 5 minutes. While stirring, add mushroom water from the hydrating process, if available; then add the clam water and clams. Remove some of the broth and dissolve in it the clam or fish bouillon cube. Stir the mixture back into the broth and add parsley, oregano, thyme, and Tabasco.

When all is thoroughly combined, stir in the potatoes and simmer the soup until the potatoes are tender. Add the half-and-half and simmer about 4 to 5 minutes more to reheat the soup.

Serve in heated bowls, garnished with the pink peppercorns and parsley.

NOTE: Clam bouillon cubes are now available in some supermarkets. If not, use a fish bouillon cube. Since the mushroom flavor is strong in this recipe, it is necessary to boost the clam flavor in order to find a balance between the two. If the cubes are not available, add a bit of salt to the soup. Any clams that will not open should be discarded.

ONIONS

Pickled Onions

The Hermitage in Ho-Ho-Kus, New Jersey, is the only eighteenth-and-nineteenth century house in Bergen County designated as a National Landmark. William Ranlett, a well-known Victorian architect, remodeled the pre-Revolutionary structure into a picturesque Gothic Revival home with steep gabled roofs, diamond-paned bay windows, elaborately carved gingerbread trim, and wide verandas—the epitome of Victorian romanticism. To raise funds to preserve this lovely structure and its contents, a charming card collection called Heritage Sampler *was published. The collection contains adapted recipes from different period cookbooks in the archives. I chose the following recipe, recommended as an accompaniment to cold roast beef or other cold cuts.*

MAKES *about 1 quart*

PREPARATION TIME: *15 minutes*

COOKING TIME: *5 minutes*

1½   *pounds small, white onions, peeled*
3   *cups vinegar mixed with 1 cup water*
¾   *teaspoon broken pieces of cinnamon stick*

¾ **teaspoon ground mace**
¾ **teaspoon whole cloves**
3 **tablespoons salt**
2 **tablespoons sugar**

Boil the onions in water for 5 minutes and drain. In a saucepan, heat the remaining ingredients until scalding hot. Rinse a crock or glass jar, and its lid, with boiling water, or use a sterilized jar, place the onions inside, and pour the vinegar over them. Cover and, when cooled, refrigerate them. They improve with age.

SORREL

Pasta with Chicken-Sorrel Sauce

Charles T. Gehring is not only the director and translator of the New Nether-land Project of the New York State Library in Albany, where he brings back to life the twelve thousand documents left to us from the Dutch period, he is also a confident cook. His vivacious personality and in-depth knowledge have made him a beloved figure in Dutch-American circles. He has an uncanny knack of connecting the present with the past. What a pleasure it is to watch him prepare his favorite Italian dishes in his cozy, cluttered kitchen and listen to the stories of his latest translation of exciting historic episodes during the Stuyvesant admin-istration! His wife Jean quietly works around him and augments the menu in such a way that every dinner at their house becomes a meal to remember. In summer, Charlie, as he is known, loves to use sorrel from his garden in the fol-lowing pasta dish.

SERVES 4

PREPARATION TIME: *about 15 minutes*

COOKING TIME: *about 15–20 minutes*

---

20 **large sorrel leaves**
 4 **chicken breast halves, sliced horizon-**
       tally into two scaloppine each
     Salt to taste
     Freshly ground pepper to taste
 1 **tablespoon olive oil**

    2   tablespoons butter
    3   shallots, chopped
    ½   cup heavy cream

PASTA

    ½   pound linguine
        Juice of ½ lemon
    3–4 tablespoons extra-virgin olive oil
        Freshly ground black pepper
        Mixture of freshly grated Romano and
            Parmesan cheeses
        Fresh flat-leaf parsley, chopped

Roll the sorrel leaves in stacks of about five, like a cigar, and cut at an angle.

Season the chicken slices with salt and pepper.

Heat the oil and butter in a skillet and sauté the chicken until lightly browned. Remove to a heated platter. Add the shallots to the skillet and cook until they glisten. Add the sorrel until it wilts. Add the cream and heat through, but do not boil. Return the chicken to the sauce and simmer it on low heat while the pasta is cooking.

Cook the pasta al dente. Spread it out on a flat pasta platter and squeeze lemon over it. Pour the oil over the pasta and toss to combine. Grind a generous amount of black pepper over the pasta and toss with cheese and parsley to taste. Serve together with the chicken and sorrel.

SQUASH

Mini-Pattypan Squash with Shrimp, Tomatoes, and Feta

Miniature vegetables became popular some years ago. Now various farms in the region grow them, not only for restaurants and caterers, but also increasingly for the general public. They make beautiful additions to crudités baskets, and they are delicious briefly steamed. I like to make hors d'oeuvres from mini-pattypan squash as follows. The recipe can be doubled or quadrupled.

MAKES *10 hors d'oeuvres*

PREPARATION TIME: *15–20 minutes*

BROILING TIME: *about 2 minutes*

---

10 mini-pattypan squash (see note)
 1 tablespoon butter
 1 small tomato, finely chopped
 1 scallion, minced
    Scant teaspoon small capers
10 shrimp (size: 36 per pound), cleaned
       and deveined
    Hudson Valley goat's milk cheese, sheep's-
    milk cheese, or feta cheese, about 2-3 ounces

Steam the squash until barely done, about 2 minutes. In a small skillet, heat the butter and fry the tomato and scallion until the tomato becomes soft and juicy; add the capers. To this mixture, add the shrimp and cook until just firm and pink, no more than 60 seconds. Take off the heat.

With a melon baller, create a hollow in each little squash. Fill with a bit of the tomato-caper mixture and top with a shrimp. At serving time, preheat the broiler and top each shrimp with a small slice of cheese. Place under the broiler just long enough to melt the cheese, which will hold the shrimp in place. Serve hot.

NOTE: If mini-pattypan squash are not available, use zucchini with a diameter of no more than 1½ inches, cut into 1-inch-thick slices. Steam and scoop out as described for the pattypans.

Spaghetti Squash with Vegetable Topping

Spaghetti squash makes excellent diet fare, or a nice change from pasta.

SERVES *4–6*

PREPARATION TIME: *about 10 minutes*

COOKING TIME: *about 40 minutes for the squash*

1	spaghetti squash (about 2 pounds)
3	tablespoons olive or vegetable oil
1	zucchini, coarsely grated
5	plum tomatoes, washed and chopped
6–8	scallions, chopped, including green part
¼	cup flat-leaf parsley
¼	teaspoon dried basil
	Salt to taste
	Freshly ground black pepper to taste
	Pinch of sugar, if necessary

Preheat the oven to 350° F. Cut the spaghetti squash in half lengthwise and bake, cut side down, in a baking dish filled with an inch of boiling water for about 40 minutes. Replenish water as needed. This squash is done when the inside can be easily separated into strands with a fork. Do not overcook.

In the meantime, heat the oil in a frying pan and add the zucchini, tomatoes, and scallions. Cook, covered, until the tomatoes are soft and juicy but the pieces still retain their shape, about 5 minutes. Add the parsley and basil. Stir and taste; season with salt and pepper and a pinch of sugar, if necessary. Cover and keep hot. When the squash is done, separate the strands into a serving bowl and top with the tomato mixture.

Zucchini-Chive Fritters

A beer batter not only is used for apple beignets or sweet fritters but also works very well for this zucchini and chives combination. Fresh chives are a must for this recipe. You can serve the fritters as hors d'oeuvres or, instead of bread, with a meal. Either way, they are guaranteed to fly away.

MAKES *20 fritters*

PREPARATION TIME: *about 15 minutes*

FRYING TIME: *about 6 minutes per batch*

2   *cups self-rising flour*
8   *ounces (1 cup) beer*
3   *small zucchini*
½   *cup finely chopped fresh chives*
½   *teaspoon minced garlic*
1   *teaspoon salt*
¼   *teaspoon freshly ground pepper*
    Vegetable oil, for deep frying

Place the flour in a big bowl and slowly stir in the beer. Cut the zucchini in half lengthwise and cut each half into 4 strips. Cut the strips across into thin pieces; add to the flour. Add the chives, garlic, salt, and pepper and stir to combine. It will seem that the dough is stiff and that there is not enough of it, but it will rise and there will be enough. Just wait. Let the dough rest for 30 minutes.

Heat the vegetable oil to 350° F. Drop tablespoonfuls of fritter dough into the hot oil and fry until golden and done inside. You might want to cut the first few in half to make sure they are done, until you get the hang of it. Serve hot or cold with a maple mustard.

SWISS CHARD

Swiss Chard Pie

When you grow Swiss chard, you really get your money's worth. It grows and you pick and it grows and you pick, and so forth; there seems to be a never-ending supply. I like it best in the following pie or quiche, but you can also cook it briefly like spinach and season it with some butter, freshly grated nutmeg, salt, and freshly ground pepper.

SERVES 6

PREPARATION TIME: *about 10–15 minutes*

BAKING TIME: *about 40 minutes*

1½ pounds Swiss chard, chopped fine, heavy
    ribs removed
3 eggs
2 cups small-curd cottage cheese
8 ounces finely shredded Monterey Jack
    cheese
¼ cup grated Parmesan cheese
½ cup toasted bread crumbs
¼ cup minced flat-leaf parsley
¼ cup minced onion
½ teaspoon salt
¼ teaspoon marjoram
    Pinch of freshly ground black pepper
    Pinch of freshly grated nutmeg
1 unbaked 10-inch pie shell, fitted into a
    10-inch deep dish pie plate

Preheat the oven to 425° F.

In a large bowl, mix cut chard and eggs thoroughly; then add the cottage cheese, the other two cheeses, bread crumbs, parsley, onions, salt, marjoram, pepper and salt and combine. Put this mixture in the pie shell. It will be heaped high, but do not worry; it shrinks as it cooks to make a very well-filled pie. Bake for 40 minutes, or until the crust is brown and a knife inserted comes out clean.

TOMATOES

Tomato Corn Relish

This relish is from Virginia Murphy, of Hurley, New York. It is easy, quick, and delicious—what more could you ask for? It goes well with burgers, chops, and ribs.

MAKES about 1½ pints

PREPARATION TIME: 10 minutes

COOKING TIME: about 30–40 minutes

1 cup coarsely cut onions
1 cup coarsely cut cucumbers
1½ cups cut tomatoes
1 hot chili pepper
½ cup sugar
1 teaspoon salt
½ tablespoon mustard seed
½ tablespoon celery seed
1 teaspoon turmeric
1 cup distilled vinegar
1½ cups corn cut off the cob, or one package
(9 or 10 ounces) frozen corn

Put all ingredients except the corn in the blender. Blend at high speed for 4 seconds. Empty into a medium-sized saucepan. Add the corn and bring to a boil. Simmer for 30–40 minutes, until thickened. Cool and serve.

Tomato, Cucumber, and Chickpea Spread

The following spread, together with some crisp crackers, is a nice addition to a summer brown-bag lunch or can be served as an hors d'oeuvre, if you wish.

SERVES *6 or more*

PREPARATION TIME: *5–10 minutes*

1 can (20 ounces) chickpeas, drained,
    juice reserved
1 teaspoon minced garlic
1 tablespoon lemon juice
    Chopped tomatoes, to taste
    Chopped cucumber, seeds removed, to taste
    Salt to taste
    Freshly ground black pepper to taste

In a blender, blend the chickpeas, garlic, and lemon juice to a rough paste. If necessary, add a little of the chickpea liquid, but do not make it wet. To this mixture add as much chopped tomato and cucumber as you like. Taste, and season with salt and pepper.

TURNIPS

Turnip Soup

Turnip soup was already popular in the nineteenth century. My recipe is quickly made in the blender. Most people will like it for its pleasant, slightly peppery taste, but don't tell them what it is, until it's eaten: turnips are generally not held in high esteem.

SERVES 4–6

PREPARATION TIME: *about ten minutes*

COOKING TIME: *10–15 minutes*

---

4 cups beef broth, homemade or canned
3 medium turnips, peeled and cut
   into chunks
1 small onion, chopped
2 tablespoons chopped parsley
   Salt to taste
   Freshly ground black pepper to taste

In a large saucepan, combine beef broth, turnips, and onion and cook until the turnips are soft, about 10–15 minutes. Stir in the parsley and put the mixture in a blender. Blend until smooth; it will take 2 or 3 batches. Taste and season with salt and pepper. Reheat and serve.

6. Fall

The subjects of the fall chapter are cheeses, doughnuts and breads, meats, game, and poultry. The fruit and vegetable harvests were discussed in the two preceding chapters.

Cheeses

A large variety of goat cheeses from Little Rainbow Chêvre or Coach Farms; rich, delicate Camembert-style and sheep's-milk cheeses from Hollow Road Farms; nutty Alpine cheese from Hawthorne Valley Farm—all these dairy products of the Hudson region are helping to change the image of American cheese forever. These cheeses are so good for snacking, pastas, or desserts, or simply combined with some crusty bread, fruit, and nuts for a wholesome meal, that recipes for them seem redundant. Nevertheless, a few cheese recipes are included in this chapter, among them one from Larry Forgione, who shares his recipe for Hudson Valley Camembert that he features in his newly opened restaurant in the Beekman Arms, in Rhinebeck, New York.

Doughnuts and Breads

Fall is traditionally the time of slaughtering, with rendered lard as a by-product. In times past, fresh lard was used for frying doughnuts. Now doughnuts, today prepared in doughnut machines, are most often fried in vegetable oil rather than lard, but these delicious fried cakes are still important elements of fall trips to the orchards in the Hudson region, where a cup of hot cider and a fresh doughnut are part of the fun.

The Dutch brought the rich forerunner of the doughnut, the *olie-koeck*, to this region. Many Americans know about the Dutch in this country from the works of author Washington Irving, who lived in the Hudson region. In *A History of New York*, published in 1809, he describes *olie-koecken* served at tea as "balls of sweetened dough . . . a delicious kind of cake, at present scarce known in this city, excepting in genuine Dutch families." In another account of a Dutch tea table Irving calls them the "doughty doughnut and the tenderer oly koek." I must explain here that the original word *olie-koecken*, which means "oil cakes," became increasingly anglicized in America and is found in many spellings such as the one above, but also as *olycook* or *olycoecks*, among others.

Recently it was possible to test Irving's powers of culinary observation when we prepared recipes for doughnuts and olycooks from a handwritten manuscript by Anne Stevenson (1774–1821), wife of Pierre Van Cortlandt II, and her mother Magdalena Douw (1750–1817). The Stevensons' doughnuts (made with flour, small quantities of sugar and butter, 1 egg, and milk) were indeed quite sturdy, while the olycooks (made with flour, yeast, a lot of butter, sugar, and 12 eggs) were toothsome and tender. It was clear that Irving had eaten his share of both and knew what he was talking about.

Stevenson's olycook recipe is marked "Albany method." The phrase indicates that it came from her relatives, the Van Rensselaer family of that city, because a very similar recipe by Maria Sanders Van Rensselaer (1749–1830) appears in her family cookbook. That recipe suggests to using "as much milk as you like," whereas Anne Stevenson is more precise and says to use "as muc[h] milk as you pleas[e], say near or quite 3 pints."

The recipe of Maria's daughter Arriet [sic] Van Rensselaer uses a dough similar to her mother's, made with lots of butter and 12 eggs. But then she suggests to "spice [the dough] with nutmeg or mace" and to "fill [it] with stewed apples or raisins." This preparation is more reminiscent of the recipe in *The Sensible Cook*, included in this chapter. We cannot ascertain if this trend continues in the family, because the recipe of granddaughter Catherine Van Rensselaer Bonney (1817–1890), though listed in the index, is missing from her cookbook.

An undated letter tucked into another Van Cortlandt family cookbook, dated 1865, shows us the Americanization of the Dutch *olie-koecken*. The writer C. T. Beck confesses to feeling unwell, dispenses with family news, and simply jots down three recipes, among which is one for "oliecooks." She suggests putting "cranberries stewed very dry . . . inside." The addition of the cranberry, a native of this country but not grown in the Netherlands, indicates that the olie-koeck has adapted itself to the New World.

But the typical New Netherland version of olie-koecken is prepared according to the "Albany method." It appears over and over again in various recipe collections, such as the handwritten cookbook manuscripts of the Huguenot Historical Society in New Paltz. Eliza Tenbrook's "ole cooke" call again for that familiar combination of flour, yeast, sugar, butter, and 12 eggs. Although another, anonymous recipe for "oly cakes" divides the ingredients in half and suggests that some mace be added, it still directs the preparation of olie-koecken according to the "Albany method."

The Dutch Reformed church was a major unifying force in New Netherland. Toward the end of the nineteenth century, church groups apparently realized that the Dutch culinary traditions were fading and attempted to preserve some of the recipes in church cookbooks. *Old Dutch Receipts*, published in 1885 by the Lafayette Reformed Church of Newark, is a good example. So is *Crumbs of Comfort* by the Young Ladies Mission Band of the Madison Avenue Reformed Church of Albany, which was published in the same year. The sentiments expressed in the introduction to the first edition of the *First Dutch (Reformed) Cookbook*, compiled by the Ladies of the Reformed Church of Pompton Plains, New Jersey, in 1889, speaks for them all. It suggests that in this collection can be found "something of the ancient hospitality—for which our venerable homes have become proverbial." It goes on to explain that "not many dishes of the olden time can be reduced to print . . . but the flavor of good old Dutch cookery is not lost, so that what we term our modern dishes may be sweetened to the taste of our childhood." All three books have recipes for olie-koecken or doughnuts.

Mrs. Charles Hamlin (née Huybertie Lansing Pruyn) also wanted to preserve knowledge of Dutch ways in America. Consequently, she spent many years collecting information about the early Dutch of Albany. In "Some Remembrances," she recalls the holiday festivities of her youth in that city. She describes olie-koecken as:

> round cakes like a small tennis ball, fried in oil. These cakes are very rich and require over 60 hours to be made properly as they must be raised twice. It is said that only a Dutch cook can put the raisins soaked overnight in brandy in the center. While hot they are rolled in fine suger.

Although in her youthful longing for a tender olie-koeck it might have seemed to take 60 hours before they were done, a time span of a mere 16 hours seems more realistic, judging from the recipe by her relative Mary Pruyn in the above-mentioned *Crumbs of Comfort*. Pruyn says that first a sponge is made, which, when risen, is combined with other ingredients. Then the dough is left to rise overnight. She warns, ''If not perfectly light early in the morning, wait till it is.''

It seems clear that many descendants of the New Netherland settlers had not forgotten the taste of the foods of their ancestors. Through dishes such as olie-koecken, coleslaw, waffles, pancakes, and especially cookies, we are reminded today of the Dutch past of the Hudson region and its influence on the American kitchen.

Meats, Game, and Poultry

Farms in the Hudson region raise beef, beefalo, goats, lamb, pigs, and fallow deer, as well as chickens, pheasants, ducks, geese, and turkeys. Augmenting this abundant variety are the many game animals, especially whitetail deer. Further, according to Ken Meskill of the New York State Department of Environmental Conservation, the region has a substantial black bear population, especially in the Catskills, one that is sizable enough to allow a hunting season. Other animals that are hunted are rabbit, hare, grouse, pheasants, wild turkey, woodcock, and several species of ducks—such as merganser, mallards, wood duck, redhead, black duck, and pintail—as well as snow geese and Canada geese. While fur-bearing animals are mostly trapped for their fur, parts of them can be eaten as well. Coyote, raccoon, gray and red fox, skunk (a favorite for coats around the turn of the century), opossum, weasel, bobcat, beaver, otter, mink, fisher, and muskrat are all hunted in the Hudson region. Weapons used for hunting are shotgun, rifle, bow-and-arrow, or traps, as are appropriate and allowed for the particular area.

Native American Customs

Native Americans in the area would close the fall gathering cycle by collecting nuts, such as hickory nuts, butternuts and black walnuts, and digging up roots. For this activity, they used a fairly thick digging stick with a point that had been hardened in the fire. The same stick was used for the breaking of the ground for planting in the spring.

In Harmen Meyndertsz van den Bogaert's journal, *A Journey into Mohawk and Oneida Country, 1634–1635*, we find a description of foods, all of them native, that may also have been typical for late fall and winter foods in the Hudson region. Here is part of Van den Bogaert's entry for December 23, 1634:

> Today we feasted on two bears, and we received today one half skipple [a dry measure equivalent to .764 bushel] of beans and some dried strawberries. Also, we provided ourselves here with bread that we could take along on the journey. Some of it had nuts, chestnuts, dried blueberries and sunflower seeds baked in it.

From Walter Hill's nineteenth-century notebook we come to understand how the settlers adapted to Native American food customs. For hunting trips they would use "a very sustaining food they had learned from the Indian, dried corn, mixed with bits of dried meat and maple sugar—called kwitcheraw."

RECIPES FEATURING:

Cheese
Larry Forgione's Hudson Valley Camembert Crisp with Apple-Pear Conserve
Lillian Cahn's Chicken with Spinach and Goat Cheese
Tyropeta Variation

Doughnuts and Breads
Country-Style Hearth Loaf
Hard Bread and Peas Porridge
Olie-Koecken
Olycooks (Albany Method)
Salinger's Apple Cider Doughnuts
Whole-Grain Bread

Meat, Game, and Poultry
Beefalo
Crusader Pork Chops
Diced Pork with Green Peppers
Foie Gras au Torchon
John Novi's Foie Gras Terrine
Jerk Chicken
Lithgow Roundup Chili
Miltie's Nuggets
Quattro's Pheasant with White Wine and Portobello Mushrooms
Rabbit Fricassee with Vegetables
Roast Venison
Rolled Beefsteak
Venison Hash with Currant Jelly
Venison Sausage

CHEESE

Larry Forgione's Hudson Valley Camembert Crisp with Apple-Pear Conserve

Larry Forgione's cooking has a straightforward message: show off past and present American cuisine at its best. He is known for such old-fashioned favorites as buttery mashed potatoes and homey chocolate pudding. No wonder he was attracted to the Hudson region, where fine fresh ingredients are readily available. In the historic setting of the Beekman Arms, which claims to be America's oldest inn, he cooks dishes with Hudson region ingredients. Although it is "not a Hudson Valley theme park," as one of his employees said, the restaurant makes a sincere effort to use local foods and produce.

This dish is a good example of Forgione's wonderful cooking. In the restaurant, the cheese triangle would be served on a bed of lettuces dressed with a wild hickory nut vinaigrette. Create your own vinaigrette with a good oil and herb vinegar, or use one of the excellent flavored vinegars made by Hudson region companies. This makes a substantial appetizer or a delicious light meal.

SERVES 4

PREPARATION TIME: *about 20 minutes*

COOKING TIME: *about 5 minutes*

---

4   *cups assorted lettuce leaves (for example,*
        red leaf, Bibb, oak leaf, watercress,
        spinach and arugula)
    Vinaigrette, to taste
    Salt to taste
    Freshly ground black pepper to taste
2   *ripe 5-ounce Hollow Road Farms square*
        Camembert cheeses
3   *sheets phyllo dough*
2   *tablespoons clarified butter (see note)*
1   *large egg, beaten lightly*
2   *tablespoons unsalted butter*
    Apple-Pear Conserve (recipe follows)

Put the lettuces in a large bowl; add enough vinaigrette to coat the greens, and season with salt and freshly ground pepper. Toss well. Divide the salad among 4 serving plates.

Cut each square of cheese into two triangles. Place one sheet of phyllo dough on a clean dry surface and brush with clarified butter. Brush another sheet with clarified butter and place on top. Repeat the procedure with the third sheet. Cut the stack of phyllo sheets into four equal strips. Place each triangle of Camembert on the bottom corner of each phyllo strip. Roll up, maintaining the "triangle." Brush with beaten egg to seal.

Heat the 2 tablespoons butter in a heavy skillet over medium heat until it begins to foam. Place the cheese triangles in the pan and sauté each side until light brown and crisp. Do not overcook or the cheese will be too liquid. Remove with a spatula and drain on paper towels.

Spoon equal amounts of apple-pear conserve over the greens and put fried Camembert on top. Serve immediately.

NOTE: To make clarified butter: In a small saucepan, melt 4 tablespoons unsalted butter over low heat. When completely melted, remove and let it stand for a few minutes, so that the milk solids settle on the bottom. Skim the golden butter fat from the top and use in the above recipe.

■·■·■·■·■·■·■

APPLE-PEAR CONSERVE

COOKING TIME: *about 5 minutes*

---

1 *tablespoon butter*
1 *crisp Granny Smith apple, peeled, cored, and diced*
1 *ripe Bartlett or Bosc pear, peeled, cored, and diced*
1 *teaspoon dark brown sugar*
1 *tablespoon cider vinegar*
1 *tablespoon halved dried tart cherries, if available*
   Pinch of allspice
   Pinch of cumin
   Pinch of freshly grated nutmeg

In a small frying pan, heat the butter and briefly sauté the diced apple and pear until slightly softened. Stir in the sugar, vinegar, and cherries. Sprinkle with the seasonings, combine, and cook for one more minute.

Lillian Cahn's Chicken with Spinach and Goat Cheese

Coach Farm of Pine Plains, New York, in Dutchess County, is another increasingly better-known producer of Hudson region cheeses. They are faithful to the traditional methods of the French farmstead cheesemaker and produce authentic, hand-ladled goat's-milk cheeses. These cheeses are featured in the finest markets and restaurants and are also sold at the Union Square Greenmarket farmers market. Lillian Cahn, co-owner with her husband Miles, shares one of her favorite recipes for chicken breast stuffed with spinach and goat cheese.

SERVES 4

PREPARATION TIME: *20–30 minutes*

COOKING TIME: *1 hour and 10 minutes*

Vegetable oil
2 cloves garlic, minced
3 scallions, minced, green part included
1 package (10 ounces) frozen spinach,
        thawed and squeezed dry
   scant ¼ teaspoon freshly grated nutmeg
4 skinned chicken breast halves,
        pounded flat
8 tablespoons goat cheese
   Fine freshly made bread crumbs, or
        commercial toasted bread crumbs
1 egg, lightly beaten with a little milk
2 tablespoons butter, melted
2 tablespoons chopped fresh dill

Heat 2 tablespoons of vegetable oil and fry the garlic and scallions until the garlic is very light brown. Remove and stir in the spinach and nutmeg.

Place the chicken breast halves on a cutting board, skinned side down. Divide the spinach mixture over the chicken breast halves, and top with 2 tablespoons goat cheese for each chicken breast. Roll each breast around the filling, making as neat and tightly closed a package as possible. Roll the package in the bread crumbs, then in the egg mixture, and then again in the bread crumbs. Place on a baking sheet and allow to rest for about 10 minutes.

Preheat the oven to 300° F.

In the meantime, heat about half an inch of vegetable oil in a frying pan. When the oil is hot, fry the coated chicken breast packages until golden brown all around. Remove them and place on a clean baking sheet. Brush with the melted butter and sprinkle with the chopped dill. Bake for 1 hour.

Tyropeta Variation

The cheeses from Hollow Road Farm in Stuyvesant, New York, have been hailed by food writers for various newspapers and magazines, including the New York Times. *Joan Snyder and Ken Kleinpeter joined forces in 1983 to create this dairy. New York State has shown its interest in their venture by giving them a grant to develop an economic model for future sheep-dairy aspirants.*

Here is their Tyropeta variation, customarily made with fresh unsalted Ricotta, which uses fresh sheep's-milk cheese. This cheese averages only 45 calories per ounce and has a fat content of 3 grams per ounce. Serve the molded cheese with some fall raspberries for a perfect seasonal dessert.

SERVES *6–8*

PREPARATION TIME: *about 10–15 minutes*

STANDING TIME: *24 hours*

4	**logs Hollow Road Farms fresh sheep's-milk cheese, plain**
2	**tablespoons honey**
1–2	**tablespoons sweet white wine or cream sherry**
	Butter, for greasing mold
⅓	**cup grated, toasted hazelnuts**

Combine cheese, honey, and wine in a food processor until well blended. Butter a decoratively shaped 1-quart mold and dust with some of the grated nuts. Add the rest of the nuts to the cheese mixture and blend thoroughly. Press the cheese firmly and evenly into the mold and chill, covered tightly, for approximately 24 hours.

To serve, dip the mold into hot water for a few seconds, then invert onto a serving plate.

Country-Style Hearth Loaf

Bread Alone, in Boiceville, New York, is a small European-style bakery, that bakes thick-crusted hearty loaves of bread directly on the wood-fired hearth. The bakery is owned by Daniel Leader, who tells an enchanting story about his beginnings:

In 1976, on my first trip to France . . . I passed the rear entrance of a quiet boulangerie. Peering through the stone entrance, I watched a bare-chested boulanger assisted by a young apprentice. Both were dressed in their humble baking shorts and sandals. I watched them work for a couple of hours mixing, kneading, shaping, rolling and finally loading their fine breads into a cavernous wood-fired brick oven. Their silence and dedication impressed [me with] a sense of love that they shared for the work they did. As they unloaded the crackling thick-crusted breads into large willow cooling baskets, I felt this work call to me.

Leader shares this recipe for great-tasting, chewy bread. It is a fun project for a cold fall Sunday. The bread will take most of the day, but it needs to be worked only once in a while. It is definitely worth the effort!

MAKES *2 loaves*

PREPARATION TIME: *about 25 minutes*

TOTAL RISING TIME: *about 2–8 hours for the sponge; about 3–4 hours for the dough*

BAKING TIME: *50–60 minutes*

1½ **cups lukewarm water at 70° F.**
3½–4 **cups Golden white flour, or a good bread flour**
1¼ **teaspoons dry yeast**
Scant tablespoon salt

In a medium bowl, combine ½ cup of the lukewarm water, ¾ cup of the flour, and ½ teaspoon of the dry yeast. Stir until very thick and sticky. Cover with a clean kitchen towel and place in a warm (75°–80° F) draft-free place until it doubles in volume and begins to collapse. This can take from 2 to 8 hours. Start checking every half hour after two hours. The longer the sponge ferments, the nuttier and tangier your breads will be.

When the sponge is ready, add the remaining cup of water. Stir with a wooden spoon until the mixture becomes loose and foams slightly. Add the remaining ¾ teaspoon yeast, the salt, and only enough of the flour to make the dough very difficult to stir.

Turn out onto a well-floured board. The dough will be quite sticky at first and difficult to work with. Dip your hands in flour to prevent them from sticking. Knead the dough by pushing it down and forward with the heel of one hand, then pulling back from the top and folding the dough over with the other. Gradually add the remaining flour as you work the dough, and knead vigorously for 15 minutes. To see if the dough is done, pull a little dough from the mass. If it springs back quickly, it is ready.

Shape the dough into a firm ball and place in a greased bowl 1½ times larger than the ball of dough. Cover with a damp, clean, kitchen towel and place in a warm (75°–80° F) draft-free place. Let rise until doubled in volume, about 1½ to 2 hours.

Deflate the dough by pulling up on the sides and pushing down in the center. Cover again with a towel and let rise for 30 minutes.

Transfer the dough to an unfloured work surface and cut into two equal pieces. Flatten each with the heel of your hand, using firm direct strokes. This releases any remaining gas and invigorates the yeast in the dough. Shape each piece into a tight ball. Line two bowls or baskets with damp, floured kitchen towels and place the loaves upside down in each bowl. Dust the top side with flour. Cover with a clean, damp towel and place in a warm (75°–80° F) place until it has increased about 1½ times in volume, about 1 to 2 hours.

One hour before baking, preheat the oven to 450° F. Just before baking, gently flip the loaves over. Score them with a sharp knife by making quick shallow cuts about ⅛ inch deep along the surface. Quickly place the loaves in the oven and spray the oven's interior walls and roof 7 or 8 times with water from a spritzer bottle, until steam is pouring from the oven. Close the oven to trap the steam and bake 3 minutes. Spray again in the same way and bake until the loaves begin to color, about 20 minutes. The steam provides a hot dampness that helps produce crisp crusts with good color. Reduce the heat to 425° F and bake until the loaves are a rich caramel color and the crust is firm, another 25 to 35 minutes. The bread is done when the bottom sounds hollow when lightly tapped or when an instant-reading thermometer reads 200° F. If the bread is not done, return it to the oven and bake for 5 more minutes. Remove and cool on a wire rack or in a basket.

Once the loaf has cooled, slice off what you want and leave the remainder standing cut side down on a flat surface. You need not wrap it in plastic. If the bread can breathe, the crust will remain crisp and chewy. The loaf will keep at least 3 days this way, if it lasts that long in your household.

Hard Bread and Peas Porridge

▪▪

The entire Hudson region is rich in revolutionary history. The assault on Stony Point by the American Light Infantry marked the end of major British activities in the north. A spacious stone house in Vails Gate, New York, best known as Knox's Headquarters, provided quarters for several American generals. In the closing months of the war, Washington's headquarters was in the Hasbrouck House in Newburgh, New York. Nearby New Windsor Cantonment was the final encampment of the Continental Army.

Bernadette Noe, Site Interpreter at Knox's Headquarters, is working on the New Windsor Cantonment Cook Book. Here are two recipes from the first chapter, which deals specifically with the foods Continental soldiers were eating at the encampment in the winter of 1782–83. The bread recipe makes one 1-pound loaf. Three such loaves are needed to be steamed with the peas porridge, of which they are an integral part. This dish would feed six hungry soldiers.

MAKES *one 1-pound loaf*

PREPARATION TIME: *about 10 minutes*

BAKING TIME: *about 4½ hours in a regular oven*

---

2 *cups whole-wheat flour*
½ *cup wheat bran*
1 *cup warm water*

Preheat the oven to 375° F.

In a bowl, sift together the flour and bran. Make a well in the middle and pour in the water. Mix thoroughly. Turn out onto a floured board and knead into a uniform loaf. Shape into a round bread. Bake in a quick camp oven 3 hours. In a regular oven, bake 4½ hours. To serve, steam with the peas porridge.

▪▪▪▪▪▪▪▪▪▪▪▪

PEAS PORRIDGE

SERVES *6 or more*

PREPARATION TIME: *about 20 minutes*

COOKING TIME: *about 2 hours*

3	*pounds salt beef or pork*
3	*cups dried split peas*
3	*tablespoons vinegar*
3	*loaves Hard Bread (see above)*

Cut the beef into ½-inch cubes and brown them in the bottom of an iron kettle or large pan. Stir in the split peas and vinegar. Lay the bread on top. Fill the kettle with water and boil briskly until the broth reduces to reach the bottom of the bread. Refill the kettle with water and simmer gently until all ingredients are tender. To serve:

Some like it hot
Some like it cold
Some like it in the pot
Nine days old

Olie-Koecken

As explained in the introduction to this chapter, olie-koecken were the rich fore-runners of the thriftier doughnut. Here is an early recipe from the 1683 edition of The Sensible Cook. *Filled with apples, raisins, and whole almonds, spiced with cinnamon, cloves, and ginger, they make a rich treat. Do not make them too small; they should be at least 2 inches in diameter. When feeding a crowd, it is better to cut them in halves or quarters than to make them in a smaller size, because it is difficult to distribute the ingredients evenly if the olie-koecken are too small.*

MAKES *about 30*

PREPARATION TIME: *about 15–20 minutes*

RISING TIME: *1 hour*

FRYING TIME: *about 8–10 minutes per batch*

½ cup lukewarm (105°–115° F) water
   Pinch sugar
3 packages dry yeast
1 stick (8 tablespoons) butter
1¾ cups raisins
4 cups flour
¼ teaspoon salt
1 tablespoon cinnamon
½ teaspoon ground cloves
½ teaspoon ground ginger
1½ cups milk
1 cup whole almonds
3 medium Granny Smith apples, peeled,
      cored, and cut into small slivers
   Oil, for deep frying
   Confectioners' sugar (optional)

Pour the warm water in a small bowl; sprinkle with the yeast and then the sugar. Let it stand for a moment; then stir to dissolve the yeast. Set aside in a warm place.

In the meantime, melt the butter and let cool. Place the raisins in a saucepan, cover with water, and bring to a boil.

Allow them to boil for 1 minute and turn off the heat. Let the raisins stand for 5 minutes and drain. Pat them dry with paper towels and mix them with a tablespoon of flour.

Place the rest of the flour in a large bowl; stir in the salt, cinnamon, cloves, and ginger. Make a well in the middle and pour in the yeast. Stirring from the middle, slowly add the melted butter and the milk. The dough should be very thick and difficult to stir. Then add the raisins, the almonds, and the apples; combine thoroughly. Allow this batter to rise for about an hour. When doubled in bulk, stir down the dough.

Heat the oil to 350° F. Scoop out a heaping tablespoon of dough and pushing it off the spoon with the aid of another spoon, carefully drop it into the hot oil. The olie-keocken should be at least 2 inches in diameter. Fry them for about 5 minutes on each side, until golden brown. Check one by cutting into it to see if it is cooked all the way through. Drain on a thick layer of paper towels. The original recipe does not tell us to sprinkle them with sugar or roll them in it, and they are very good plain, but if you prefer you can dust them with confectioners' sugar.

Olycooks (Albany Method)

Here is a scaled-down version of Anne Stevenson's recipe. The original, in the archives of Historic Hudson Valley would make more than a hundred olycooks. Anne Stevenson Van Cortlandt lived at the Van Cortlandt Manor in Croton-on-Hudson, New York. The manor, administered by Historic Hudson Valley and open to the public, has a big, cozy kitchen with a large hearth, a beehive oven, and many of the original cooking implements, including waffle and wafer irons and period pieces such as large wooden cookie molds. As discussed in the introduction to this chapter, the Stevenson recipe, probably derived from the Van Rensselaer family in Albany, is, I believe, the direct forerunner of the American doughnut.

MAKES 25–30

PREPARATION TIME: *about 15 minutes*

RISING TIME: *1 hour*

FRYING TIME: *about 8–10 minutes*

¼ *cup of warm water (105°–115° F)*
3 *packages yeast*
   Pinch of sugar for the yeast
1 *stick (8 tablespoons) butter*
¾ *cup sugar*
3 *eggs*
1 *cup milk*
4 *cups flour*
   Oil, for deep frying
   Additional sugar, to coat finished product

Pour the water in a small bowl; sprinkle with the yeast and then the pinch of sugar. Let it stand for a moment and stir to dissolve the yeast. Set aside in a warm place.

In a large bowl, cream together the butter and ¾ cup sugar. One at a time add the eggs and combine. Add the milk and the yeast.

Slowly stir in the flour and combine thoroughly. Let the dough rise until doubled in bulk, about 1 hour.

Heat the oil to about 350° F. Scoop out a heaping tablespoon of dough and, pushing it off the spoon with the aid of another spoon, drop it carefully into the hot oil. Cook slowly on one side until a deep brown; then turn it and cook the other side. Check one olycook by cutting it in half to see if it is cooked all the way through. Remove it and drain on a thick layer of paper towels. Roll in sugar to coat. Cool and serve.

Salinger's Apple Cider Doughnuts

Many of the orchards in the Hudson region sell apple cider doughnuts. It is a Hudson region specialty. Here is the recipe of Maureen Salinger of Salinger's Orchards, known not only for a wide variety of apples and other fruit but also for her excellent freshly baked pies and muffins.

MAKES *about 2 dozen*

PREPARATION TIME: *about 10 minutes*

RESTING AND DRYING TIME: *one hour and 10 minutes*

FRYING TIME: *4–6 minutes*

3½–4½	cups all-purpose flour
½	cup whole-wheat flour
1	tablespoon baking powder
½	teaspoon baking soda
½	teaspoon salt
¼	teaspoon freshly grated nutmeg
1	teaspoon ground cinnamon
2	eggs
½	cup light brown sugar
½	cup granulated sugar
6	tablespoons shortening, melted
1	cup apple cider
	Vegetable oil, for frying
	Cinnamon-sugar (optional)

In a large mixing bowl, combine 3½ cups all-purpose flour, the whole-wheat flour, and the baking powder, baking soda, salt, nutmeg, and cinnamon. In the bowl of an electric mixer, combine 2 eggs and the two sugars. Gradually stir in the melted shortening and the cider. At low speed, beat in the flour mixture. Chill for 1 hour.

If the dough is still too soft and sticky, stir in up to a cup of all-purpose flour to make a soft dough that can be patted out to a ½-inch thickness. Cut with double cutter or two different-sized circles, to create the hole in the middle. Allow the doughnuts to dry for 10 minutes.

Heat at least 2 inches of oil to 375° F in a large skillet or kettle. Slide the doughnuts into the hot oil with the aid of an oiled spatula. Fry 2–3 minutes on each side, turning once. Remove onto a thick layer of paper towels. Cool slightly and roll in cinnamon-sugar, or serve plain. Serve warm or at room temperature.

Whole-Grain Bread

The following recipe is for experienced bread bakers who like a challenge. This rather complicated recipe comes from the 1991 culinary competition of the Dutchess County Fair, New York State's second largest fair, in Rhinebeck, New York. Contestants had to follow the recipe exactly, and their submitted samples were judged by the usual standards of taste, texture, and appearance. This recipe makes a beautiful large loaf of hearty, fiber-filled whole-grain bread.

MAKES *one 3¼-pound loaf.*

PREPARATION TIME: *about 35 minutes*

RISING TIME: *2 hours and 15 minutes*

BAKING TIME: *50–60 minutes*

2	cups rye flour
1	cup unprocessed bran
½	cup wheat germ
About 4¼	cups whole-wheat flour
3	tablespoons sugar
4	teaspoons salt
2	packages dry yeast

¾   cup milk
1   stick (8 tablespoons) butter or
      margarine
⅓   cup dark molasses
2   eggs
2   tablespoons yellow cornmeal
1   teaspoon caraway seed

In a large bowl, combine the rye flour, bran, and wheat germ and 3 cups of the whole-wheat flour. Set aside.

In the bowl of an electric mixer, combine the sugar, salt, and yeast and 3 cups of the flour mixture.

In a 2-quart saucepan over low heat, heat the milk, butter, and molasses and 1 cup water until very warm (120°–130° F). (The butter does not need to melt.) With the mixer at low speed, gradually beat liquid into the dry ingredients until just blended. Increase the speed to medium; beat 2 minutes, occasionally scraping the bowl. Reserve 1 egg white; beat in the remaining eggs and 2 cups of the flour mixture. Continue beating 2 minutes, occasionally scraping the bowl. With a spoon, stir in the remaining flour mixture and additional whole-wheat flour (about ¾ cup) to make a soft dough.

Lightly flour a surface with whole-wheat flour; turn the dough onto the surface. Knead until smooth and elastic about 10 minutes, adding more whole-wheat flour, of the remaining ½ cup of flour, while kneading, as needed. Shape the dough into a ball; place it in a greased large bowl, turning the dough to grease the top. Cover and let rise in warm place (80°–85° F), away from draft, until doubled, about 1 hour. (The dough is doubled when 2 fingers pressed lightly into dough leave a dent.)

Punch down the dough. Turn it out onto a surface lightly floured with whole-wheat flour and cover it with a bowl for 15 minutes; let the dough rest. Sprinkle a baking sheet with cornmeal.

Shape the dough into an oval and taper the ends; place it on a baking sheet. Cover with a clean kitchen towel; let it rise in a warm place until doubled in bulk, about 1 hour.

Preheat the oven to 350° F.

Cut three diagonal slashes on the top of the loaf. In a cup, mix the reserved egg white with 1 tablespoon water. With a pastry brush, brush the bread with the egg white mixture. Sprinkle the bread with caraway seed. Bake 50–60 minutes until the bottom of the loaf sounds hollow when lightly tapped, or an instant-reading thermometer reads 200° F. Remove and let cool on rack.

MEAT, GAME, AND POULTRY

Beefalo

Beefalo is genetically ⅜ bison and ⅝ domestic cattle. Parentage on full-blood beefalo must be proved in order to register with the American Beefalo World Registry. Approximately 50,000 such animals have so far been registered.

Beefalo tastes like beef, yet it has the nutritional values of bison; low fat, low calories, and low cholesterol. Samples of ground beef from beefalo and ground beef purchased in a supermarket were tested by Certified Laboratories in New York City; the results shown are for a normal 4-ounce serving.

	Ground Beefalo	Ground Beef
Protein	20.35%	16.6%
Fat	3.65%	24.8%
Calories	129.6	329.6
Cholesterol	20.8 mg	602.0 mg

Beefalo cooks the same as beef, with two exceptions. Because of its low fat content, it continues to cook longer than commercial beef after it has been removed from the heat source. It is therefore suggested that the cooking time be reduced by ⅖. Beefalo also defrosts quicker than Western grain-fattened beef.

Sandra and Roger Corlew, of Corlew Beefalo Farm in Argyle, in Washington County, New York, have raised beefalo for sixteen years. They have currently a herd of about fifty animals, which are raised naturally—without growth stimulants or hormones. Sandra says she cooks beefalo like beef, but over the years she had learned "to cook the beefalo patties frozen, roasts partially thawed, and steaks frozen. Because of the leanness, they are juicier if cooked frozen," she asserts. She also suggests that, when grilling, you use a lower heat than usual and do not overcook. Customers tell her that beefalo "tastes like beef used to taste years ago."

Crusader Pork Chops

For eighteen years, Roger Gabrielsen, of Purdys, New York, sailed up and down the Hudson on the tugboat Crusader. *The tug would push or tow Red Star/ Hess Oil gas or oil barges. Gabrielsen, now retired, would be on board for two weeks and then have two weeks off. During a working day, he would prepare three meals for six people. "They ate very well," he says. For breakfast he served them pancakes, bacon, eggs or "anything they liked." Lunch consisted of a soup and often pork chops. Steaks were frequently part of the dinner menu, with desserts such as bread pudding. The crew liked his Norwegian specialties. At one time, he owned a Norwegian restaurant, where he served many hearty dishes, of which the fruit-stuffed pork chops that follow are an example.*

SERVES *8*

PREPARATION TIME: *about 10–15 minutes*

BAKING TIME: *2 hours and 50 minutes*

---

12 ounces mixed dried fruits (apples,
    apricots, and prunes)
8 thick (2 inches) rib pork chops, each with
    a pocket (see note)
Salt to taste
Freshly ground pepper to taste
8 thin lemon slices

Soak the dried fruits overnight in water to cover.

The next day, preheat the oven to 350° F.

Drain and dry the fruits with paper towels. Cut them into small pieces. Divide the fruits over the 8 pork chops, and firmly stuff them into the pockets. Season the chops with salt and pepper. Place the seasoned pork chops in one layer on a baking sheet or if necessary two baking sheets with a rim. Top each chop with a lemon slice. Cover with aluminum foil and bake for 2½ hours. Uncover and baste with the juices. Continue to bake for another 20 minutes. During those last minutes watch the chops carefully for burning.

NOTE: The butcher will prepare these for you.

Diced Pork with Green Peppers

Soy sauce is not a product logically associated with the Hudson region. Yet in Middletown, New York, is Mandarin Soy Sauce, a manufacturing facility with a capability of producing upwards of 1,800,000 gallons of naturally brewed soy sauce per year. Here is a pleasantly spicy recipe for their product. Serve the pork dish with brown rice, broccoli, and a cucumber salad.

SERVES *2–4, depending on accompaniments*

PREPARATION TIME: *about 15 minutes; marinade: at least 30 minutes*

FRYING TIME: *about 3 minutes*

- ⅔ **pound pork loin**
- 1½ **tablespoons soy sauce**
- 1½ **tablespoons cornstarch**
- 3 **cups vegetable oil, for deep frying**
- 1 **cup green pepper, cored, seeded, and diced (in ½-inch square pieces)**
- 3 **tablespoons diced hot red pepper**
- 3 **tablespoons chopped scallions**
- 15 **slices garlic**

SEASONING SAUCE

- 2 **tablespoons soy sauce**
- 1 **tablespoon dry white wine**
- ½ **teaspoon sugar**
- ½ **teaspoon salt**
- 1 **teaspoon cornstarch**
- ¼ **teaspoon sesame oil**
- ¼ **teaspoon black pepper**

Cut the pork into ⅔-inch cubes. Combine with the 1½ tablespoons soy sauce and the 1½ tablespoons cornstarch and marinate for at least 30 minutes.

In a small bowl, thoroughly mix the ingredients of the seasoning sauce.

In a wok, heat the 3 cups oil to 300° F. Drain the diced pork and fry for about 15 seconds. Remove and set aside. Pour out the oil from the pan except for 3 tablespoons and reheat. Stir-fry the green pepper, hot pepper, scallion and garlic for about 10 seconds. Then add the pork and the seasoning sauce. Stir over high heat until the sauce has thickened and the pork is cooked through, about 4 minutes. Transfer to a heated platter and serve as indicated above.

Foie Gras au Torchon
•.

Ariane Daguin, daughter of renowned two-star French chef André Daguin, is co-owner of D'Artagnan in Jersey City, New Jersey, the first company in American to make and market true fresh foie gras. While studying at Barnard and working part-time in a gourmet shop, she met her future partner George Faison, and together they have made a success of their business. Silky, smooth foie gras is the fatted liver of ducks or geese. To some not familiar with foie gras, it seems to have little liver taste, because the most frequently asked question about their American foie gras is: "Is there liver in it?"

Here is Daguin's recipe for duck liver poached in a kitchen towel. She suggests that you serve the foie gras with country-style bread and the best Sauternes or Champagne you can afford. Duck fat can be purchased at some gourmet shops.

SERVES *10–12*

PREPARATION TIME: *about 30 minutes*

COOKING TIME: *50 minutes*

STANDING TIME: *3 days*

---

1   *whole foie gras at room temperature*
1   *tablespoon salt*
1   *teaspoon white pepper*
5   *pounds duck fat*

•.•.•.•.•.•.•.•.

Devein the foie gras at room temperature, gently pulling off the main vein of each lobe. These veins run vertically with their base at the bottom of the lobes. It is better *not* to devein than to break the liver in pieces as you do this. Season both lobes with the salt and pepper.

In the meantime, melt the duck fat in a large pot and bring it to a temperature of 212° F. Use an instant-reading thermometer to check. Place the liver at one end of a clean 30- by 20-inch kitchen towel and roll it tightly. To make a tight package, twist the overlapping ends of the towel firmly in opposite directions and tie them with kitchen string. Place the tied foie gras in the duck fat so it is entirely covered. Cook at a constant 212° F for 50 minutes. Remove and refrigerate the liver at once. Wait three days before unwrapping it to slice and serve it.

John Novi's Foie Gras Terrine

John Novi is the chef and proprietor of the DePuy Canal House, in High Falls, New York. The Depuy Canal House is a restored building that goes back to 1797. Built by Simeon DePuy, it was a particularly popular spot with the workers on the Delaware and Hudson canal, which was started in 1825. The present restaurant is decorated with many charming canal memorabilia.

Novi is an exuberant American nouvelle cuisine cook as well as a staunch supporter of the local Hudson region growers, whose dishes incorporate elements of many different cuisines. An example is a winter offering of beggar's bag tied with edible Chinese gourd string: steamed moo shu flour pancake filled with Cajun sausage and sauerkraut served in hot-and-sour broth.

John Novi likes to cook foie gras. He contributed this recipe for a terrine, which at some later date he hopes to market through his adjacent store. He suggests serving the small terrines with crackers or toast and a raspberry mustard made by mashing equal parts of fresh raspberries and Dijon mustard.

SERVES *8*

PREPARATION TIME: *about 20 minutes*

BAKING TIME: *10–14 minutes*

½   pound foie gras
2   cups egg whites
    White pepper or Tabasco, to taste
2   tablespoons brandy
    Salt to taste

Preheat the oven to 350° F.

Break the liver in half and remove all the veins and excess fat. Also see the instructions in the previous recipe. Save the best half for slicing and quick sautéing. Take the scraps and other whole pieces and put them in a blender. Add the egg whites, pepper, brandy, and salt and purée until smooth. Pour into eight 2-ounce individual molds or terrines, placed in a hot water bath. Cover the dish, but leave space between the cover and top of the terrines. Steam for the first 8 minutes at 350° F, then reduce the oven temperature to 300° for the remaining 6 minutes, until just lightly firm in the middle when touched. The mixture will rise like a soufflé, but it will settle and just fit the little molds. Be careful not to increase the heat, which may cause them to "blow up." To unmold the small terrines, place an inverted plate on top of the mold and turn both upside down; the foie gras should come right out. Serve hot as described above.

Jerk Chicken
••.

Who picks all the wonderful fruits grown in the Hudson region? Since the 1940s many apple growers have turned to Jamaicans to harvest their crops. These skillful workers come here to earn as much money as they can by picking some 100 to 120 bushels a day. Malty Hunt of Trinityville, Jamaica, is one of them. For years, he has worked at Indian Ladder Farms, in Altamont, New York. In addition to his skills as a picker, he says he is a good cook. He gave me the directions from which I put together the following recipe for a very simple version of a Jamaican favorite. It has just the right amount of spiciness, and the sauce makes it special.

SERVES 4

••.••.••.••.••.••.••.

PREPARATION TIME: *about 10 minutes; marinade: 1 hour or more*

GRILLING TIME: *about 40–45 minutes*

1	teaspoon cayenne pepper
1	medium onion, chopped fine
2–3	cloves garlic, minced
1	large tomato, chopped fine
3	pounds chicken, cut in serving pieces
2	tablespoons vegetable oil
	Salt to taste
	Freshly ground pepper to taste

In a large bowl, combine the cayenne, onion, garlic, and tomato. Add the chicken and spoon this mixture over the chicken pieces. Marinate for 1 hour.

In the meantime, heat the grill. When hot, brush off and reserve onion mixture and place the chicken on the grill, about 5–6 inches above the coals. Grill for about 40–45 minutes, turning the pieces as necessary.

In a medium frying pan, heat the oil and add the onion mixture. Fry for a few minutes over medium heat; then add a dash of water, reduce the heat, and simmer for 5 minutes. Season with salt and freshly ground pepper. Pour this sauce over the chicken when done.

Lithgow Roundup Chili

Whitetail deer are difficult to keep in herds and cannot be sold legally. That's why Eliot Clarke raises fallow deer at Lithgow Deer Farm, in Millbrook, New York. He has a herd of three hundred animals, which are sold as breeding stock all over the United States and as meat to local restaurants. The deer graze in the summer and are fed corn, grain, and hay in the winter. Once a year, the animals are rounded up to be weighed and given shots. The roundup is performed with the help of lots of volunteers. At the end of the day, Susie Clarke serves the following chili with an unusual, lively taste, full of cumin flavor.

SERVE *6–8*

PREPARATION TIME: *about 15 minutes*

COOKING TIME: *about 30–40 minutes*

---

3   *pounds ground venison*
1   *medium onion, chopped*
2   *cloves garlic, minced*
1   *can (12 ounces) tomato paste*
1   *can (29 ounces) tomato purée*
1½ *tablespoons Dijon mustard*
1½ *tablespoons ground cumin*
1   *tablespoon ground coriander*
2   *tablespoons chili powder*
4   *cans (15 ounces each) dark red kidney
        beans, drained*
    Salt to taste
    Freshly ground pepper to taste
    Dried red pepper flakes, for garnish
    Sour cream, for garnish
    Grated cheddar cheese, for garnish

In a large kettle, brown the venison, onion, and garlic. Pour off excess fat, if any. Add tomato paste, tomato purée, mustard, cumin, coriander, and chili powder. Mix well. Stir in the kidney beans and heat through. Season with salt and freshly ground pepper to taste. Serve with red pepper flakes, sour cream, and grated cheddar cheese.

Miltie's Nuggets

Fresh eggs and organically grown chickens have gained Three Brothers Egg Farm in Ulster Park, New York, a wide reputation. This recipe, for which you can use any boneless chicken meat, is named for owner Milton Tsitsera. Serve these delicious, crunchy morsels with your favorite Chinese duck sauce or honey mustard. You'll never buy the fast-food version again!

MAKES *about 16 pieces*

PREPARATION TIME: *about 15 minutes*

FRYING TIME: *about 15 minutes*

> 4 **boneless chicken thighs, or breasts, or combination, cut into 1½ inch cubes**
> **Salt to taste**
> **Freshly ground pepper to taste**
> 1 **large egg, lightly beaten with 1 tablespoon water**
> About ½ **cup seasoned (Italian) toasted bread crumbs**
> About ¼ **cup vegetable oil, for frying**

Season the chicken pieces with salt and freshly ground pepper. Using a fork, dip each nugget into the beaten egg and then into the flavored bread crumbs. Heat enough oil to cover the bottom of a large skillet. When the oil is hot, brown the chicken pieces, without crowding, on one side. Turn and brown the other sides. Cook until light brown in color, for 15 minutes total. Keep the cooked chicken warm while frying the remaining pieces.

Quattro's Pheasant with White Wine and Portobello Mushrooms

Quattro's Game Farm in Pleasant Valley, New York, is another one of the many farms represented at the Greenmarket farmers markets in New York City. Along with their chickens, they sell game birds such as ring-necked pheasant, Milan white pheasant, Embden geese, wild turkey, mallards, and muscovy ducks, as well as their eggs. The farm is run by Carmella and Frank Quattrociocchi and their two sons, Salvatore and Frank. Daughter-in-law Joyce gave me her recipe for pheasant, which came from her grandmother. Make it with Portobello mushrooms—their intense mushroom flavor is well worth the extra expense.

Since the late 1930s Andrew DePoala and his family have been growing mushrooms in the Hudson region, including Portobello mushrooms, but also white cultivated mushrooms and creminis. They sell to local stores and wholesalers. In this recipe, we combine the products of two of the region's family businesses. Serve with rice and a big salad of mixed greens.

SERVES 4

PREPARATION TIME: *about 15 minutes*

COOKING TIME: *about 1 hour*

½	cup olive oil
2½–3	pounds pheasant, quartered
1–1½	pounds Portobello mushrooms
1	medium onion, sliced very thin
4	large cloves garlic, crushed
½	cup Hudson region dry white wine
2	tablespoons fresh parsley, finely chopped
	Salt to taste
	Freshly ground pepper to taste
½	cup chicken or pheasant broth

Rabbit Fricassee with Vegetables

There are many wild rabbits in the region, and some people also raise rabbits for their own and limited commercial use. Nevertheless, most of us have to make do with the frozen supermarket rabbits. I like to prepare a fricassee with rabbit, and add some vegetables to the sauce. Then all that is further needed is either boiled rice or mashed potatoes to make a good but simple meal.

SERVES 4

PREPARATION TIME: *about 15 minutes*

COOKING TIME: *about 35–40 minutes*

½	**cup flour**
	Salt to taste
	Freshly ground pepper to taste
2½–3	**pounds fresh rabbit (thawed if frozen)**
3	**tablespoons vegetable oil**
1½	**cups chicken broth**
1	**pound tiny onions, peeled and left whole**
1	**pound carrots, scraped and cut into 1-inch strips**
2–3	**tablespoons fresh lemon juice**
⅓	**cup fresh parsley, chopped**
	Cornstarch, mixed with water (optional)
	Lemon wedges for garnish

Combine flour, salt, and pepper in a paper or plastic bag. Add a piece of rabbit and coat it thoroughly by shaking the bag. Remove and proceed with the other pieces.

In a frying pan, large enough to hold the pieces in a single layer, heat the vegetable oil and brown the rabbit pieces on all sides. Add the chicken broth, cover the pan, and simmer for about 25 minutes. Then add the onions, carrot strips, and lemon juice. Cook for another 10–15 minutes or so. Taste and adjust seasoning and add the parsley. The sauce may be thickened with cornstarch, if you prefer. Heat through and serve, garnished with lemon wedges.

Roast Venison

Over the years I have been the recipient of many packages of game meat because my friends know how much I enjoy cooking (and eating) game. Here is my way of preparing venison. The results are best if you use an instant-reading thermometer. Serve with parsleyed potatoes, stewed cranberries, and steamed baby vegetables, buttered and lightly seasoned with salt and freshly ground pepper. I have also served the thinly sliced roast cold as an appetizer, together with a salad of mixed greens, enlivened with nasturtium blossoms.

SERVES *4–6*

PREPARATION TIME: *5 minutes; marinade: 36–48 hours*

COOKING TIME: *no more than 15 minutes per pound*

---

 1   *venison roast, 2–3 pounds*
10   *juniper berries*
 2   *bay leaves*
     *Sliced onions, enough to thickly cover
        the roast*
 1   *bottle dry red Hudson region wine*

Two days before you want to serve the roast, place it in a bowl and add juniper berries and bay leaves. Cover with onion slices and pour in enough wine to cover. Marinate for 2 days, turning the roast every 12 hours.

Preheat the oven to 425° F. Remove the onions from the marinade and place in a shallow roasting pan. If no instant-reading thermometer is available, insert a standard meat thermometer and place the roast on top of the onions. Discard the marinade. Roast the meat until the thermometer registers 125° F. Remove from the oven, cover, and let rest for 10 minutes. The roast will continue to cook. Serve rare. If rare meat really appalls you, then cook until the thermometer registers 140° F, cover, and let stand 10 minutes. Do not cook over 140 degrees! With a sharp knife, cut the meat in very thin slices. Serve as described above.

Rolled Beefsteak

George Washington, the Marquis de la Fayette, and other notables visited the Hermitage in Ho-Ho-Kus, New Jersey. Aaron Burr was married there in 1782. The house was remodeled in 1847 as a Gothic Revival house for the Rosencrantz family, who made it their home from 1807 to 1970. The rolled beefsteak recipe that follows comes from Hermitage Sampler, *a fund-raising booklet. It was very creatively adapted from a period cookbook that belonged to "Lillie" Charlotte Caroline Dennis (1846–1910). The meat is spread with a pungent mixture of crumbs, tomato, and fresh basil; then it is rolled and gently braised. In the last minutes of cooking, various vegetables are added to make a toothsome meal in one pot. Serve with baked potatoes.*

SERVES 4

PREPARATION TIME: *about 30 minutes*

COOKING TIME: *about 50 minutes*

	Butter, margarine, or oil
1¾–2	pounds boneless flank steak
½	cup toasted bread crumbs
1	large ripe tomato, chopped fine
2	tablespoons minced fresh basil leaves
	Salt to taste
	Freshly ground pepper to taste
1	can beef broth, or about 1½ cups home made broth
	Cornstarch, mixed with water (optional)
5	cups chopped vegetables (such as broccoli, carrots, lima beans, collard greens, snap beans, green pepper, onion, mushrooms, potato, celery, zucchini)

In a large heavy pan with a tight-fitting cover or a Dutch oven, brown the butter or heat the oil, and brown the meat on both sides. Remove the meat from the pan. Let it cool enough to handle.

Meanwhile, in a small bowl, combine the bread crumbs, tomato, and basil. Season the meat on both sides with the salt and pepper; then spread with the tomato mixture. Roll the meat up jelly-roll fashion and tie in several places. Put it back in the pan and pour in 1 cup of the beef broth. Tightly cover the pan. Gently braise for 30 minutes, turning occasionally. After 30 minutes, add the vegetables and more broth if that seems necessary. Cook for another 20 minutes. Cut into the meat to see whether it is done to your liking. If so, remove the meat to a cutting board and cut it into ¾-inch slices. Reshape each slice if the filling falls out during the cutting. Place the meat on a deep platter and surround it with the vegetables. Keep warm. Reheat the pan juices and thicken them with cornstarch, if desired. Pour the gravy over the sliced meat and vegetables.

Venison Hash with Currant Jelly

The annals of the Steuben House, in River Edge, New Jersey, which probably dates back to 1713, are a lesson in American history. The house is part of a site that includes two other houses, a barn, an iron-swing bridge called New Bridge, and the wharf New Bridge Landing, a major transshipment point in the eighteenth and nineteenth centuries. A grist mill was erected on the site prior to 1710. By 1744, owner Jan Zabriskie shipped flour weekly to New York City. Pig and bar iron from the Ramapo Mountains was carted to the nearby wharf for shipment to market.

On November 20, 1776, six thousand British and Hessian troops crossed the Hudson River at the Lower Cloister Landing to attack Fort Lee. Washington rode out from his headquarters in Hackensack and led the fleeing garrison of the fort over the New Bridge, a wooden drawbridge at the time. This action saved a large part of the American army from entrapment on the peninsula between the Hudson and Hackensack rivers. The old wooden span that carried them to safety was later dubbed, ''The Bridge That Saved a Nation.''

Jan Zabriskie, Junior, was accused of passing military intelligence to the British. In 1783, his estate was given to Major General Baron von Steuben in gratitude for his service to the Continental Army, hence the name of the house. It was sold numerous times since then and eventually came back into the Zabriskie family. It is now owned by the Bergen County Historical Society, which displays in the house such items as a Dutch-style kast *(cupboard) of cherry wood, cabinet-work, an oak settle, and a particularly outstanding collection of slip-decorated redware pie dishes by George Wolfkiel (1805–1867). Its collection makes the Steuben House a unique showcase of local manufacture and use.*

From notes in the archives of the society, I adapted the following recipe for leftover venison. It makes a delicious second go-round for the game meat, but the recipe can also be prepared with beef, if you prefer. Serve it with mashed potatoes, red cabbage, and applesauce for a homey, comforting meal.

PREPARATION TIME: *about 10 minutes*

COOKING TIME: *about 10 minutes*

Butter, margarine, or oil for frying
1 *large onion, sliced, or more*
Leftover gravy
Beef or veal broth, if needed
*Butter mixed with flour for thickening,
   as needed*
Leftover cooked venison, chopped
Currant jelly, to taste
Salt to taste
Pepper to taste

For two cups chopped leftover venison use 1 onion, 1 cup gravy, 2 tablespoons flour, and 1 tablespoon butter.

In a skillet, lightly brown the butter or heat the oil. Add the onion slices and fry until golden brown. Stir in the gravy and add some broth if necessary. Bring to a gentle boil and drop in pieces of the flour-and-butter mixture, stirring until the gravy thickens. Add the chopped venison and heat through. Stir in the currant jelly a tablespoon at a time. Taste and season with salt and pepper; add more currant jelly, if necessary. Serve as described above.

Venison Sausage

Ground venison is very lean; some ground pork needs to be added to make a good sausage mixture. But when you make your own, you can control how much. The following patties are quick and easy to make and are very tasty for breakfast, brunch, or a quick snack.

MAKES *16 patties*

PREPARATION TIME: *about 10 minutes*

FRYING TIME: *about 8 minutes*

---

3   **pounds ground venison**
1   **pound ground pork**
2   **cups toasted bread crumbs**
2   **teaspoons salt**
1   **tablespoon ground allspice**
1   **teaspoon ground pepper**
½   **teaspoon thyme**
½   **teaspoon sage**

Combine all ingredients and shape into patties. Fry as needed. Use anytime. These patties freeze well.

7. Winter

▪▫

The subjects of this chapter are fireplace cooking, pancakes, soups, and stamppot. The homey, warming, satisfying, and sustaining dishes in this chapter, dishes that will fortify you against piercing winds and heavy snows or revive your spirit after a day of skiing or skating, are the kind of foods I cook at home at this time of the year. Most are family recipes. Winter food is Dutch cooking at its best, and this kind of cooking fits in perfectly with the climate of the Hudson region. The recipes make use of the winter vegetables that have been grown here for centuries.

Fireplace Cooking

The chapter begins with recipes for fireplace cooking. Lighting a fire adds a festive touch to any occasion, and cooking on that same fire adds even more to the general sense of relaxation and fun. The cooking need not be limited to roasting chestnuts or toasting marshmallows. Instead, some quite sophisticated fare can be created, and the cook need never depart for the kitchen!

It was a logical extension of my interest in historical cooking to prepare some dishes in our own fireplace. Ours is large (4 feet wide, 3 feet high, and 1½ feet deep), but the general instructions will make clear that you can prepare some food in almost any size fireplace. We learned how to do it the hard way, but after some burned pots, some messy spills, and a few blisters, we are now rather good at fixing a meal over the fire with a minimum amount of fuss or mess.

Fireplace cooking is the most fun with two people—one to cook and one to tend the fire. For us the choice is easy. My husband is a fire freak and known for his spectacular, carefully built fires. We have a great time cooking together, solving problems as we go along. Foods, especially breads, cooked this way have an irresistible flavor. When dinner is served, we eat by candlelight and the light of the fire and grin conspiratorially at each other while we taste our latest creation. Afterward, as we enjoy the last of our wine, we sometimes companionably nod off. It is a relaxing and fun way to spend a winter's evening.

Carefully read and reread the general instructions before you start, and you should not have any major problems.

GENERAL INSTRUCTIONS FOR FIREPLACE COOKING

Safety first. Have your chimney cleaned and checked on a regular basis. Preferably, wear woolen clothing, which smolders rather than burns. Avoid synthetics, even when treated; they flare quickly. Keep hair tied back and out of the way.

Food takes about the same time to cook over the fire as it does on the kitchen stove, once you have learned how to manage a fire. It is not harmed at all by standing in a warm place, waiting to be served, so there is no need to feel anxious or rushed if it is done sooner than you expected. Nor is there need for anxiety if it takes longer; the cooking itself is part of the fun. Therefore, invite to fireplace meals only those friends who can get into the spirit of the occasion.

Almost anything you can do on the stove or in the oven can be done in the fireplace, provided you have the equipment. For dishes that create little mess and do not need a great deal of effort, fireplace cooking is best done with a lot of liquid. We prefer to braise or stew our dishes, or use the bag method of cooking, and we use the Dutch oven for baking.

As you get more experienced you might be tempted to fry or even deep-fry foods over the fire. These methods require constant care and attention. They should not be attempted until after experience has been gained by using other cooking methods. I think these cooking techniques are much better employed outside when you go camping. Another temptation might be to simply use the charcoal grill or hibachi indoors. This is only safe when placed in a fireplace with proper upward draft. You need to be very careful about carbon monoxide fumes when using charcoal indoors. I would not recommend it.

About an hour before you plan to start cooking, build a fire in one corner of the fireplace, light it and replenish it with wood as it burns down. This fire will supply the coals or embers, which will produce a long-lasting, steady heat source. Hardwoods such as ash or oak work well, and fruit woods are particularly good. Avoid soft woods, such as beech and pine, which produce creosotes. They make the pots hard to clean and give the food a nasty flavor.

Just remember that the food is not cooked over flames but over coals from the fire as it is burning down. These coals will glow at first, then turn gray as they cool, but they will keep the heat for a long time. When you have a good supply of coals, take several shovelfuls and create as many "burners" as needed to cook the meal by heaping the embers in small piles on the stone floor of the fireplace, away from the main fire. The cooking pots are set over these "burners." If the pot has legs, it is set right over the coals. If not, it is placed on a trivet with legs over the coals. Lacking a trivet, use four bricks. Place a stack of two bricks on either side of the coals and put the pot on them.

The equipment for fireplace cooking is quite minimal. Start with an old pot, four bricks to support the pot if it does not have legs, oven mitts, and a long-handled fork and spoon. You can expand your inventory with cast-iron or aluminum pots and trivets. My husband and I now have acquired a very handy lid-lifting gadget that stabilizes the lid while removing it. You might be able to find cookware at tag sales, flea markets, and hardware and camping goods stores.

For roasting, a tin oven, sometimes called a reflector oven or even a Dutch oven, is used. It contains a spit for meat and the food is cooked by the reflected heat of the fire. It gives delicious results. Unfortunately, we found that it is just a little too easy to get spills from it on the carpet in the living room, so we do not use it inside. What we do use is the true Dutch oven, which looks like a large cast-iron pan with a flat lid on which coals are heaped. Some Dutch ovens have concave lids; these pots are buried in the coals. When preheated, the Dutch oven becomes a fireplace oven in which we bake our bread. Keep in mind that bread baking requires more heat on top than on the bottom.

Although most cast-iron cookware has been preseasoned to resist sticking, for water-based cooking it is advisable to season the utensil before first use. Wash it out with soap and water and dry completely. Coat it with unsalted fat (preferably suet) or vegetable oil and place it in a slow (300° F) oven for about 3 hours. Remove it from the oven and wipe off excess fat with paper towels. It is a miserable, smelly job, but it must be done to prevent your pots from rusting. Fortunately, you only have to do it once! Another solution is to consider buying aluminum pots. Shaped like cast iron, they are lighter and require no seasoning. If you use your regular pans for fireplace cooking, borrow the old scout trick of soaping the outside of the pot. This will prevent the soot from sticking. Clean with a soapy steelwool pad. You might also consider dedicating certain cookware to fireplace use and skip cleaning the outside each time.

The recipes that follow are meant to be prepared in a living-room fireplace. Preparation of the dishes is done in the kitchen; only the essential equipment and ingredients are brought to the fireplace. The object is to accomplish the task with the least amount of effort or mess.

Pancakes

Traditionally, pancakes are a main course and not a breakfast food in the Netherlands. Pancake recipes, and the pans for frying them, were brought by the settlers to New Netherland. The Dutch even adapted them to native foodstuffs, as you can see in the recipe for Pumpkin Cornmeal Pancakes in Chapter 4.

A comfort food, like mashed potatoes, Dutch pancakes will appear on the table when anyone in the family needs cheering up. I make these plate-sized flapjacks without baking powder and incorporate such fillings as Gouda cheese, cored apple slices, or bacon. Because they are made without baking powder, they are sturdy rather than fluffy. A bowl of soup and a sweet pancake or a savory pancake and a salad make inexpensive and quick yet hearty meals that taste particularly good in the colder weather.

Because the Dutch are so fond of pancakes, they have devised all sorts of variations in size and filling. The smallest ones, *poffertjes*—or silver-dollar pancakes, as they are called in this country—require a special pan with indentations in which the batter is poured. The next size up are "drie-in-de-pan," three small pancakes fried in one pan. Filled with a combination of chopped apples and currants or raisins, these yeast pancakes fit nicely into an American brunch menu. *Flensjes* are 6- to 7-inch pancakes, the same size as a French crêpe but a little thicker. A favorite way of serving them is stacked with homemade applesauce between the layers and heavily dusted with powdered sugar. Finally, there is the plate-sized pancake with assorted fillings, featured in Dutch pancake restaurants for lunch as well as dinner.

Soups

I give you two recipes, both my mother's, for winter meal soups. Her version of pea soup is richly filled with carrots, leeks, meats, and sausage. Her other winter soup is made with kidney beans, well seasoned with fried onions and a good red wine.

Stamppot

Included in this chapter are recipes for the most popular Dutch stamppot dishes. A stamppot is different from a one-pot meal or stew in that all ingredients are mashed together to a fairly smooth consistency. My mother always said that the Dutch are "lazy eaters," and the popularity of these meals seems to prove her right! Judging by the favorable comments I have received over the years when I published these recipes in my column, I have found that Americans can easily come to like these dishes as well.

RECIPES FEATURING:

Fireplace Cooking
Ash Potatoes
Carrots, Parsnips, and Parsley
Fireplace Stew
John-in-the-Bag
Penny Loaves
Currant and Raisin Rice
Sunday Cabbage

•.•.•.•.•.•.•.•.

Pancakes
Apple Pancake
Bacon Pancake
Cheese Pancake
Stacked Small Pancakes with Applesauce
Three-in-the-Pan Pancakes

Soups
Mother's Pea Soup
Mother's Kidney Bean Soup with Red Wine

Stamppot
Potato, Carrot, Onion, and Beef Stamppot
Potato and Chicory Stamppot
Potato, Kale, and Smoked Sausage Stamppot
Potato, Bean, and Bacon Stamppot
Potato, Sauerkraut, and Smoked Sausage Stamppot

FIREPLACE COOKING

Ash Potatoes

You can put potatoes in the hot coals without covering them with foil. When baked, they will be charred on the outside but light and fluffy on the inside. I like to eat the potato skin and therefore prefer the method that follows.

For all fireplace cooking, be sure to read the general instructions in the introduction to this chapter.

SERVES 4

PREPARATION TIME: *3 minutes*

BAKING TIME: *about 45 minutes*

Scrub four baking potatoes, prick them with a fork in several places, and wrap them in heavy-duty foil. Place them on the side of the fire and cover them with coals. Turn them after 20 minutes and replenish the coals. Check for doneness after 40 minutes by sticking a fork in a potato through the foil. They may take up to an hour, depending on their size.

Carrots, Parsnips, and Parsley

A simple, but ever so tasty vegetable dish. The cooking water can be used for stew or soup.

For all fireplace cooking, be sure to read the general instructions in the introduction to this chapter.

SERVES 4

PREPARATION TIME: *5–10 minutes*

COOKING TIME: *15–20 minutes*

---

1 *pound carrots, scraped and sliced*
1 *pound parsnips, scraped and sliced*
Large handful of parsley, chopped
Salt to taste
Freshly ground pepper to taste
Sugar, to taste
Butter, to taste

In a small cast-iron pot, combine the carrots, parsnips, and most of the chopped parsley. Keep some for garnishing the finished dish. Add water to about half way up the side of the pot and bring to a boil on the stove. In the meantime, prepare a "burner" in the fireplace. When the water boils, place the pot, uncovered, on the "burner." Cook for about 15 minutes. Check if the vegetables are done to your liking. Drain. Season the vegetables with salt, freshly ground pepper, a little sugar, butter, and the rest of the parsley.

Fireplace Stew

Here is a proper fireplace stew with winter vegetables. Serve it straight from the pot with whole-grain bread and butter.

For all fireplace cooking, be sure to read the general instructions in the introduction to this chapter.

SERVES 4–6

PREPARATION TIME: *about 25 minutes*

COOKING TIME: *about 30–40 minutes*

---

1   *large leek*
4   *tablespoons vegetable oil*
2   *pounds top round, cut into 1½-inch cubes*
2   *medium onions, thinly sliced*
2   *cloves garlic, minced (optional)*
1   *pound carrots, sliced*
    Salt to taste
    Freshly ground pepper to taste
½   *teaspoon dried marjoram*
1   *celery root (celeriac), about 8 ounces, cut*
        into ¼-inch cubes
6   *medium potatoes, peeled and cut into chunks*
    Half of a 6-inch green cabbage, cut into
        1-inch slices
    Leftover beef gravy
    Beef broth
    Water, if necessary

Cut the leek into thin slices, using as much of the green part as possible, and wash thoroughly.

On the kitchen stove, heat a 10-inch cast-iron pot and add the oil and half of the meat cubes. Brown them on all sides and remove from the pan. Proceed with the second batch the same way. Remove and add the onions and garlic, if used. Brown them lightly and remove. Return all the meat cubes to the pot and place the onion-and-garlic mixture on top. Then make a layer with carrots. Lightly sprinkle with salt, pepper, and marjoram and top with the celery root cubes and leek slices. Again, sprinkle lightly with salt, pepper and marjoram. Top with potatoes and a final layer of cabbage. Season again. The pot will be filled to the top.

Combine leftover gravy, beef broth, and water so that you have enough to fill the pot ¾ of the way up. Bring the pot to a boil on the stove. In the meantime, prepare a "burner" in your fireplace and place the covered pot on top. Check after about 25 minutes to make sure the pot does not cook dry. Continue to cook until done to your liking, about 30–40 minutes.

John-in-the-Bag

Bag cooking in water is an alternative method to slow braising or stewing. Not much can go wrong as long as you keep the water at a simmer. The following bread resembles a raisin pumpernickel. It is delicious warm or cold, slathered with butter and topped with mild cheese or a plain Coach Farm goat cheese. Children often do not like the candied peel in this bread; it tastes fine without it. My recipe is used for demonstrations of hearth cooking at the 1832 Jacob Blauvelt House of the Rockland County Historical Society in New City, New York.

For all fireplace cooking, be sure to read the general instruction in the introduction to this chapter.

MAKES *1 loaf*

PREPARATION TIME: *about 20 minutes*

RISING TIME: *about 30 minutes*

BOILING TIME: *2 hours*

DRYING TIME: *30–40 minutes*

2	cups all-purpose flour, more if needed
1¼	cups buckwheat flour
½	teaspoon salt
2	eggs
1	cup milk
2	tablespoons dark brown sugar
2	packages dry yeast
¼	cup candied lemon peel, minced (optional)
1	cup dark raisins, firmly packed
1	cup currants, firmly packed
1	20-inch square cloth or towel

In a large mixing bowl, sieve the two flours and the salt. Remove one cup of this mixture and set aside. Make a well in the middle of the remaining flour mixture and break the eggs into it.

Warm the milk and sugar to about 110° F; stir to combine. Sprinkle the yeast over the mixture and set in a warm place until bubbly. Then add it to the flour mixture.

Start stirring from the middle until the batter is smooth and thick. Turn it out on a floured board and knead the rest of the flour into it, incorporating the lemon peel, raisins, and currants as you go along. The dough will be slightly sticky; if you cannot handle it, add a bit more all-purpose flour.

Rinse a cloth or towel several times to remove any soapy residue and wring out tightly. Spread it on the counter and generously rub with flour. Place the dough in the center of the cloth and tie the cloth together with string. Be sure to leave enough room for the dough to rise.

Place the bag on a baking sheet and let it rest in a warm spot by the fire until doubled in bulk, about 20–30 minutes.

In the meantime, prepare a "burner" in the fireplace. Put a large pot of water on it and bring to a boil. When the dough has doubled in bulk, hang the bundle in this pot of boiling water; tie the string to one of the pot's handles and cover the pot. Do not let any part of the cloth hang over the sides of the pot or it might catch fire. Gently keep the water boiling for 2 hours. Remove the bundle. Hold it over the pot to drain and put it in a bowl. Carefully open up the bundle and turn out the bread onto a baking sheet. Place the bread by the fire for about 30–40 minutes, turning it occasionally so it dries on all sides. Serve as described above. Refrigerate leftovers.

Penny Loaves

Penny loaves, so called because they were once supposed to have been sold for a penny, have good flavor and a chewy crust. This recipe has been developed over years of hearth cooking to become virtually foolproof. The loaves are baked in a Dutch oven set on hot coals, with a layer of coals on the lid, or with "fire above and below," as some old recipes read. The recipe also has instructions for baking in a regular oven; baking times are about the same. The recipe makes 2 loaves, but if your Dutch oven is not large enough to accommodate both, bake one in a regular oven and one over the fire. It is fun to compare them.

Deborah Hobson, gifted cook and historic site assistant at Crailo State Historic Site in Rensselaer, New York, has been using my recipe for several years. Visitors to the warm and cozy basement kitchen always marvel when these delicious-smelling loaves appear from the Dutch oven.

For all fireplace cooking, be sure to read the general instructions in the introduction to this chapter.

MAKES *2 loaves*

PREPARATION TIME: *about 20 minutes*

RISING TIME: *the first, about an hour; the second, about 45 minutes*

BAKING TIME: *20–30 minutes*

> 4 cups all-purpose flour
> 2 cups whole-wheat flour
> 3 packages dry yeast
> 1–2 teaspoons salt
> 2¼ cups milk
> 2 tablespoons honey
> 3 tablespoons butter

Combine 3 cups of the all-purpose flour with the whole-wheat flour, the dry yeast, and the salt. In a saucepan, heat the milk, honey, and butter to 120–130° F; add them to the flour mixture and blend thoroughly.

Turn the dough out onto a floured board. Add the final cup of all-purpose flour and knead until the dough is smooth and elastic, about 8–10 minutes. Form the dough into a ball and place it in a greased bowl, rotating the dough to grease the entire ball. Let the dough rise, covered, in a warm place for about 1 hour, until doubled in bulk. Punch the dough down, divide it in half, and shape into two balls. Set them to rise again for about 45 minutes.

About 10 minutes before they are ready, prepare a "burner" in the fireplace and place the Dutch oven on it to heat through. When the loaves are ready, reshape them into oblongs, so they will fit side by side in the Dutch oven. Sprinkle the bottom of the Dutch oven with cornmeal, place the loaves on top, and close the lid. Bread baking requires more heat on top than on the bottom, so put a thick layer of coals on top of the lid. Bake for about 20 minutes.

Very carefully remove the lid. If you are afraid of spilling the coals into the pot, then brush them off first. The loaves are done when they are nicely browned, and the loaves sound hollow when the bottoms are lightly tapped; an instant-reading thermometer should read 200° F.

NOTE: The instructions are for preparing the bread by hand, but it can also be made very well in an electric mixer equipped with a dough paddle. Follow the manufacturer's instructions on bread dough preparation.

Currant and Raisin Rice

•.•..•.•..•.•..•.•..•.•..•.•..•.•..•.•..•.•..•.•..•.•..•.•..•.•..•.•..•.•..•.•..•.•.•.

You can divide this rice dish in half and use one half as a savory side dish, the other half as a dessert. When the rice mixture is cooked, season one half with salt and pepper and the other with some sugar and a little cinnamon and stir in a bit of cream.

For all fireplace cooking, be sure to read the general instructions in the introduction to this chapter.

SERVES 4–6

PREPARATION TIME: *3–5 minutes*

COOKING TIME: *about 20 minutes*

1	**cup raw long-grain rice**
½	**cup currants**
½	**cup raisins**
	Salt to taste
	Freshly ground pepper to taste
2–4	**tablespoons butter or margarine, to taste**

Rinse a clean kitchen towel to remove any soapy residue and wring very dry, or use a double layer of cheesecloth. Place towel or cloth in a bowl and put the rice, currants, and raisins in the middle. Tie off the cloth about 4 inches above the contents.

Prepare a "burner" in your fireplace. Fill a pot ¾ full of water and bring it to a boil on the "burner." When it boils, carefully slide in the rice bundle and tie it to the pot handle. Do not let any of the cloth hang over the side of the pan. Gently boil for about 20 minutes.

Remove the bundle and place in a colander set into a large bowl. Let it drain for 5 minutes. Open the bundle and scrape the rice,

•.•..•.•..•.•..•.•..•.

currants, and raisins into a bowl. Add salt, freshly ground pepper, and butter; mix thoroughly. As suggested above, instead of salt and pepper, sugar and cinnamon may be used, and this rice combination could be served as dessert with some cream added.

Sunday Cabbage

The final recipe for fireplace cooking comes from a handwritten manuscript cookbook of the Philips family, dated 1847. Anton Philips was the founder of the world-famous Philips (Norelco) factories in the latter half of the nineteenth century. This recipe was a favorite for Sunday dinner, hence the name. Sunday Cabbage—together with carrots, parsnips, and parsley and one of the two breads above—makes a memorable Sunday dinner indeed.

For all fireplace cooking, be sure to read the general instructions in the introduction to this chapter.

SERVES 4–6

PREPARATION TIME: *about 25 minutes*

COOKING TIME: *about 2 hours*

---

1 green cabbage, about 2 pounds
2 pounds ground beef or veal
3 slices bread, soaked in ¼ cup milk and
      squeezed fairly dry
2 eggs
1 medium onion, minced
2 teaspoons salt
¼ teaspoon freshly ground black pepper
¼ teaspoon freshly grated nutmeg
1 20-inch square cloth or towel

Carefully separate the entire cabbage, leaf by leaf, and wash. Bring a large pot—the same pot you will use later on in the fireplace—of water to a boil and drop the separated leaves into it to wilt them, about 3–5 minutes. Remove them from the water with tongs and cool. Save the water in the pot.

Prepare a "burner" in your fireplace and transfer the pot with water to the "burner." Bring the water back to a boil.

In the meantime, mix the ground beef with the bread, eggs, onion, and seasonings. Knead with your hands until the mixture is well combined.

Rinse a cloth or towel to remove any soapy residue and wring dry. Place the cloth in a bowl. Starting with the outside cabbage leaves, layer meat and cabbage until all the ingredients have been used up, ending with a layer of cabbage.

Tie the cloth together with kitchen twine to form a ball. Carefully slide this bundle into the boiling water. Tie it to the handle of the pot. Do not let any part of the cloth hang over the side of the pan. Gently cook the cabbage for 2 hours. Remove slowly to drain and place in a colander set in a large bowl. Allow to drain for 5 minutes. Open the cloth and carefully remove what will look like a whole steamed cabbage. Cut into slices to serve.

PANCAKES

Apple Pancake
■·■·:·■·:·■·■·:·■·:·■·■·:·■·:·■·■·:·■·:·■·■·:·■·:·■·■·:·■·:·■·■·:·■·:·■·■·:·■·:·■·

Try a steaming bowl of Mother's kidney bean soup followed by an apple pancake for a quick and satisfying winter meal. These plate-size flapjacks can also be cut in wedges and shared. For a real pancake meal in my house, I fry up one of each—one apple, one cheese, and one bacon—and we share. Once you get the hang of it, you'll make your own filling combinations.

MAKES *1 large pancake (serves 1, 2, or more, depending on how it is served)*

PREPARATION TIME: *3–5 minutes*

FRYING TIME: *about 12 minutes*

---

1   *cup all-purpose flour*
1   *cup milk*
1   *egg*
    Butter or margarine, for frying
1   *medium Golden Delicious or Mutsu (also
        called Crispin) apple, peeled and cut
        into ½-inch slices or chopped*

■·■·:·■·:·■·■·:·■·:·■·

For ease in pouring, especially if you make more than one pancake, place the flour in a 4-cup measuring cup. Combine milk and egg and stir into the flour a little at a time, to make a smooth batter.

In a 9-inch frying pan melt enough butter or margarine to amply coat the pan. Pour in the batter. Swirl the pan to distribute evenly. Top with the apple slices. Over medium to low heat, fry until solid on top and brown on the bottom. Shake the pan occasionally to make sure the pancake does not stick. Slide it out carefully onto a plate and turn it over with the help of a flat lid, slide back into the pan, and brown on the other side, or, toss the pancake up in the air and turn it over in proper flapjack style.

When the pancake is done, remove to a plate, eat the whole thing, or cut it into wedges and share. Sugar, cinnamon-sugar, or pancake syrup and butter make nice toppings. The pancake can be kept warm in a 300° F oven.

Bacon Pancake

The following pancakes are not as heavy as you might think. Just drain off the bacon fat before pouring in the pancake batter. They are especially delicious when served with some maple syrup.

MAKES *1 large pancake (serves 1, 2, or more, depending on how it is served)*

PREPARATION TIME: *8–10 minutes*

FRYING TIME: *6–8 minutes*

---

6   slices bacon, cut into 1-inch pieces
1   cup flour
1   cup milk
1   egg
     Salt to taste
     Freshly ground black pepper to taste

In a 9-inch frying pan cook the bacon until brown. Drain off excess grease but leave enough to amply coat the pan.

For ease in pouring, especially if you make more than one pancake, place the flour in a 4-cup measuring cup. Combine milk and egg and stir into the flour, a little at a time, to make a smooth batter.

Pour the batter over the bacon pieces, swirling the pan to distribute evenly. Cook over medium to low heat until the pancake is solid on top and brown on the bottom. Shake the pan occasionally to make sure the pancake does not stick. Slide it out carefully onto a plate, turn it over with the help of a flat lid, slide it back into the pan, and brown the other side, or toss the pancake up in the air and turn it over in proper flapjack style.

When the pancake is done, remove it to a plate, eat the whole thing, or cut into wedges and share. Serve as described above.

Cheese Pancake

As much as I like to use Hudson Valley cheeses, for the next pancake you need a Gouda. It stays together and melts to the right chewy consistency. The curry powder adds a bit of piquancy.

MAKES *1 large pancake (serves 1, 2, or more, depending on how it is served)*

PREPARATION TIME: *3–5 minutes*

FRYING TIME: *about 12 minutes*

---

  1 *cup flour*
  ½ *teaspoon curry powder*
  ⅛ *teaspoon freshly grated nutmeg*
  1 *cup milk*
  1 *egg*
3–4 *ounces Gouda cheese, cut into small pieces*
    Butter or margarine, for frying

For ease in pouring, especially if you make more than one pancake, place the flour, curry powder, and nutmeg in a 4-cup measuring cup. Combine milk and egg, and stir into the flour, a little at a time, to make a smooth batter. Stir in the cheese pieces.

In a 9-inch frying pan melt enough butter to amply coat the pan. Pour in the batter. Swirl the pan to distribute it evenly. Over medium to low heat, fry until it is solid on top and brown on the bottom. Shake the pan occasionally to make sure the pancake does not stick. Slide it out carefully onto a plate and turn it over with the help of a flat lid, and brown on the other side. Or toss the pancake up in the air and turn it over in proper flapjack style.

When the pancake is done, remove it to a plate; eat the whole thing or cut into wedges and share. If necessary, keep the pancake warm in a 300° F oven.

Stacked Small Pancakes with Applesauce

Flensjes are thin, but not as thin as crêpes. These dessert pancakes were always a hit the morning after one of my daughter's slumber parties. The girls would eat them with sugar and butter on top, and applesauce on the side. My husband would devour his share rolled up with raspberry jam inside and with a heavy dusting of confectioners' sugar. They are good singly or, as presented here, stacked with homemade applesauce in between. A great brunch dish!

SERVES 4–6

PREPARATION TIME: *5 minutes*

FRYING TIME: *4–5 minutes per pancake*

1¼ *cups all-purpose flour*
2 *cups milk*
2 *eggs, lightly beaten*
  Butter, for frying and topping
  Confectioners' sugar
  Applesauce

Make the batter in a 4-cup measuring cup for ease in pouring. Place the flour in the cup; stir in the eggs and then the milk, a little at a time. Stir with a whisk until smooth and all the milk has been used up. This quantity will yield 3⅓ cups batter and should make about 10 pancakes.

Melt some butter in a 7-inch crêpe pan. Use about ⅓ cup batter and swirl it around to cover the bottom. Brown the pancake on both sides. Remove it to a plate set in a 300° F oven and spread it with a few tablespoons of applesauce. Continue in the same manner until all pancakes are fried and stacked with applesauce. Keep warm until ready to eat. To serve, dust with confectioners' sugar and cut into wedges.

Three-in-the-Pan Pancakes

•▪•

I used to cook with the children in my daughter's elementary school, the Lewisboro School in South Salem, New York. One day I made Three-in-the-Pan pancakes with them. Gregory Cowles—then a little boy with a huge appetite, now six feet of skin and bones—who had eaten at least ten, turned to me with his round little face smeared with butter and sugar and said, ''You can come back anytime.''

MAKES *about 18 small pancakes*

PREPARATION TIME: *about 10 minutes*

STANDING TIME FOR BATTER: *1 hour*

FRYING TIME: *3–4 minutes for each batch*

---

   2   **packages dry yeast**
   ¼   **cup lukewarm water (105–115° F)**
   ½   **teaspoon sugar**
   2   **cups all–purpose flour**
       Pinch of salt
   1½ **cups lukewarm milk (105–115° F)**
   1   **cup currants or raisins**
   2   **medium Granny Smith, Mutsu (also
          called Crispin), or other cooking
          apples, peeled, cored, and chopped**
       Confectioners' sugar
       Butter or margarine

•▪•▪•▪•▪•▪•

Sprinkle the yeast over the ¼ cup of warm water. Sprinkle ½ teaspoon sugar over it and let it stand for 2 minutes; then stir. Leave in a warm place for 5 minutes until bubbly.

In a deep bowl place the flour and salt. Make a well in the middle and add the yeast mixture. Start stirring from the middle, adding the lukewarm milk a little at a time and stirring until the batter is smooth. Add the currants and chopped apples and combine. Allow the batter to stand in a warm place for about 1 hour.

Heat enough butter or margarine in a large frying pan to amply coat the bottom and pour in a little batter for each of the 3 small pancakes. Fry on both sides until golden brown and serve them hot, heavily dusted with confectioners' sugar and with just a small pat of butter on top.

SOUPS

Mother's Pea Soup

Pea soup is not only wonderfully warming and filling but also pretty, with its colorful vegetables and pink meats in a green base. This is one of my mother's best recipes. Serve hot with plenty of pumpernickel bread and butter.

SERVES *8 or more*

PREPARATION TIME: *20 minutes*

COOKING TIME: *4 hours and 45 minutes*

---

1 large ham bone with some meat on it, or 3 pounds soup bones plus a marrow bone, if available
1½ pounds loin end pork chops
2 pounds green split peas, rinsed and picked over
2 large leeks
4 large carrots, scraped and chopped
4 large potatoes, peeled, washed, and diced
2 onions, chopped
3 large ribs celery and at least 3 tablespoons celery leaves, chopped

> 1 pound smoked sausage (such as Kielbasa
>   or smoked turkey sausage)
>   Salt to taste
>   Freshly ground pepper to taste
> 1 large handful fresh parsley, washed and
>   chopped

In a large soup pot, bring to a boil in 1 gallon of COLD water, the hambone, or the soup bones and marrow bone. Skim the surface carefully to remove the foam and other impurities. Simmer for 2 hours. Add the chops. Bring to a boil again. Skim. Simmer for another hour. Remove the pan from the heat and cool. Refrigerate overnight.

The next day take off and discard any hardened fat. Cut off any usable meat, set aside, and discard the bones. Pour the broth through a sieve back into the pan.

Add the split peas to the broth and cook for about an hour until they are soft.

Meanwhile, cut the leeks into thin slices, including as much of the green part as possible, and wash thoroughly.

Add the leeks, carrots, potatoes, onion, and celery. Stir occasionally; this soup tends to burn at the bottom of the pot. Cook for about 30 minutes, then add the whole smoked sausage and the cut-up meat. Gently simmer everything for another 10–15 minutes. Taste; season with salt and pepper. Remove the sausage, cut it into slices, and return it to the soup, together with the chopped parsley.

Mother's Kidney Bean Soup with Red Wine

Like pea soups, bean soups have always been favorites for winter meals. This one is best made from scratch. Use a good dry red wine for the soup and drink the rest of the bottle with your meal. Serve with slices of pumpernickel-raisin bread and butter. A cored apple, baked with a spoonful of currant jelly in the hollow, makes a perfect dessert.

SERVES *6 or more*

PREPARATION TIME: *about 20 minutes at various intervals*

COOKING TIME: *about 3½ hours*

---

3   *pounds soup bones*
1   *pound beef such as chuck steak, or end*
        pieces from a roast, or whatever else
        you have on hand
1   *pound dry kidney beans, rinsed and*
        picked over
2   *medium bay leaves*
3   *whole cloves*
2   *tablespoons vegetable oil*
1   *large yellow onion, chopped*
½   *cup dry red wine*
    Worcestershire sauce, to taste
    Salt to taste
    Freshly ground pepper to taste

In a large soup pot, combine bones, meat, and 12 cups cold water. Bring to a boil and skim the surface carefully to remove the foam and other impurities. Reduce the heat and simmer the broth for about 2½ hours. Remove from heat. Cool and then refrigerate overnight.

The next day, remove the hardened fat and strain the broth through a sieve back into the rinsed pot. Cut any usable meat into small pieces and set aside. Add the kidney beans to the broth. Bring to a boil and allow to boil for 2 minutes. Turn off the heat and let the beans soak for 1 hour. Bring back to a boil; then add the bay leaves and cloves. Cook for about 1 hour, until beans are tender.

In the meantime, heat the oil and fry the chopped onions until light brown and limp. Set aside. When the beans are done, stir in the onions.

Remove the cloves and bay leaves. Purée the mixture in a blender; you will need to do this in several batches. Pour the purée back into the pot; stir in the red wine and the meat pieces. Taste and season with Worcestershire sauce, salt, and pepper.

STAMPPOT

Potato, Carrot, Onion, and Beef Stamppot

The origins of this typical one-pot meal go back as far as the liberation of the City of Leyden on Sunday, October 3, 1574, during the eighty-year war between the Dutch and the Spanish. Legend has it that the Spanish lifted their siege of the city in such haste that they left their cooking pots filled with a hearty stew behind. The hungry people of Leyden quickly retrieved them; and this stamppot has been on the menu for October 3 ever since! In those early days, the dish would not have contained the potatoes that are now an integral part of it, since potatoes were not generally eaten in Europe at the time. In Dutch, the dish is called hutspot, *or hodgepodge. Serve steaming platefuls, accompanied by some good, grainy mustard. Chocolate pudding with whipped cream makes a nice homey dessert.*

SERVES 4

PREPARATION TIME: *about 15 minutes*

COOKING TIME: *about 2 hours*

1	*pound boneless chuck steak*
1½	*pounds soup bones*
2	*pounds potatoes, cut into chunks*
1	*pound carrots, cut into strips*
2	*medium onions, cut into rough chunks*
1	*teaspoon salt*
¼	*teaspoon freshly ground pepper*
1	*teaspoon Worcestershire sauce*

The day before serving, bring 6 cups cold water, the meat, and the bones, to a boil in a large pan. Skim the surface carefully to remove the foam and other impurities. Simmer for about 1½ hours.

Strain the broth and discard the soup bones. Cut the meat into bite–size pieces and set aside.

Let the broth and meat cool and refrigerate separately.

The next day discard any hardened fat from the broth and

measure the broth; you will need 4 cups. Add water, if necessary. Pour the broth into a stove-to-table kind of pan, add the potatoes, carrots, and onions. Cook for about 30 minutes, until the vegetables are tender.

Coarsely mash the mixture with a potato masher, if you like. Add the meat together with the salt, pepper and Worestershire sauce and heat through. Taste and adjust seasonings, if necessary. Serve straight from the pot.

Potato and Chicory Stamppot

Chicory is a fresh-tasting, crunchy addition to this one-pot meal. Authentically, the dish is made with fried salt pork, but I give you the option to use melted butter or margarine. This stamppot is particularly good when served with a juicy pan-fried hamburger. Fruit salad makes a simple dessert.

SERVES 4

PREPARATION TIME: *about 15 minutes*

COOKING TIME: *about 25 minutes*

---

3 pounds potatoes, peeled, washed, and
    cut into chunks
½ pound salt pork OR 6 tablespoons hot
    melted butter or margarine
  Hot milk
  Salt to taste
  Freshly ground pepper to taste
1 pound chicory, washed and cut into
    ¼-inch strips
1½ tablespoons vinegar

Boil the potatoes until tender.

In the meantime, cut the salt pork into ¼-inch cubes. Fry them until crisp and brown and set aside. This takes about 20 minutes.

Mash the potatoes with some milk and season them with the salt and pepper to taste.

Put the chicory on top of the potatoes, sprinkle the fried pork cubes over it and as much of the pork grease as you like, OR use hot melted butter. This will wilt the chicory. Add the vinegar and stir everything thoroughly. Taste and adjust seasoning.

Potato, Kale, and Smoked Sausage Stamppot

The next stamppot is a particular winter favorite. Dutch people who are away from home crave this kind of dish. Even those who frequent the finest restaurants will tell you nostalgically that stamppot with kale exemplifies Mom's best food, and they'll eat it when they can get it. Kale is a real winter vegetable and tastes best when harvested after a frost. Serve the dish with a green salad with vinaigrette dressing (the salad is not part of the tradition but goes well with it.) Do not forget to put some good mustard on the table. Sweet oranges and cookies make a nice dessert for this family meal.

SERVES 4

PREPARATION TIME: *about 15 minutes*

COOKING TIME: *about 35 minutes*

1½   *pounds fresh curly kale or 2 packages (10 ounces each) frozen kale, thawed*
2   *pounds potatoes, peeled, washed, and cut into chunks*
1   *pound smoked sausage or Kielbasa*
½   *cup milk*
4   *tablespoons butter or margarine*
    Salt to taste
    Freshly ground pepper to taste

Strip the greens off the stems. Wash the greens, cut them fine, and boil them for 15 minutes in 2 cups of water. Then add the potatoes and more water if necessary. Frozen kale can be cooked together with the potatoes. When the potatoes and kale have come to a boil top with the sausage. Boil until the potatoes are tender. Take out the sausage and keep warm. Drain the mixture if necessary and mash the potatoes and kale together. Add the milk, the butter, and salt and pepper to taste. Each serving gets a part of the sausage.

Potato, Bean, and Bacon Stamppot

Another recipe for stamppot combines little white marrow beans, which turn pink when they are cooked, with French-cut pole or green beans, potatoes, and bacon. The Dutch name of this recipe is ''Naked Children in the Grass,'' the pinkish marrow beans being the children and the cut pole beans the grass. In many Dutch families, mine included, it is eaten on New Year's Day to offset the aftereffects of too many toasts to the New Year. It is a very old recipe and was originally made with green beans that had been preserved for the winter by salting.

The dish is filling, but if you prefer you can serve a smoked sausage with it. Cook the sausage together with the potatoes and the green beans so none of the flavorful juices are lost.

SERVES 4–6

PREPARATION TIME: *about 20 minutes*

COOKING TIME: *2–3 hours for the marrow beans; 20–30 minutes for the rest of the dish*

½ *pound marrow beans (small dried white beans), rinsed and picked over*
½ *onion*
2 *pounds potatoes, peeled, washed, and cut into chunks*
1 *pound pole beans, cut on a slant (French cut), OR 2 packages frozen French-cut green beans, thawed*
1 *pound smoked sausage (optional)*
1 *pound bacon, finely cut*
½ *stick (4 tablespoons) butter or margarine*
½ *cup light cream or milk*

¼ teaspoon *freshly ground black pepper,*
  or more
  Salt to taste

Place the marrow beans in a large saucepan and pour in water to about 1 inch above the beans. Bring to a boil. Turn off the heat and let them soak for 1 hour.

Add the onion and simmer 2–3 hours. Marrow beans tend to need a lot of time, but do not overcook; they should be tender but not mushy. Drain and set aside.

Boil the potatoes and pole or green beans together until tender. Place the sausage, if used, on top when the potatoes and vegetables have come to a boil. Drain and save the cooking water. Set aside the beans, potatoes, and sausage, if used, but keep them warm.

In the same pan, lightly brown the bacon pieces. Drain off most of the fat and discard or save for another purpose. Melt the butter or margarine into the bacon and add the potatoes and pole beans, cream, pepper and more salt if desired. Mash with a potato masher until creamy, then stir in the marrow beans. If the mixture is too thick, you can thin it with some of the reserved potato/bean water. Serve the sausage separately.

Potato, Sauerkraut, and Smoked Sausage Stamppot

The preparation of sauerkraut, or salted and fermented cabbage, is a food preservation technique from the days when vegetables were salted and packed into crocks for wintertime use. When you make a recipe with sauerkraut, a lot depends on the quality of the kraut. I find the best comes from stores that specialize in German foods, such as Karl Ehmer. Before cooking, taste the sauerkraut. If it seems too sour or salty, give it a quick rinse.

SERVES 4

PREPARATION TIME: *about 10 minutes*

COOKING TIME: *about 30 minutes*

    2   pounds potatoes, peeled, washed,
            and cut in half
    1   pound sauerkraut, rinsed if
            necessary
    1   sweet-sour apple, peeled, cored,
            and finely chopped
    1   pound or more smoked sausage,
            such as Kielbasa
About ½ cup milk
    3–4 tablespoons butter
    6–8 slices bacon, fried to a crisp and
            crumbled (optional)
        Salt to taste
        Freshly ground black pepper to
            taste

Place the potatoes in a large pan and pour in water halfway up the potatoes. Mix the sauerkraut and apple and place on top. Bring to a boil, then add the sausage. Cover the pan and gently boil for about 25–30 minutes, until the potatoes are tender. Remove the sausage and keep warm. Drain, then mash the potato-sauerkraut mixture and blend in the milk and butter. Stir in the crumbled bacon, if used. Taste and season with salt and pepper. Each serving gets a part of the sausage.

8. Holiday Treats and Other Favorites

•:•

The subject of the final chapter is holiday treats and other favorites of the different ethnic groups in the Hudson River region.

The Hudson River region is one of great ethnic diversity. It has among its inhabitants representatives of each of the seventy-one groups mentioned on the census forms. From the 1980 census figures—the 1990 census figures were not yet available at the time of this writing in spring 1992—I composed a list of its largest ethnic groups. They are African-Americans, Dutch, English, French, Germans, Hispanics, Hungarians, Irish, Italians, Jews, Poles, and Russians.

Ethnic recipes are shown off at their best at holiday time. There might not be enough time during the year to cook or bake the way our grandmothers or great-grandmothers did, but for holidays or special occasions, time is set aside to re-create the tastes of our ancestors.

Some people like to re-create a whole holiday dinner menu just the way it was served in the past, while others use a family recipe to make a single dish that reveals their culinary roots. This shared remembrance brings the family closer together and creates a sense of continuation. Anna Gould, Duchess of Talleyrand-Perigord, was an example of the first group and habitually repeated the traditional family Christmas dinner at Lyndhurst, in Tarrytown,

•:•:•:•:•:•:•:•:•:•:•

railroad baron Jay Gould's great estate along the Hudson. Here is her menu as served to 5 guests at 2 P.M. on Christmas Day 1958. According to Lyndhurst's curator, Henry Duffy, it was the same as that of the 1880s.

A relish tray of assorted olives, celery hearts, carrots, and radishes, preceded a clear homemade chicken consommé served with puff pastry sticks. After a fish course, the traditional turkey was served with all its trimmings, followed by salads and then an equally traditional dessert of Christmas plum pudding with hard sauce and a rather odd—for the occasion, that is—addition of stewed pears.

RECIPES FEATURING THE FOLLOWING ETHNIC GROUPS:

African-American
Sweet Potato Pie

Dutch
Tea Cookjes
Baker Thiebe's New Year's Cakes

English
Old English Drop Cookies

French
Hasbrouck Coconut Cake

German
Great-grandmother Siefert's German Pound Cake

Hungarian
Ethel Szylvássy's Palacsinta

Irish
Aunt Annie's Boiled Raisin Cake

Italian
Matilda Cuomo's Apple Pie

Jewish
Cannot-Fail Passover Cake

Polish
Chruŝciki

Puerto Rican
Epiphany Rice-Flour Dessert

Russian
Sweet Apple Pirog

AFRICAN-AMERICAN

Kwanzaa is an African-American family celebration that increasingly gains in popularity all over America. It was founded in 1966 by Maulana "Ron" Karenga. This nonreligious holiday is celebrated from December 26 to January 1.

According to *Kwanzaa: Everything You Always Wanted to Know But Didn't Know Where to Ask,* by Cedric McClester, the Kwanzaa celebration contains the following seven symbols. Each is identified in the Kiswahili language, chosen because it is a nontribal African language spoken in a large part of the African continent.

Mazao (fruit and vegetables)

Mkeka (place mat)

Kinara (candle holder for seven candles: one black, three red, and three green)

Vibunzi (ears of corn reflecting the number of children in the home)

Zawadi (gifts)

Kikombe Cha Umoja (community unity cup)

Mishumaa Saba (the seven candles)

Celebrants espouse seven principles, which not only are the cornerstones of the holiday but also function as a guide to daily living: unity, self-determination, collective work and responsibility, cooperative economics, purpose, creativity, and faith. Each day, one of the principles is observed.

Lovette Harper of Croton-on-Hudson, New York, has celebrated Kwanzaa since 1968 and particularly likes the giving, the sharing, and the intergenerational aspects, especially the storytelling, which is very much a part of this growing tradition. She sees Kwanzaa as "a truly ethnic celebration, an opportunity for African-Americans to develop a special holiday which cuts across all religious lines."

Sweet Potato Pie

Food is very much part of the Kwanzaa holiday. Mrs. Harper said that sweet potato pie is often on the menu, because it is not only an appropriate seasonal choice but also a particular favorite among African-Americans. She likes to reduce the fat and sugar content of the recipe, however, and suggests making it with egg whites and half the amount of butter and sugar of the standard recipes.

SERVES *6–8*

PREPARATION TIME: *15 minutes*

COOKING TIME: *25–30 minutes*

BAKING TIME: *40–50 minutes*

- 4 **medium sweet potatoes, peeled, washed, and quartered**
- 2 **tablespoons butter or margarine**
- ½ **cup dark brown sugar, firmly packed**
- ½ **cup condensed skimmed milk**
- 1½ **teaspoons finely grated lemon peel**
- 1 **teaspoon vanilla**
- 1 **teaspoon cinnamon**
- 3 **egg whites**
- 1 **unbaked 9-inch pie shell, fluted with ½-inch rim**

Preheat the oven to 425° F.

Boil the sweet potatoes until soft. Drain and mash them. Set aside.

In a mixing bowl, beat together the butter and the sugar until light and fluffy; add the milk, lemon peel, vanilla, and cinnamon and finally the mashed sweet potatoes.

In another bowl, beat the egg whites until thick but not dry and fold into the filling mixture. Pour the filling into the pie shell and place in the middle of the oven. Bake for 10 minutes; then reduce the temperature to 350° F and bake for about 30–40 minutes, until a knife inserted in the center comes out clean. Remove from the oven and let cool.

DUTCH

Tea Cookjes

▪▪•▪

The Dutch of the Hudson region are represented in this chapter by two recipes, which makes the total of our ethnic culinary representation a baker's dozen. Appropriately so, because legend has it that it was a Dutch baker who introduced the custom of giving thirteen cookies for the price of twelve.

The first recipe comes from the handwritten cookbook of Maria Sanders Van Rensselaer (1749–1830), whose home, Historic Cherry Hill, in Albany, New York, is open to the public. The house was lived in by five generations of the same family. Each generation left its influence on the house and grounds with alterations to the structure and additions of personal belongings. The house and its contents are preserved today, resembling the way the last generation left them.

Maria Van Rensselaer's recipe is the oldest Dutch-American cookie recipe that I am aware of. Its almost anglicized name "Tea cookjes" perfectly illustrates how the American word "cookies" evolved from the Dutch koekjes. *When you look at the very simple ingredients—the recipe reads: "½ lb butt ¾ Sugar 1 tea cup water as much flour as it takes"—you can hardly imagine that these cookies would be any good. Believe me, they are! Here is my adaptation.*

MAKES *10 dozen small cookies*

PREPARATION TIME: *about 15 minutes*

BAKING TIME: *12–14 minutes*

---

   2   *sticks (½ pound) butter, softened*
1½   *cups sugar*
 ¾   *cup cold water*
3½   *cups flour*

Preheat the oven to 350° F.

This recipe is easiest when made with an electric mixer. Cream the butter. Add the sugar, a little at a time, and continue creaming. Add the water alternately with the flour.

Take the dough out with a spatula, wrap, and refrigerate for an hour.

Roll into ½-inch balls, which will make little dot-shaped cookies. Or roll into slightly larger balls and press them down with the

▪▪•▪▪•▪▪•▪▪•▪▪•▪

bottom of a glass that has been dipped (lightly!) in flour. Or make some of each. Bake until lightly browned on the bottom. They are charmingly plain, and very good!

Baker Thiebe's New Year's Cakes

▪·

While the Tea Cookjes recipe may be the first Dutch-American cookie recipe, this recipe is certainly one of the last remaining recipes. The custom of making New Year's cakes (the old English word for cookies) was brought here by the Dutch settlers in the seventeenth century. These cakes were part of the New Year's celebration, which involved congratulatory visits to relatives, neighbors, and friends on New Year's Day, at which time New Year's cakes were served. By mid-nineteenth century, this custom had been adopted by Americans of other ethnic origins.

In his diary entry of January 1, 1861, John Ward of New York City describes his New Year's day calls in the company of his brother Press, who ''insisted on making very few calls'' that year. He reports that they made thirty-three visits and describes in detail what subjects were discussed with his hostesses. To put this number in perspective, after his return from the war five years later, he and his friend Benjamin Church called on one hundred seven houses.

The ladies would stay home to receive, while the gentlemen went calling. Gleaming silver and china were used for the tables, which were laden with the best the household had to offer. In An Albany Childhood, *Huybertie Pruyn, talking about her youth in the 1880s, recalls that various ''messenger boys, newsboys with calendars, postmen, policemen and many others'' also would come to wish the family a happy new year, and each would receive a paper bag containing four New Year's cakes.*

Baker Otto Thiebe, of Third Avenue, in Albany, still baked these cookies in his bakery at that address until his death in 1965. His daughter Elfrieda Textores told me that he rolled them very thin and baked them to a pale color. Many people in the area happily recall buying his cookies at 30 cents a dozen. Here is a smaller version of his recipe.

MAKES *at least 12 dozen, depending on size*

PREPARATION TIME: *about 20 minutes*

BAKING TIME: *about 8–10 minutes*

▪·▪·▪·▪·▪·▪·▪·▪·▪·

1	pound light brown sugar, sifted or use granulated brown sugar
1	teaspoon baking soda
1	teaspoon salt
1	egg, lightly beaten
1¼	cups margarine
8½	cups flour
1	cup milk
2	tablespoons caraway seed

In a large bowl, combine the sugar, baking soda, salt, and egg and stir to dissolve the sugar, making sure no brown lumps remain. Set aside.

In another bowl, use a pastry blender to cut the margarine into the flour until the mixture resembles coarse meal.

Slowly stir the milk into the sugar mixture and pour it through a sieve into the flour and butter. Add the caraway seed. Let the dough rest for a while before rolling it out.

Preheat the oven to 300° F.

Roll the dough out as thin as possible, to less than ¼ inch. Cut with a 4-inch oval cookie cutter, if available, or cut into 4-inch rounds and place on greased baking sheet.

Bake for 8–10 minutes, until the cookies have a very pale color.

ENGLISH

Old English Drop Cookies

Newcomb, New York, located almost at the base of Mt. Marcy in the heart of the Adirondacks, is the northernmost town in the Hudson region. From the town of Newcomb, it is only 14 miles to the base of the mountain and the beginnings of a hiking path up to the source of the Hudson, Lake Tear of the Clouds, so named by surveyor Verplanck Colvin in the early 1870s. The great river is not much more than a babbling brook at this point, but if the black flies do not chase you off, you can follow it up for about 10 miles to its origins in the tiny lake halfway up Mt. Marcy. Native Americans called that great peak "Tawahus," or, "He splits the sky."

*The Totten and Crossfield's Purchase was the beginning of colonial develop-
ment in the Newcomb area. Its deed, written on animal skin and signed by five
Native American nations, is now kept at the capitol in Albany. Lana Fennessy,
who contributed the next recipe, can trace her ancestry back to the beginnings of
the town, founded on March 15, 1828, and has recorded its chronicles in* The
History of Newcomb. *It can be cold way up there in the north. It was 25° F
below at the time she wrote me the note accompanying this recipe, which has
been in her family for a long time. These cookies are favorites for any occasion,
but especially at Christmastime, when they make a very nice addition to the holiday cookie tray.*

MAKES *6–7 dozen, depending on size*

PREPARATION TIME: *10 minutes*

BAKING TIME: *12 minutes*

---

2   *cups light brown sugar*
1   *cup cold coffee*
2   *cups raisins*
1   *teaspoon baking soda, dissolved in
      1 tablespoon water*
1   *teaspoon baking powder*
3   *cups flour*
1   *cup shortening, preferably butter*
2   *eggs*
1   *teaspoon freshly grated nutmeg*
1   *cup chopped nuts (I use almonds)*

Preheat the oven to 375° F.

In a large bowl, combine all ingredients and drop by the teaspoonful on greased baking sheets. Bake for about 12 minutes,
until golden brown.

···········

FRENCH

Hasbrouck Coconut Cake

Huguenot Street in New Paltz proudly lays claim to being "the oldest street in America with its original houses." The land was settled by twelve Huguenot families. They came here by way of Die Pfaltz, the Rhenish Palatinate in Germany. The Pfaltz served as their initial refuge from persecution, hence the name New Paltz. The Hasbrouck family was one of the original settlers. They came here in 1674 via Die Pfaltz from a small place near Calais, France. Descendant Kenneth E. Hasbrouck is now the Director of the Huguenot Historical Society. His wife Alice has done a yeoman's job in transcribing the handwritten cookbook manuscripts that are in the Society's archives. Mrs. Hasbrouck says in the introduction of her book As Our Ancestors Cooked:

> *These are recipes which, as cherished possessions, were handed down from mother to daughter. They were also sometimes exchanged between friendly neighbors at sewing bees, church suppers and like events. Many that survive were scribbled on scraps of paper and tucked away with other household notes such as directions for dyeing flax or making soft soap.*

Among those recipes is one for "Cocoanut Cake," marked M. A. Hasbrouck, and dated September 4, 1852. It came from the recipe book of Kenneth Hasbrouck's great-grandmother. He believes it was given to his ancestress by her first cousin Margaret Ann Hasbrouck, who later married John McGee and had eight children.

The recipe reads:

> *1 lb. cocoanut (coconut), 1 lb. sugar, ½ lb. flour, ½ lb. butter and 6 eggs. Grate the cocoanut the day before using. Separate the whites and yolks and beat each.*

I adapted the recipe as follows, using commercial, sweetened coconut without adding further sugar. If you wish, you can make it with fresh coconut, grating it the day before use to dry it slightly, and using 1 pound of sugar as indicated in the original recipe.

SERVES *10*

PREPARATION TIME: *15 minutes*

BAKING TIME: *about 35 minutes*

6   eggs, separated
2   sticks (½ pound) butter
2   packages (7 ounces each) sweetened
      coconut flakes
1¾ cups flour

Preheat the oven to 350° F.

In the bowl of an electric mixer, beat the egg whites until stiff. Remove and set aside.

In the same bowl, beat together the butter and coconut, then add one egg yolk at a time and beat after each addition. With a spatula in an under-over motion fold in the stiffly beaten egg whites.

Spoon this batter into a lightly greased 10-inch tube pan and bake for about 35 minutes (check after 25 minutes), until very light brown and a knife inserted in the center comes out clean. Remove and cool.

This dense, wonderful cake goes very well with cinnamon ice cream or a fruit sherbet.

GERMAN

Great-Grandmother Siefert's German Pound Cake

Dorothy Fox of Mamaroneck, New York, is a dynamic and involved volunteer. She cooks and especially bakes for all sorts of fund-raising occasions, such as the annual Beaux Arts festival of the Westchester Women's Clubs or for TWIGS, the fundraising organization of the United Hospitals. One of her favorite recipes is her great-grandmother's German pound cake. It sells for $20 at the TWIGS bake table. Dottie, as she is known, says she also uses the recipe for funerals. When an unexpected tragedy occurs "you always have sugar, butter, flour, and eggs in the house, so you can immediately bake a cake and bring it over," she told me.

The cake recipe was discovered in Dottie's mother's attic. It was hand-written in German and was translated by Dottie's daughter, who actually located the recipe and was studying German at the time. While translating, she called her mother because she was quite concerned that the recipe called for only four ingredients and no flavoring. Although Dottie has adapted the recipe to modern techniques—the original said to beat the batter by hand for 2 hours—she has found that the cake is best when it is made with only those four ingredients, without additional flavorings such as lemon or vanilla.

SERVES *at least 10, if not 20*

PREPARATION TIME: *about 35 minutes*

BAKING TIME: *3½ hours*

---

1   *pound butter*
1   *pound eggs (2 cups)*
1   *pound sugar (3⅓ cups)*
1   *pound flour (4 cups)*

Cream together the butter and sugar.

For the next step Dottie suggests putting a plastic bag over the mixer so that you can turn the mixer on as high as possible without dough flying out. Add the eggs and beat at least ½ hour or until batter is very light and fluffy.

Fold in the flour.

Spoon the dough into a well-buttered 10-inch tube pan. Place the cake on the lowest rack of a cold oven and turn the oven on to 250° F. Bake the cake for 2½ hours at 250° F from the time you put it in the oven. Then raise the oven temperature to 300° F and bake for 1 hour more, but check after 30 minutes. The cake is done when a knife inserted in the center comes out clean.

Remove and let cool. When cool, remove from pan and sprinkle with sifted confectioners' sugar. Slice as thinly as possible, offering 2 or 3 very thin slices per serving, instead of 1 thick slice. The cake can be presliced and put in freezer bags. Take out a few slices as needed; they defrost quickly.

HUNGARIAN

Ethel Szilvássy's Palacsinta

In the 1950s, Seventy-ninth Street between First and Second Avenues was the heart of Hungarian life in New York City. Arpad Hamid had his bakery there, and Helen Wankowicz, née Szilvássy, lived down the street with her parents in another brownstone. Hamid was known for his mouth-watering pastries and delicious cookies, such as chocolate cookies or little white cookies with apricot filling. Later he moved his shop to Washingtonville, New York, where many still remember his wonderful baked goods.

Unfortunately, no matter how hard his son Allan tried to find any of his recipes, it was to no avail. In the process of his search, he turned to Helen Wankowicz, now of Yonkers, New York, the daughter of his parents' friends, to see if she might shed some light. Although Helen has vivid memories of "Arpad's Pastries," as his shop was called, she could not give any recipes. Instead, she offers a recipe for the popular Hungarian dessert pancakes, palacsinta, which her mother made all her life. In fact, she made them so frequently that she would not measure, but just use "a little of this and a little of that." Fortunately, one day Helen asked her mother to measure the ingredients so she could write them down. Her mother died not long thereafter.

Helen has modernized the recipe just enough to suit present-day circumstances, but essentially it is still the way Ethel Szilvássy used to make it for any festive occasion, or when company was coming. Helen feels "they are the best palacsinta you'll ever eat." If there is a moral to this story, it is that we should all follow her example and record precious family recipes when we can!

MAKES *16–18 palascintas*

PREPARATION TIME: *10 minutes*

STANDING TIME: *30 minutes*

FRYING TIME: *about 5–6 minutes*

> 2 *cups lowfat milk*
> 7 *heaping tablespoons (about 1 cup) flour*
> 4 *eggs*
> 2 *tablespoons sugar*
> 1 *scant teaspoon salt*
> 1–2 *tablespoons light rum*
> About ½ *cup vegetable oil*

Apricot jam
Confectioners' sugar
Finely chopped walnuts

In a blender, combine the milk, flour, eggs, sugar, and salt. Blend for 3 minutes; then add the rum and blend again. Pour the batter into a bowl and let it stand for 30 minutes.

Heat an 8-inch frying pan or crêpe pan and add ½ tablespoon of the oil. Pour in about ¼ cup of batter and swirl the pan to cover the bottom. Fry the pancake until the top is bubbly; then carefully turn with a spatula and fry the other side for about 2 more minutes, until done. Remove the pancake to a platter and keep hot.

Repeat the procedure in the same manner with the rest of the batter. When all pancakes are done, spread them with apricot jam and roll them. At this point, they can be frozen. (Reheat by placing them in a toaster oven set at 300° F for 10 minutes, or until heated through.)

To serve, place two palacsinta on a plate in crisscross fashion, and sprinkle with confectioners' sugar and finely chopped walnuts.

IRISH

Aunt Annie's Boiled Raisin Cake

Grace Hunter of New City, New York, supplied an Irish recipe that has been ''in the family close to one hundred years.'' Her first cousin Firth Fabend adds some background information on their family. She writes:

> *Our Irish ancestors settled in Haverstraw in around 1850—refugees, no doubt, of the potato famines in Ireland. Haverstraw attracted a huge Irish population in the nineteenth century, mainly because jobs were plentiful in the brick and calico mills. Our immigrant ancestors were Tom and Rose McGuire, whose granddaughter, Elizabeth, was our grandmother. We have a photograph of Rose (she seems to be in her late 30s), and though dressed in her best silk and well-coifed, with crystal drop earrings, she looks, to me,*

painfully sad. I don't think life was much easier in Haverstraw than it was in Ireland. Let's hope she at least had the means to buy the ingredients for a sweet holiday treat!

The wonderful, intense spicing of this cake and the creamy frosting make it very special. It is, indeed, a treat for any festive occasion.

SERVES *8 or more*

PREPARATION TIME: *about 10 minutes*

BAKING TIME: *40–60 minutes, depending on what kind of pan is used*

---

1 *cup sugar*
2 *tablespoons lard or margarine (not butter)*
1 *cup raisins*
1 *teaspoon ground cloves*
1 *teaspoon cinnamon*
½ *teaspoon freshly grated nutmeg*
1 *apple, peeled, cored, and cubed*
2 *cups flour*
1 *scant teaspoon baking soda*
1 *full teaspoon baking powder*
2 *pinches of salt*
1 *egg*

ICING

---

1 *package (3 ounces) cream cheese, at room temperature*
1 *teaspoon vanilla extract*
   Enough confectioners' sugar to make a creamy paste, about ⅓ cup

---

In a medium saucepan, combine 1½ cups water, sugar, lard or margarine, raisins, seasonings, and apple. Boil for 5 minutes. Remove and let cool.

Preheat the oven to 350° F.

Sift the flour with the baking soda.

When the apple mixture is cool, stir in the flour/baking soda mixture, baking powder, salt, and egg, if used.

Spoon the dough into a 7-inch tube pan and bake for about 40 minutes. If a 7-inch tube pan is not available, use a 9-inch square pan and increase baking time to about 1 hour, until a knife inserted in the center comes out clean. Remove and cool on a rack until cool enough to touch.

In the meantime, make the icing. In a small bowl, combine the cream cheese, the vanilla, and enough confectioners' sugar to make a creamy paste. When the cake has cooled sufficiently, ice it in a decorative pattern. Store, tightly covered, in the refrigerator or in an airtight container.

ITALIAN

Matilda Cuomo's Apple Pie

To represent the Italian community of the Hudson region I made the obvious choice of Matilda Raffa Cuomo, who resides in Albany as First Lady of the State of New York. She graciously contributed a favorite of the governor and the Cuomo family, made with the official New York State fruit, the apple. In her letter, she adds:

> *The Hudson Valley Region is one of the finest and oldest apple-producing regions in the world, known for the quality and variety of its apples. It is home to traditional varieties such as McIntosh, Delicious, Golden and Cortlandt as well as the very popular new variety, the Empire, which was developed here in New York State.*

Susan Brown of the New York State Agricultural Experiment Station in Geneva, New York, adds a footnote. The Empire apple was the result of scientific breeding and is a cross of the McIntosh and the Delicious. The apple became available in 1966.

Mrs. Cuomo's exceptionally good apple pie recipe, with its oatmeal crumb topping, uses another New York State product, maple syrup. As discussed in the first chapter, the state is either number one or two in maple production, depending on the harvest.

SERVES *6–8*

PREPARATION TIME: *about 20 minutes for the filling*

BAKING TIME: *40–50 minutes*

1¾–2 *pounds apples, peeled, cored, and sliced*
¼ *cup dark brown sugar*
¼ *cup granulated sugar*
¼ *teaspoon cinnamon*
¼ *teaspoon freshly grated nutmeg*
1½ *tablespoons flour*
    Grated zest of ½ lemon
1 *tablespoon fresh lemon juice*
1 *unbaked 9-inch pie shell, fluted with*
    ½-inch standing rim
2 *tablespoons butter*
3 *tablespoons maple syrup*

CRUMB TOPPING

¼ *cup dark brown sugar*
¼ *cup granulated sugar*
½ *cup flour*
½ *teaspoon cinnamon*
½ *stick (4 tablespoons) butter*
½ *cup rolled oats*

Preheat the oven to 450° F.

In a large bowl, toss the apple slices with the two sugars, cinnamon, nutmeg, flour, lemon zest, and lemon juice until well combined. Arrange apple slices in a packed ring around the rim of the pieshell; then pile others loosely in the center, which should be higher than the sides. Dribble the maple syrup over the filling and dot with butter.

Prepare the crumb topping: Combine the two sugars, flour, and cinnamon in a small bowl. With a pastry blender, cut in the butter until the mixture resembles very coarse meal; then stir in the oats. Sprinkle the topping evenly over the pie. Bake for 10 minutes at 450° F; then reduce the temperature to 350° F and continue baking 30–40 minutes longer, until the crust is done and the apples are tender. Serve warm or cold with your favorite cheese, á la mode, or with whipped cream.

·ˑ·ˑ·ˑ·ˑ·ˑ·ˑ·ˑ·

JEWISH

Cannot-Fail Passover Cake

Passover is a joyous time, a time when families come together to celebrate traditions and enjoy traditional foods. The Seder (dinner) is a teaching meal during which various foods are served that have symbolic meaning to Jews worldwide. The Hagaddah, a book that contains songs and the explanation of the traditions in question-and-answer form, is read in turn by everyone present. As the Hagaddah explains, the foods help Jewish people recall their historic passage from slavery to freedom.

The maror, the bitter herbs (usually horseradish), are a reminder of the bitterness of slavery; the zeroa, the roasted bone, is a symbol of the pascal lamb the Israelites offered on the eve of their departure from Egypt. Charoset is a pleasant tasting mixture of apples, wine, nuts, and cinnamon, representing the mortar used by the Israelites to build the great pyramids and cities of Egypt. Karpas are the greens—usually parsley—dipped in a dish of salt water to recall the tears shed by the Hebrew slaves. Beitzah is the roasted egg, a symbol of the sacrificial offering. Three pieces of matzoh also are part of the Seder ritual. They represent the three historic categories of the Jewish people: the Kohanim, or priestly class; the Levites, or the priests' assistants; and Yisrael, or the populace.

The late Marilyn Scheffler, beloved educator and leader in the Westchester Jewish community, who inspired and founded the religious school at Temple Shaaray Tefila, was always willing to explain Jewish traditions and customs to me for my columns. She gave me the family recipe that follows. The cake is appropriate for Passover, or for any time you want a spectacular finale to a memorable meal. Serve it with sugared fresh strawberries. As its title indicates, it indeed cannot fail, provided you bake it in an ungreased tube pan.

SERVES *8*

PREPARATION TIME: *about 15 minutes*

BAKING TIME: *50 minutes*

---

   7   *eggs*
 1½ *cups sugar*
 1½ *teaspoons grated lemon zest*
 1½ *tablespoons fresh lemon juice*
  ¾ *cup potato starch, sifted*
      Dash of salt

Preheat the oven to 350° F.

Separate 6 eggs. Beat 6 egg yolks and 1 whole egg; add the sugar, lemon zest, and lemon juice. Beat well. Gradually add the potato starch; mix very well. Beat the 6 egg whites until stiff but not dry. Fold gently into the egg-sugar-potato starch mixture, ⅓ at a time.

Pour the batter into a 10-inch *ungreased* tube pan and bake for 50 minutes, or until a knife inserted in the center comes out clean. Turn the pan upside down and let it cool on its little legs; but, failing those, fit the tube pan over a filled liter soda bottle.

Serve as indicated above.

POLISH

Chruściki

During the 1940s, most of the Serafin clan lived within several blocks of one another in the middle of the Polish district of Yonkers. Grandma Serafin, the family matriarch, ruled the clan from the top floor of the three-family house that was also occupied by two of her offspring and their families.

Her granddaughter Elaine Frankonis, now of Watervliet, New York, remembers well how several weeks before each Christmas holiday, her daughters, daughters-in-law, and female grandchildren would begin gathering on Saturdays in Grandma's large railroad-flat kitchen to join in the ritual of making chruściki, light flaky strips of fried dough that would melt in the mouth and leave telltale signs of their powdered sugar topping that clung to their faces and clothes ''like the remains of an indoor snowstorm.''

Grandmother Serafin, of course, was in charge of organizing and assigning duties as well as operating the frying kettle. Dropping the delicate strips of dough into the kettle of hot Crisco was the most crucial part of the entire operation and therefore had to be left to the most experienced chruściki maker. Left too long in the hot oil, the pastry would taste like burnt toast. (It is almost impossible for them to be underdone, Elaine adds.) The final test of one's expertise was to be able to lift the thin, bubbling strip of dough from the boiling oil without scarring a hand or having the pastry crumble before it reached its place alongside the dozens of others already cooling on the rows of flattened, oil-absorbing brown paper bags.

The jobs of the daughters and daughters-in-law centered on mixing, kneading, and rolling out the dough in thin sheets that covered the entire surface of the white metal table. Elaine and her cousins, depending on age, dexterity, and experience, were assigned the tasks of rolling the pastry wheel to cut the strips of dough or folding one end of each strip through a center slit to form a sort of bow, or dusting the cooling pastries with powdered sugar. She sighs nostalgically:

> *And behind the sounds of mixing and kneading and rolling and frying was the constant hum of conversation, the sharing of generations of gossip and rumors and stories and laughter—perhaps the truly essential ingredients for those melt-in-your-mouth treats that my relatives used to create, for I have not had any as fine since.*

Here is the original recipe for these Polish treats.

MAKES *40–50 pieces*

PREPARATION TIME: *about 30 minutes*

FRYING TIME: *about 2 minutes*

---

3   cups flour
1   teaspoon baking powder
½   cup sugar
1   stick (8 tablespoons) unsalted butter,
        softened
8   ounces sour cream
1   egg
1   tablespoon brandy or rum (optional)
    Crisco or vegetable oil, for frying
    Confectioners' sugar

Sift and mix together the flour, baking powder, and sugar. Make a well in the center of the flour mixture and add the butter, sour cream, egg, and brandy, if used. Mix well.

Knead on a floured board until the dough "blisters." Roll out very thin. Cut into 2- by 4-inch strips; then slit each strip in the center and pull one end through.

Heat the Crisco or oil to 350° F and fry the chruściki until light brown. Remove with a skimmer or slotted spoon. Drain on absorbent paper and sprinkle with confectioners' sugar.

PUERTO RICAN

Epiphany Rice-Flour Dessert

Food historian Yvonne Ortiz of Jersey City, New Jersey, is presently researching five hundred years of Puerto Rican cuisine. In addition, she is very active in changing the image of Hispanics in the food industry. "They are no longer dishwashers or prep cooks," she asserts, and to this end she has founded the Association of Hispanic Culinary Professionals.

She shares a recipe for Epiphany, January 6, known as "Three Kings' Day" in Puerto Rico. It is a holiday of great significance in the island's food culture, the day when children get their presents. Before they go to bed they will cut some grass and put it in a box under their bed for the Kings' camels. Needless to say, in the morning they find presents in return.

Ortiz talks about some of her memories of the day:

> I remember when I was growing up in the island going over to my mother's parents' house for a feast. My grandfather would have a pig ready to roast and my grandma would be busy in the kitchen making rice with green pigeon peas, and desserts. One of my favorite holiday dishes is this simple rice flour and coconut milk combination. My father would climb in a palm tree and get a few coconuts. My job was to extract the milk from the pulp. I did not mind because I got to drink the fresh coconut water.

My family and I found this custard positively addictive. She advises you to use canned milk if coconut milk is not available for the following recipe. Rice flour can be purchased in Hispanic food stores or in natural food stores.

SERVES 6

PREPARATION TIME: *about 5–10 minutes*

COOKING TIME: *10–12 minutes*

- 3 cups coconut milk (see note)
- ½ cup sugar
- ½ teaspoon salt
- 6 strips fresh lemon zest
- 1 teaspoon butter or margarine
  Ground cinnamon, to taste
  Freshly grated nutmeg, to taste
- ½ cup sifted rice flour

In a large saucepan, combine the coconut milk, sugar, salt, lemon zest, butter, and spices. Bring to a boil. Remove from the stove. Add the rice flour gradually, whisking all the time. Return the pan to the heat, reducing it to medium-low. Cook while stirring until the custard gets thickened according to your taste. Remove the lemon zest and pour the custard into a glass bowl or individual cups. Dust with cinnamon and nutmeg. Refrigerate at least 1 hour before serving.

NOTE: Coconut milk comes in 14-ounce cans; use two cans.

RUSSIAN

Sweet Apple Pirog

Nikolai Burlakoff is the managing director of the Half Moon Visitor Center and New Netherland Museum in Liberty State Park in Jersey City, New Jersey. The Half Moon, a 78-foot full-scale replica of Henry Hudson's ship, is open to the public.

Burlakoff, a trained folklorist and historian, brings a unique mix of personal experience and academic training to the questions of cultural preservation. He is a first-generation immigrant from a Russian background and came to this country at age eleven. He remembers well the special dishes of his homeland, which his mother continued to cook for him, and has many of her recipes. Not all of them are as precise as one would wish. He cites a notation on one of them for a pastry: "Knead until it is soft and hard."

For his name day, Saint Nicholas Day, which falls in the Russian calendar on December 19, his mother would make him either the traditional krendel, a pretzel-like pastry, or a sweet apple "pirog." He explains about the "pirog" that it is the central dish in a Russian name-day celebration. The usually rectangular "pirog, prepared from a yeast dough, was filled with anything from salmon to apples"; Burlakoff adds that "it always was the richest and most complex pie that finances, time of year, and the cook's skill could produce" and that the term "immeninyi [name day] pirog" still "refers to something that is particularly opulent and beautiful." Beginning in the late nineteenth century, he goes on, the "pirog" was increasingly "supplemented and then replaced by sweet dough products." Laughingly, he adds that a nineteenth-century Russian author had once described "a pirog that was so rich, it had a filling in each corner."

This recipe makes a very dense, solid apple cake, full of lemon and cardamom flavor.

SERVES *12–16*

PREPARATION TIME: *50 minutes, including refrigeration time*

BAKING TIME: *about 1 hour and 45 minutes to 2 hours*

1	**whole egg**
2	**egg yolks**
2	**sticks (½ pound) unsalted butter, softened**
8	**ounces sour cream**
1¾	**cups sugar**
1	**tablespoon potato starch**
	Zest of 1 lemon
	Juice of ½ lemon
1½	**teaspoons ground cardamom**
6–7	**cups all-purpose flour**
1	**egg yolk**

FILLING

2	**tablespoons butter**
3	**pounds Granny Smith apples, peeled, cored, and thinly sliced**
¼	**cup sugar**

Preheat the oven to 325° F.

Thoroughly butter a 10-inch springform pan and set aside. In a large bowl, combine the egg, yolks, butter, sour cream, sugar, potato starch, lemon zest, lemon juice, and cardamom. Beat together until combined and until the batter foams lightly. Add 6 cups of the flour, a cup at a time, and beat dough until smooth and pliable. If it is still too sticky, add some more flour. Divide the dough into 5 parts and refrigerate for 20 minutes.

In the meantime, make the filling. In a large frying pan, melt the 2 tablespoons butter and add the apple slices. Sauté the apples for just a few minutes, sprinkle with the ¼ cup sugar, remove the pan from the heat, and drain.

When the dough has been refrigerated for 20 minutes, remove from the refrigerator.

Roll each dough part into a ball and then into a circle to match the diameter of the 10-inch springform pan. Transfer a circle of dough to the pan. Cover the dough with apple slices. Place another dough circle on top and repeat the layering procedure until all apples and dough are used. Brush the top dough layer with the egg yolk.

Place the pirog in the middle of the oven and bake for 1 hour and 45 minutes. Test for doneness by inserting a knife in the very middle of the cake. If the knife comes out clean, the cake is done. It will probably take closer to 2 hours.

Bibliography

 The following works are among those consulted in preparation of *Foods of the Hudson*

Adams, Arthur G. *The Hudson: A Guidebook to the River.* Albany: State University of New York Press, 1981.

Alexander, Robert S. *Albany's First Church: And It's [sic] Role in the Growth of the City.* Albany: First Church, 1988.

A Taste of History: With a Collection of Reminiscences and Receipts of Dutchess County. Poughkeepsie: Friends of the Glebe House, 1976.

Boyle, Robert H. *The Hudson River: A Natural and Unnatural History.* New York: W.W. Norton & Company, 1969.

Carmer, Carl. *The Hudson.* New York: Farrar & Rinehart, 1939; New York: Fordham University Press, 1989.

Crumbs of Comfort. The Young Ladies Mission Band of the Madison Avenue Reformed Church of Albany, 1885.

Come to the Fair: A Cookbook. New York Unit—the Herb Society of America.

Cruger, Eliza. Handwritten cookbook dated January 1829. Archives Boscobel Restoration, Inc., Garrison-on-Hudson, N.Y.

Danckaerts, Jasper. *The Journal of Jasper Danckaerts: 1679-1680.* Edited by J. Franklin Jameson. New York: Charles Scribner Sons, 1913.

Exceptional Desserts. Staff of the Westchester Exceptional Childrens' School, Purdys, N.Y.

Fenessy, Lana. *The History of Newcomb.* Belfast, M.E.: North Country Press,

First Dutch (Reformed) Cookbook. Ladies of the Reformed Church of Pompton Plains, N.J., 1889.

Gehring, Charles T. and William A. Starna, eds. and trans. *A Journey into Mohawk and Oneida Country: 1634-1635.* Syracuse: Syracuse University Press, 1988.

Greig, Sandy and Marion. *Family Recipes: The Greig Farm.*

Guide to Adirondack Trails: High Peak Region. 10th ed. Glens Falls: Adirondack Mountain Club, 1980.

Hamlin, Huybertie Pruyn. *An Albany Girlhood.* Edited by Alice P. Kenney. Albany: Washington Park Press Ltd., 1990.

―――. "Some Remembrances." MacKinney Library Albany Institute of History and Art.

Hasbrouck, Alice Jackson, ed. *As Our Ancestors Cooked.* New Paltz: Huguenot Historical Society, 1976.

Hasbrouck, Alice Jackson, ed. *Recipes from Locust Grove.* Poughkeepsie: Young-Morse Historic Site, 1991.

Heinbach, Ellen Boraz and Gale Gibson Kohlhagen. *Hippocrene U.S.A. Guide to West Point and the Hudson Valley.* New York: Hippocrene Books, 1990.

Hermitage Sampler. HoHoKus, N.J.: The Hermitage.

Hill, Walter. Notebook. Manuscript. New York State Historical Association, Cooperstown, N.Y.

Hudson Valley Guide. Hudson River Valley Association.

Hudson, Henry. Journal. As quoted in *New World*, book III, by Johannes De Laet.

Hurley's Corny Cookbook. Hurley Heritage Society, N.Y.

Irving, Washington. *A History of New York.* Edited by Edwin T. Bowden. New York: Twayne Publishers Inc., 1964.

Jameson, J. Franklin, ed. *Narrative of New Netherland: 1609-1664. Original Narratives of Early American History.* New York: Barnes & Noble, Inc., 1967.

Kalm, Peter. *Travels in North America: The English Version of 1770.* Edited by Adolph B. Benson. 2 vols. New York: Dover, 1966.

Kellar, Jane Carpenter, Ellen Miller, and Paul Stambach, eds. and comp. *On the Score of Hospitality: Selected Receipts of a Van Rensselaer Family Albany, New York 1785-1835.* Albany: Historic Cherry Hill, 1986.

McClester, Cedric. *Kwanzaa: Everything You Always Wanted to Know But Didn't Know Where to Ask.* New York: Gumbs & Thomas, 1990.

Morash, Marian. *Victory Garden Cookbook.* New York: Alfred A. Knopf, 1982.

Mrs. Lefferts Book, Manuscript cookbook, archives Lefferts House, Prospect Park Alliance, Brooklyn, N.Y.

Mulligan, Tim. *The Hudson River Valley: From Saratoga Springs to New York City.* 1992-93 ed. New York: Random House, 1991.

Nesbitt, Henrietta. *The Presidential Cookbook.* New York: Doubleday, 1951.

New York State Guide to Farm Fresh Food: Metro Region 1990-1991. State of New York Department of Agriculture and Markets.

New York State Guide to Farm Fresh Meats. New York State Department of Agriculture and Markets.

O'Callaghan, E. B., ed. *Documents Relative to the Colonial History of the State of New York.* Volume I. Albany: Weed Parsons & Company, Printers, 1856.

Old Dutch Receipts. Lafayette Reformed Church of Newark, 1885.

Philips family manuscript cookbook, dated 1847.

Rickett, H. W., ed. *Botanic Manuscript of Jane Colden: 1724 - 1766.* Garden Club of Orange and Dutchess Counties, 1963.

Saving Grace: A Collection of Recipes and Graces. Bedford: St. Matthew's Church, 1980.

Rose, Peter G. *Festive Chocolate.* White Plains: Peter Pauper Press, 1986.

———. *The Sensible Cook: Dutch Foodways in the Old and the New World.* Syracuse: Syracuse University Press, 1989.

Simpson, Jeffrey and Ted Spiegel. *An American Treasure: The Hudson River Valley.* Tarrytown: Sleepy Hollow Press, 1986.

Specialty Food Directory. New York State Department of Agriculture and Markets.

•.•.•.•.•.•.•.•.

Stevenson, Anne and Magdalena Douw. Untitled manuscript. Tarrytown: Library Historic Hudson Valley.

The Fifth Annual Marketplace Tasting: Foods & Wines of the Northeast Region. New York Chapter of the American Institute of Wine & Food.

Turco, Peggy. "Indian Life on the Hudson River." *Sea History.* (Summer 1991): 17–18.

Van der Donck, Adriaen. *A description of the New Netherlands.* Edited with an Introduction by Thomas F. O'Donnell. Syracuse: Syracuse University Press, 1968.

Ward, John. Diary as quoted in Susan E. Lyman, "New Year's Day in 1861." *New York Historical Society Quarterly*, vol. 26, no.1, (January 1944): 21-28.

Wilstach, Paul. *Hudson River Landings.* Indianapolis: The Bobbs-Merrill Company, 1933.

Index

•:•:•:•:•:•:•:•:•

•.•.•.•.•.•.•.

•.•.•.•.•.•.•.